An Open Work

AF813628

An Open Work
At Home with Marco Zanuso in Midcentury Milan

Shantel Blakely

THE MIT PRESS
Cambridge, Massachusetts . London, England

The MIT Press
Massachusetts Institute of Technology
77 Massachusetts Avenue
Cambridge, MA 02139
mitpress.mit.edu

© 2026 Massachusetts Institute of Technology

All rights reserved. No part of this book may be used to train artificial intelligence systems or reproduced in any form by any electronic or mechanical means (including photocopying, recording, or information storage and retrieval) without permission in writing from the publisher.

The MIT Press would like to thank the anonymous peer reviewers who provided comments on drafts of this book. The generous work of academic experts is essential for establishing the authority and quality of our publications. We acknowledge with gratitude the contributions of these otherwise uncredited readers.

This book was set in Haultin by Jen Jackowitz. Printed and bound in the United States of America.

Publication of this book was made possible by funding from the Graham Foundation for Advanced Studies in the Fine Arts and from the Scholarly and Creative Works Subvention Fund at Rice University.

Graham Foundation

RICE OFFICE OF RESEARCH
Creative Ventures Funds

Library of Congress Cataloging-in-Publication Data
Names: Blakely, Shantel author
Title: An open work : at home with Marco Zanuso in midcentury Milan / Shantel Blakely.
Description: Cambridge, Massachusetts : The MIT Press, 2026. | Includes bibliographical references and index.
Identifiers: LCCN 2025054926 | ISBN 9780262054799 paperback
Subjects: LCSH: Zanuso, Marco—Homes and haunts—Italy—Milan | Zanuso, Marco—Criticism and interpretation
Classification: LCC NA1123.Z365 B59 2026
LC record available at https://lccn.loc.gov/2025054926

10 9 8 7 6 5 4 3 2 1

EU Authorised Representative: Easy Access System Europe, Mustamäe tee 50, 10621 Tallinn, Estonia | Email: gpsr.requests@easproject.com

To my parents,
Allison Blakely and Shirley Reynolds Blakely

Contents

Ambiente

Marco Zanuso (1916–2001), an architect in practice in late twentieth-century Milan, established his reputation between 1945 and 1980. Educated at the Milan Polytechnic during the rationalist era, under Fascism, he entered practice after World War II and saw his first buildings realized in the Italian Republic, with its focus on democratic discourse and on new political and economic structures, new institutions. By the end of the century Zanuso would see a number of his designs built across the city, including residences, office buildings, and private-sector institutional projects. Meanwhile he was prolific as a designer for industry. He designed several factories, built in the provinces, and was one of a small group of architects who applied themselves to the design of furniture and objects of everyday use. For architects to design small objects was not a new phenomenon, but these architects' focus on the mass production of objects, on the consumer rather than the architecture client, represented an expanded scope of practice.

Zanuso was one of the youngest of Milan's modernist architects right after the war. The importance of his career has been acknowledged at least since the 1990s, when he was the subject of an exhibition at the Milan Triennale. Since then, the literature has been enlarged by a number of essays on the architect and his work. The variety of scales at which Zanuso worked is mirrored in a split in this literature, in which some scholars have tended to consider him as primarily a designer while others have foregrounded his architectural work. This book instead focuses on a single project, the apartment Zanuso designed for his family in Milan, in which strategies of both architect and designer were brought to bear. In tracing connections among Zanuso's designs across the gamut of scales, it locates the furniture piece and *arredamento* (furnishing plan scheme) as intersectional works through which he fulfilled the roles of many disciplines, including the architectural tasks of shaping, qualifying, and differentiating spaces as well as design tasks of responding to new imperatives of cultural continuity amid the spread of mass production. Zanuso as architect-designer, understood by way of this approach, offers a model of practice that remains relevant today, when architects often find themselves challenged by the need to reexamine and enlarge their repertoire of concepts and methods in response to the conditions and constraints of building production.

Some notable architects in late twentieth-century Italy, such as Ernesto Nathan Rogers (1909–1969) and Aldo Rossi (1931–1997), are known for how they addressed the potential of architecture in theoretical writings. Zanuso, a close associate of Rogers and a sometime mentor of Rossi, was more inclined to research and experimentation. He wrote constantly throughout his career and was known for his speeches at conferences, but he preferred to explore architecture's potential in practical terms, working closely with mentors, peer collaborators, and young architects in his office on projects, exhibitions, and public dialogues. Zanuso's collaboration with others outside architecture, including manufacturers and structural engineers, was decisive in his practice.

While this book cannot include an adequate history of architecture in Milan during the first postwar decades, it begins with a sketch of the city as a means to situate Zanuso in relation to the architectural discourse and social themes of that time and place. The site of the Zanuso apartment in Milan is the point of departure, for it touches in meaningful ways on the architecture of the city, the history of its architecture, and the dynamics of the cultural milieu to which Zanuso belonged.

* * *

As in many Italian cities, the center of Milan is the Duomo, the city's cathedral. From the Duomo's rooftop terraces, which are publicly accessible, on a clear day you can see Monte Rosa, the 15,203-foot (4,634-meter) peak on the Italian-Swiss border. The views are due to Milan's situation 50 kilometers south of the border on a roughly triangular plain between the Alps and Apennines that crosses Italy from Turin to Udine, from Como in the northwest to Bologna and Rimini to the southeast. Milan was not traditionally a destination for foreign tourists, who tended to set their sights first on Rome, Florence, or Venice in the Grand Tour that was common among certain classes (including architects) from the seventeenth century onward; but Milan was a stop along the way for visitors who crossed the Alps from northern Europe. Roman Milan, called Mediolanum, was a hub in a road network that connected Italy to Gaul and crossed the peninsula from Piacenza to Rimini and other points to the southeast; but the *cardo* and *decumanus*, north-south and east-west roads whose intersection was typically central in Roman cities, are not easily distinguished in the street pattern of Milan today. Nor does Milan have the street pattern of a Roman city, often a rectangular grid. Instead, many of the curved streets that cross the city center are the former canals that once facilitated transfer of goods between two rivers that descend from the Alps, the Ticino to the west and the Adda to the east, both of which empty into Italy's largest river, the Po.[1]

In a bird's-eye view, Piazza Castello, 20, the site of Marco Zanuso's family apartment, sits in one of six blocks that make up the zone known as Foro Buonaparte (figure 1.1). Built according to the Beruto Plan of 1884, Milan's first master plan, constructed in the late 1800s in a U-shaped curve around the Castello Sforzesco, the Foro Buonaparte defined the border between the Castello and the rest of the city. At first glance suggestive of a revision of the entire city street pattern into concentric rings, this group of city blocks is in fact a singularity.

The Foro Buonaparte, along with the Duomo, is one of several monumental fragments in the web of streets. These landmarks have served as the standard for monumental urban works for recent generations of Milanese architects.[2] The unification of Italy in 1861–1870, which brought to a close a series of changes in sovereignty since medieval times, saw a new class of entrepreneurs converging in the city. Like Piazza Duomo, which was designed by architect Giuseppe Mengoni (1829–1877) and built in the 1870s by clearing away medieval buildings in front of the cathedral, the

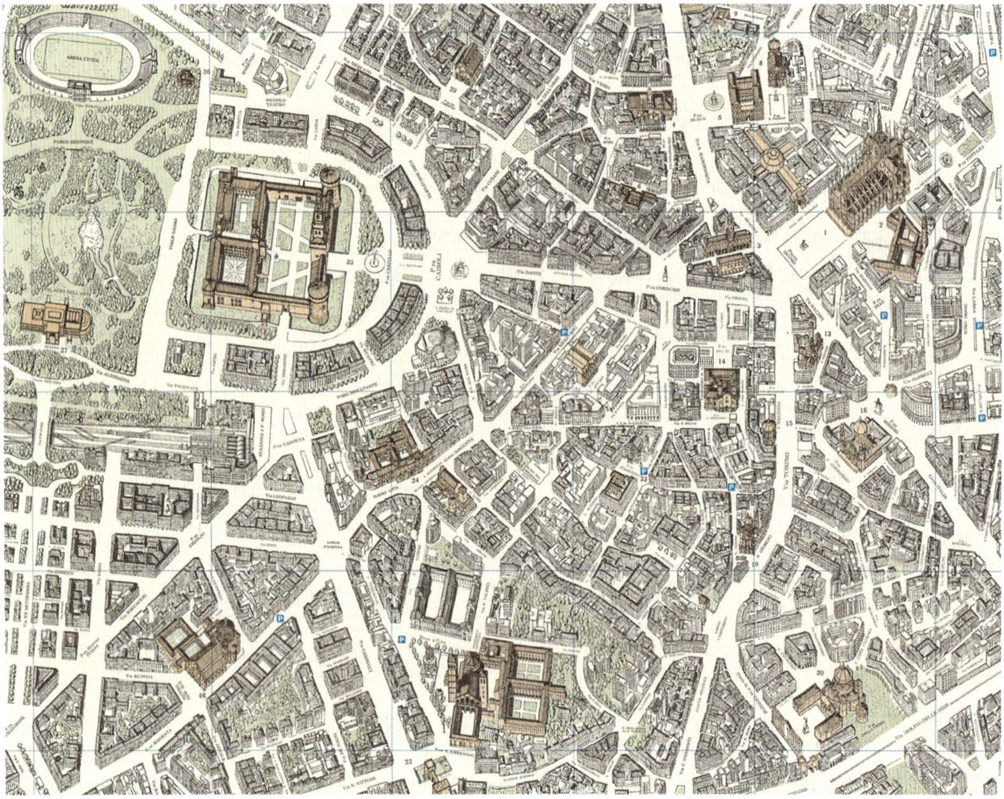

Figure 1.1 Giovanni R. Dradi, bird's-eye view map of Milan, 2015, detail. © Giovanni Dradi Heirs 2025. All rights reserved.

Foro Buonaparte was constructed in the late nineteenth century by members of this upper *borghese* class, many of them engineers who had arrived in recent decades. These newcomers, along with members of Milan's aristocratic class, established major industrial firms, often in small towns in the area around Milan, and commissioned new institutional, residential, and office buildings in the late 1800s.[3] The architects they worked with, too, from Camillo Boito (1836–1914), Milan's most celebrated architect of the time, to the lesser-known Giovanni Battista Bossi (1864–1924), the architect of Piazza Castello, 20, tended to have a background that included engineering.[4]

The Foro Buonaparte shows characteristic traits of architecture in nineteenth-century Milan, above all an apparent mixture of two temperaments, decorative and technical—a duality that is demonstrated by one of Milan's best-known buildings, Mengoni's Galleria Vittorio Emanuele II, completed in the 1870s with an interior decorated with neoclassical ornaments and glass mosaics, beneath an innovative roof made of iron and cast glass. The first proposal for the Foro Buonaparte site, an undeveloped area around the massive medieval Sforza castle, showed a strongly decorative sensibility. Its neoclassical *parti* assembled diverse functions, including government offices, schools, and a museum as well as residences, and connected them by a circular loggia around the castle. This first forum plan, drawn by the architect Giovanni Antolini (1753–1841), was presented in 1801 to the Napoleonic government and is strongly evocative of academic French architecture of the time, though scholars have argued that its resemblance to the work of Claude-Nicolas Ledoux (1736–1806) is more likely due to the influence of Roman sources on both architects.[5]

While the curve in the built Foro Buonaparte and to some extent its programming draw on this early scheme, the built forum was also a manifestation of the Regolamento Edilizio del Comune di Milano of 1889, a building code that set guidelines for its buildings' dimensions and configurations. Previous regulations had been oriented mainly to *ornato*, or the suitable appearance of buildings as seen from the public domain.[6] The Regolamento Edilizio shared some of the same concerns as the Ornato Fabbriche, the document it superseded; for instance, it indicated which building surfaces must be decorated and specified the kinds of materials that could be used on the parts that faced the street (Art. 43). But the Regolamento paid more attention to the pragmatics of the functioning city. It set standards for security, construction safety, the heights and projections of balconies or terraces, the heights of buildings, the placement of gutters and dripstones, the use of cisterns, the access to utilities for repair, the prohibition against obstructing streets, the provision of toilets with adequate light and ventilation, and other such details. The attention to these factors expressed a concern not only for aesthetics but also for public health and the navigability of public thoroughfares. The code also specified the responsibilities of building owners and the procedures for inspection, licensing, and fees for the approval of designs and for construction and inhabitation.[7]

Piazza Castello, 20 was commissioned around 1890 by Pietro Gadda, a lawyer descended from a family that specialized in silk production, who had moved to Milan from Novara in the late 1800s with his young family.[8] The site, at the intersection of Piazza Castello and Via Lanza, was two blocks north of the Foro's central axis (figure 1.1). The design, which is associated by signatures on permit drawings with the architect Giovanni Battista Bossi, reflects both of the tendencies that characterize the Foro Buonaparte itself, with some details that place it in a longer lineage of Lombard architecture and others that identify it as a manifestation of the functional city fabric that was prioritized by the 1889 Regolamento. From the outside, in its general characteristics the building resembles a Lombard palazzo whose details allude to Renaissance models such as the Palazzo Farnese in Rome (Antonio da Sangallo, 1517). In the building permit elevation, dated 1893, Bossi delineated the shape of the frame around each window opening, the shadows that would be cast by the cut stones, and the texture of the brick infill around the stone features, analogous to the palazzo type (figure 1.2). The Renaissance allusion is also sustained by the rustication of masonry that distinguishes the ground-floor and mezzanine (first-floor) levels from the upper facade, which is finished in brick with stone trim. The ceiling height on the second floor is about 18 inches (0.5 m) higher than on other floors. This difference, and the occurrence of a balcony facing Piazza Castello on that level only, are suggestive of the *piano nobile*, another key characteristic of the palazzo type (figure 1.3).

Although the Gadda residence was a sizable urban residential building on a prestigious street, the drawings that were submitted to the city in a building permit application show that, in its details, the building was modest and sober compared to other

Figure 1.2 Giovanni Battista Bossi, elevation, Piazza Castello, 20, Milan, 1893. Fondo Ornato Fabbriche. © Comune di Milano, Archivio Storico Civico e Biblioteca Trivulziana, Milan. All rights reserved.

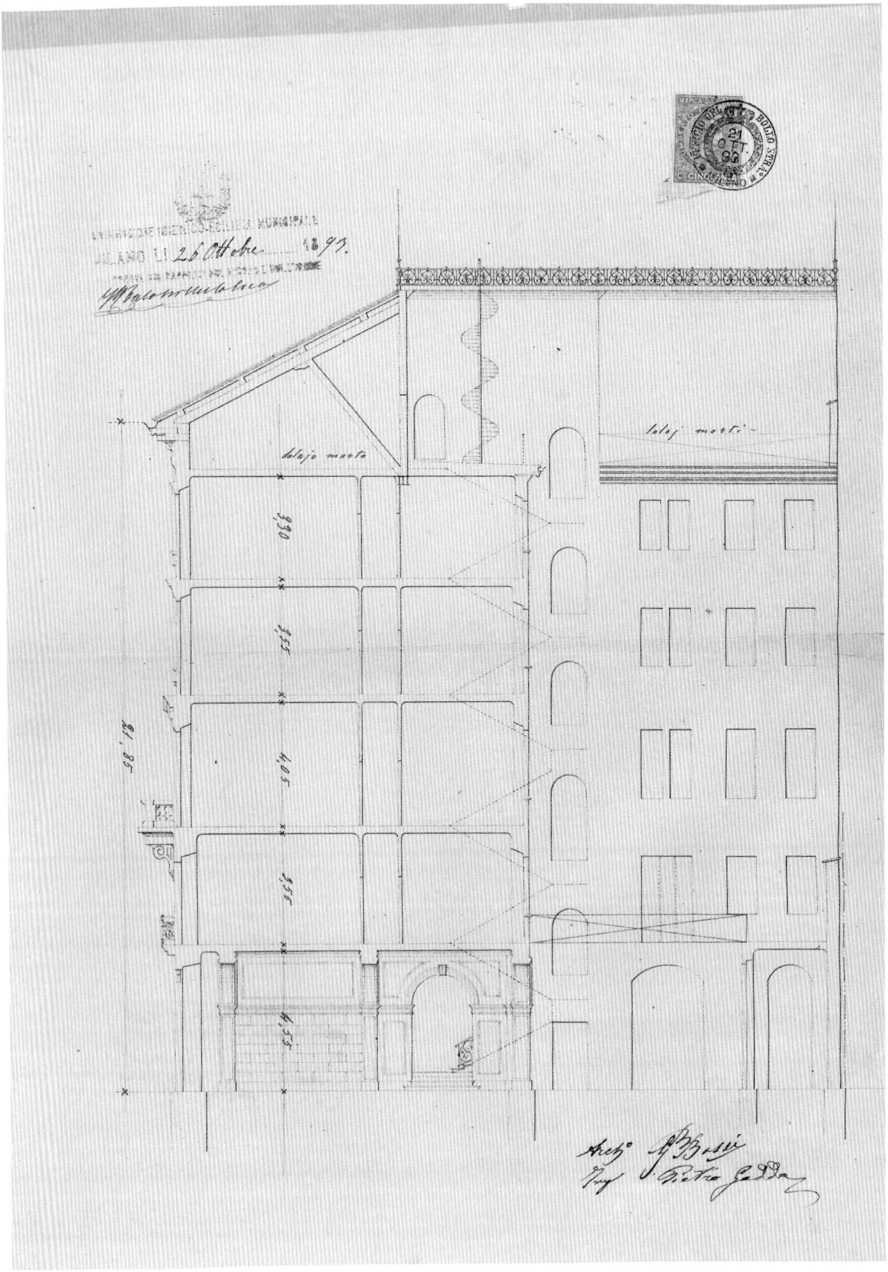

Figure 1.3 Giovanni Battista Bossi, section, Piazza Castello, 20, Milan, 1893. Fondo Ornato Fabbriche. © Comune di Milano, Archivio Storico Civico e Biblioteca Trivulziana, Milan. All rights reserved.

buildings on the same street. Other buildings designed by Bossi, constructed elsewhere in Milan, were also more ornate, including the Casa Galimberti (1905), a celebrated example of the Liberty style with mural decorations in ceramic and paint and dramatic wrought-iron window grilles by master ironworker Mazzucotelli. Moreover, Piazza Castello, 20 more closely resembles a multifamily apartment building than a single-family palace. The typical apartment floor plan, marked "Primo piano" (first floor) in the permit drawing set, shows a dining room, marked "sala manger," about 22 feet (7 meters) square, as the largest in a series of en suite chambers. Otherwise there is no single room in the design that would have accommodated a gathering of several families (figure 1.4).

Notwithstanding its noble stylistic allusions, Piazza Castello, 20 seems intended as a well-built but unremarkable part of a broader urban fabric with consistent qualities. The Foro Buonaparte's component palazzos resemble one another, and its blocks resemble other blocks constructed around the same time elsewhere in the city, including a zone to the west between the Cadorna rail station and the church of Santa Maria delle Grazie. The Foro Buonaparte's six blocks were specifically described by the Regolamento, including the specification that their facades should resemble one another and that their cornice height, which forms a continuous datum around the piazza, should be at most 22 meters above ground level.[9] As required by specific passages in the 1889 Regolamento, their facades, each no less than 14 meters long, form a continuous curved plane along the arc of the avenue, with all exposed surfaces elaborated in a decorative manner (figure 1.5). The curve of this plane is accordingly registered in the eave of no. 20 and in the attic apartment's Piazza Castello-facing wall.

The attic apartment at Piazza Castello, 20 was made available to Marco Zanuso in the 1940s by Piero Gadda Conti. Gadda Conti was a writer and critic, but his family included members of the engineering profession that had played an important role in the industrialization of Milan. His father was Giuseppe Gadda, a son of Pietro Gadda who had commissioned the building in 1890. Already a young adult when the family moved in, Giuseppe Gadda had studied engineering first at Novara and then at the Milan Polytechnic. In companies formed with classmates from the Polytechnic, he would play a role in the industries of energy and electrical machinery in the Milan region. The attic was an initially peripheral space that by 1950 had been made partially inhabitable by a

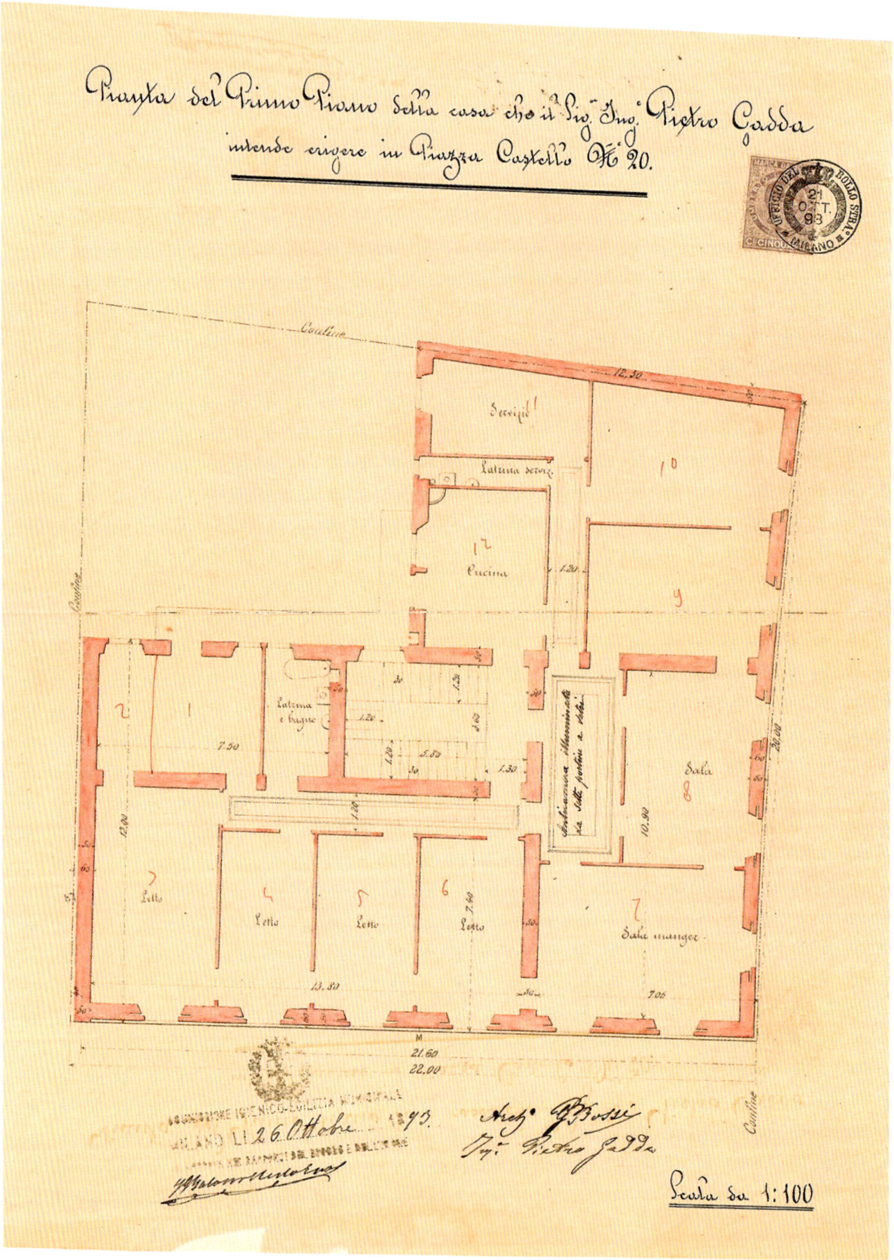

Figure 1.4 Giovanni Battista Bossi, first-floor plan, Piazza Castello, 20, Milan, 1893. Fondo Ornato Fabbriche. © Comune di Milano, Archivio Storico Civico e Biblioteca Trivulziana, Milan. All rights reserved.

Figure 1.5 Piazza Castello, 20, Milan, 2024.

renovation that had brought a portion of it up to code. The exact details of the arrangement between Gadda Conti and Zanuso are not known, but in a city that was extensively destroyed by wartime bombing, housing was scarce and the conversion of attic space into apartments was common.

Zanuso had just begun his career when he moved to Piazza Castello following the end of World War II, but he was already completing his first architecture projects, including the renovation of a vacation home near Lago Maggiore (with Gianni Albricci) and the design of a new office building on Via Senato in Milan (with Roberto Menghi). During the first few years after the war, he worked with the company Arflex on Lady, a chair with a metal frame and foam rubber cushions (figure 1.6). He also designed a chair made of bent metal and repurposed canvas tarpaulins which he exhibited in 1947 at the Milan Triennale, the recurring exhibition that took place in the Palazzo dell'Arte, a 1933 building whose construction for that purpose not far from Foro Buonaparte had reinforced the cultural significance of the Foro area in a distant allusion to Antolini's vision for it. Zanuso also submitted his iron-and-canvas chair to a competition for "low-cost" seating at the Museum of Modern Art in New York. A prototype of the chair is visible in early photographs of Zanuso's home.[10]

Architecture culture in Milan between 1945 and the 1960s was made up of architects who had mostly trained at the Milan Polytechnic. 1934 was the first official year of educational reforms that added classes in technology and hard sciences such as geology and chemistry to the architecture curriculum, which had included math and physics since 1875. Meanwhile, the school remained primarily a school of engineering and technical subjects; when Zanuso arrived as a student in 1934, the ratio of students of architecture to students of engineering and technical subjects hovered around one to nine.[11] The Milan Polytechnic of the 1930s, as it had been in the 1890s, was a place where architects and engineers were educated side by side, and the architects regarded themselves as solvers of problems, like engineers, even as they were instructed by professors like Gaetano Moretti (1860–1938), an architect associated with the decorative Floreale style.

In this light it is perhaps natural that postwar Italian architecture culture should have been characterized in part, at the beginning, by the architects' anticipation of a role in cooperation with the government of the Italian Republic, analogous to

Figure 1.6 Brochure for the Lady chair, produced by Arflex. Fondo Marco Zanuso, Archivio del Moderno, Balerna.

the professional structure of architecture in the Fascist era, when the education of architects had been minutely specified by the Ministry of Education as part of a structured path into a profession with assurance of access to competitions for major public works. Although these hopes were soon disappointed, the tone of expectation would persist among architects in Zanuso's circle at least until the late 1950s.[12] Zanuso was a close associate of one of the most vocal and prolific theorists of architecture during this period, Ernesto Nathan Rogers, and collaborated with Rogers as assistant editor during Rogers's directorship of *Domus* in 1946–1947 and *Casabella* in 1954–1957.

The expectation of a new vibrant post-Fascist architecture culture was not the only historical force that motivated these architects. They were also at work during Italy's transition from a primarily agricultural economy to a mainly industrial one. Although the first industrial firms and the beginnings of modern infrastructure arrived in Italy in the nineteenth century, due to the efforts of the engineering and entrepreneurial classes discussed earlier, large-scale industrialization came relatively late to Italy, whose economy had been cut off from the rest of Europe under Mussolini. The transition to an industrial economy in Italy, between 1945 and the 1960s, came several decades after the analogous change in Great Britain, Germany, and the United States. Zanuso and other architects found a new relevance to a broad public at a moment when mass production manufacturing was beginning, causing demographic changes in the work force, and families in Milan and across Italy were returning to their homes and rebuilding their lives after the war.

In order to distinguish between, on one hand, the architects' self-representation, their orientation toward their discipline, and their assumption that they would be part of shaping a new future for Italy, and on the other hand the actual impact of their activities on Italian households, it is essential to bear in mind what was happening (and not happening) in the wider social history of Italy at the time. Italian industry had begun to expand in earnest only after the end of Fascism, ending a period of relative cultural and economic isolation and driving the economy after World War II; but the beginning of this phase in 1945 did not mean that a robust consumer base was immediately present, even if architect-designers like Zanuso were preparing for one, and even if imagery of the entrenched consumer society in America was pervasive in

Italian popular culture from the 1950s onward. There would not be a large and robust middle-class consumer base in Italy comparable to the American one until the 1980s.[13]

As the influential architecture critic Manfredo Tafuri noted in the 1980s, reflecting on this period, the early postwar architects would not have been able to see their actual position in the overall system. The architects "could not know," he wrote, "that, even though they thought they were acting like the Magi and were presenting their own engagement as a gift to the newly elected, their message was being distorted by the language of a plan whose docile tools they had become. But in the years right after the war, this aspect of the situation could not have been perceived."[14] Tafuri is perhaps too charitable here, for the dependence of architects on an economic expansion ought to have been evident in the preponderance of showrooms, trade fairs, new hotels, automobile infrastructure, and similar manifestations of capitalistic development that filled the pages of surveys of new architecture from the 1950s onward.

The association with commercial activity is at best hidden in plain sight in a survey of new architecture in the book *Milano oggi*, edited by the architect Giò Ponti (who was also the longtime editor of *Domus*) and published in 1957.[15] Ponti's Milan is described in terms of centers of business, museums, rail stations, theaters, and schools, but also storefronts; Ponti did not view the commercial culture as distinct from the expansion of culture more broadly. Several projects by Zanuso included in the book situate him in the ranks of the architects who were collectively giving expression to Milan's cultural renewal and "verve," as Ponti calls it, citing the British journalist Robert Furneaux Jordan in his introduction. Meanwhile the images of architecture in *Milano oggi* show nothing of the gritty reality of industrial expansion that many experienced, which one can see in books such as *Milano, Italia* (Milan: Lerici, 1959) by photojournalist Mario Carrieri, or in films such as *Rocco and His Brothers* (1960) by Luchino Visconti, *Miracolo a Milano* (1951) by Vittorio di Sica, or *Tutto a posto e niente in ordine* (English title *All Screwed Up*, 1974) by Lina Wertmüller, which responded to the poverty and joblessness that persisted for years while Milan struggled to accommodate a massive migration of job-seekers from rural areas in Italy.

The Milanese architects' entanglement with capitalism was not lost on a younger generation of architects who emerged as vocal critics, and the pursuit of modernism during Italy's modernization and reconstruction came to an end with the critique and rejection of that approach in the early 1970s. Too young to have held professional roles during the war and reconstruction, these critics looked at their discipline with a keen awareness of defining features of their own lifetimes, including the potent system of capitalist production, both in the built environment and industrial production, and the architect's marginal and to their minds problematic role in that system.

Zanuso's parking garage in Via Chiaravalle was among the new buildings referenced in one such critical article in 1968, along with buildings by Franco Albini and Franca Helg, Ignazio Gardella, and others. The critics pointed out that the architects, while trying to improve the form of the city and propose alternative constructive logics and modes, had little scope to bring relief from worsening congestion and traffic, or from the shortage of affordable housing that meant students could not live in the city center; the authors cited a protest in June 1968 in which students had occupied a hotel in Piazza Fontana, site of a recent architectural competition seeking proposals for redevelopment. The pursuit of "quality" in buildings coincided with a process of the architect's instrumentalization by the land-holding elites.[16] A historical benchmark for the cultural shift among architects is the Milan Triennale of 1973; critical texts associated with the exhibition relegated modern architecture, identified in Italy as "rationalism," to history, while installations and exhibits took as their theme the depredations of capitalism.

The choice made by Zanuso and other Italian architects to insert themselves in the expanding economy and become involved in industrial design is one of the most distinctive aspects of postwar Italian architecture, one that could only have happened in close proximity to both the commercial world and the realm of production, both of which are present in Milan. Zanuso's choice to pursue industrial design, embraced early in his career, reflected a longstanding personal attraction to machines that had been intensified by his service on cruisers in the Italian naval forces, which entailed a new intimacy with machines and weaponry.[17] But in comments on design, Zanuso invariably linked mass production with its capacity for diffusion, noting the potential for the mechanization of production to multiply the number of products that can be produced in a given time. For him, the scale and timing of production, the labor involved, and the cost of the product were the attractive differences between the industrial and the older artisanal modes of production. In addition to designing objects, he advocated for prefabrication in building construction and designed two partially prefabricated projects that were built in Milan in the 1960s, working with the engineer Giovanni Varlonga.[18]

Zanuso was not alone in expanding his practice along these lines. Others in this category by 1950 included Ignazio Gardella, Vittoriano Viganò, Franco Albini, the BBPR partnership, Angelo Mangiarotti, Ettore Sottsass, Achille and Pier Giacomo Castiglioni, Anna Ferrieri Castelli, and Alberto Rosselli, who would later edit the journal *Stile Industria*.[19] Italian design was widely understood as design by artisanal methods, that is, procedures in which a specific technique, often involving hand labor, is prioritized over factors such as production time and scale. A key point of reference for American perceptions is *Italy at Work*, an exhibition that opened in Brooklyn, New York, in 1950, and became the point of departure for several American museum collections of modern Italian objects.

In fact, the momentum behind industrial design in Italy had been building among architects in Milan since the 1930s, inspired by parallel developments abroad, particularly in the United States and Great Britain. While industrial manufacturing began in Italy on a large scale only after the Second World War, the design of objects for serial manufacture was a theme in the discourse on architecture beginning in the 1930s, parallel to the subject of housing. Among the relevant precursor exhibitions in Milan were the Casa Elettrica of Figini and Pollini (1930); the low-income housing project by Piero Bottoni and Enrico Griffini (1933); and an exhibition at the Triennale of 1936, directed by the architect Giuseppe Pagano. These were part of an effort of a group of architects, including Pagano and Bottoni, to push forward a modern style that would overtake the traditionalist tendencies that were preferred by the government and much of the public.[20] Of particular relevance to the Zanuso apartment is the outlook of architect Francesco Monotti, who imagined that all of Italy might become an exhibition:

> Anything can be, or rather must be, the subject of an exhibition, and nowadays we see that even houses are shown in considerable numbers at the Triennale. Our

> salvation lies precisely in widening the concept of an exhibition to the utmost extent possible. Little by little the whole of Italy must become an exhibition, that is, a model for all other countries, in every form of life, and thus in creation and action.[21]

The Zanuso apartment would be at once a family home and a design project, at once a work of architecture, a furnished interior, and a collection of object designs. Beyond that, through photography and publication Zanuso's apartment became a platform through which he could articulate and share ideas. Zanuso first had his living space photographed in the late 1940s, with a number of images taken by Gian Battista Colombo and others, many of which went unpublished (figure 1.7). The entire apartment was published in Italian architecture journals in 1950, 1958, 1962, and 1967; on other occasions individual images appeared in the popular press, which Zanuso monitored by way of a press clippings service, Eco della Stampa.[22]

Through images of his apartment, Zanuso exhibited to a wide audience both his furniture and object designs and his way of placing them in response to the problem of living in a small apartment with sloping ceilings. The multiple iterations of the dwelling as it was enlarged in stages invite us to think of the actual apartment as a support within which the architect could elaborate ideas, not just a fixed entity. Certain details in the photographic negatives are reminders of the distinction between the reality and its published representations. A standing light fixture in the cropped margin of a view of the *soggiorno*, the tear in the wallpaper in an undoctored view of the bedroom, and radiator covers that were excluded from images of the *studio* all indicate a thinking process that went on behind the scenes and behind the camera. Such evidence of editing places the emphasis more on the apartment's configuration and configurability than on the fixed design.

As noted above, Zanuso did not create in writing a conceptual glossary or theoretical framework that would help the reader to comprehend his personal outlook on the world of design and production, as some architects have done for their architecture. Although he wrote essays, the designs themselves remain the most rewarding objects of interpretation. But such objects as a chair, a desk, a bookshelf, and a building were outcomes of different questions. In any case, as mass production objects, i.e., consumer

Figure 1.7 Marco Zanuso in 1949. Photo Giancolombo © Archivio Giancolombo, Milan. All rights reserved.

products, they had to be somewhat autonomous in order to be suitable for placement in many different rooms. Zanuso's objects tend to bear little resemblance to one another superficially. Individually or sometimes in small series, each represents a different foray into the world of production, as if he avoided the temptation to "solve" production as a whole but decided instead to confront questions of design and production one problem at a time.

This study of the Zanuso apartment adopts an analogous strategy of going room by room. In the itinerary through the apartment that gives the book its division into chapters, furniture pieces are considered individually, in combination and in relation to works outside the home. While all four stages of the apartment's evolution are considered, a special emphasis is placed on the 1962 version, which was accompanied by a text in which Zanuso, interviewed by another architect, described the method behind his furnishing plans (see the chapter "Letto"). The narrative unfolds through a movement from one object to the next. Each chapter starts by stepping into a room, beginning by crossing the entrance threshold into the *ingresso*.

Ingresso

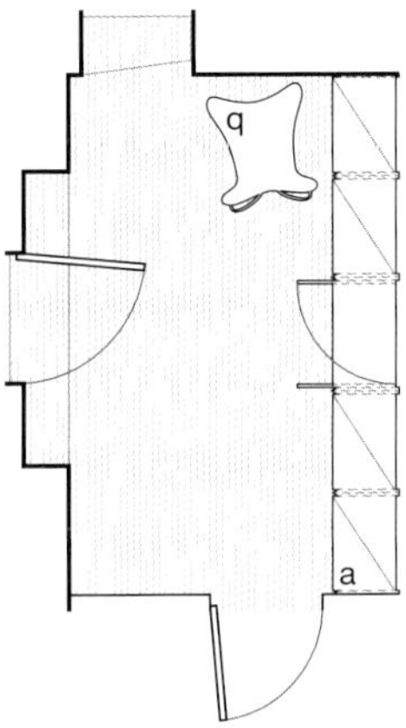

Figure 2.1 Plan of *ingresso* in 1962.

To arrive at the front door of the Zanuso apartment, you would pass through the large street-facing door of Piazza Castello, 20. You would find the entrance to the residences in the passageway between the street and courtyard and step through a discreet door into the shaft of an open-well stair with an elevator in its rectangular central opening. At the top, you would find the front door directly opposite the elevator. Once inside, having crossed the boundary between public space and private home, as of 1962 you would stand in a rectangular room the width of a hallway. Standing on the sisal carpet, whose ridges extended forward into the *studio*, you would face a pair of symmetrically placed bookcases to which a few light fixtures with transparent glass globes were attached. You would take advantage of the provided hooks for a coat and hat. Light from the windows of the *studio* would filter through the door in front of you and the transom above.

The *ingresso* is the simplest room in the Zanuso apartment, hardly more than a vestibule, but it has a distinct role. A separate entrance vestibule has intrinsic value as an expansion of the threshold, a place where guests and residents can pause before crossing into the private home and settling down in a specific part of it. But this room was not only a hallway that connected the two wings of the apartment; it was also a small multipurpose space.

From the beginning there was an *ingresso* or *anticamera* on Zanuso's floor plans, but in the 1962 publication of the apartment, the *ingresso* was reintroduced as a rectangular space at the center of the floor plan. In retrospect, this was also the first appearance of the overall floor plan that would ultimately define this apartment, with most of the interior walls at right angles to one another, creating nearly square spaces. At the smaller scale, there are traces in the *ingresso* of Zanuso's attitude toward the architectural potential of furniture. This chapter considers the *ingresso* as a sample of the design approach that operated across the apartment, entailing the integration of the wall configuration and furniture into a serviceable functional space.

The Zanuso apartment developed through successive excavations from the original roof, entailing the removal of selected timbers in the structure, the construction and relocation of partitions, and the addition and substitution of furniture. In the plan published in 1950, the apartment was a suite of rooms in an enfilade configuration, one opening onto the next (plate 32). The entrance vestibule was a rectangular room to the left of the stairwell, with its long axis parallel to the stairwell's. A second stair led from this *anticamera* (antechamber) to a flat terrace on the building's roof, above the kitchen. From the *anticamera*, with the entrance door at one's back, doorways led to the kitchen on the left and to the bedrooms and bathroom on the right. One could enter the living room either from the children's bedroom or from the antechamber itself, making a sharp 180-degree turn to the right toward Via Lanza. The apartment in 1950 ended at a diagonal wall aligned to timber members that extended from the stairwell core to the building's corner.

Already in the plan published in 1958, the apartment had an entrance door in the wall of the communal stairwell, centered, in a position identical to the entrance door in the apartments below. This doorway was cut in one of the half-meter-thick masonry walls around the stairwell, which contributed bracing to the building and extended above the cornice and through the attic and roof. The 1962 plan would introduce a rectangular *ingresso*, enclosed between walls that aligned with the sides of the communal stairwell (plate 34). By contrast, the 1958 entrance hall, located in the same position, formed a wedge shape in plan. By a door at the narrow end of the room, through the former entrance hall, one reached the children's rooms and kitchen, while a door at the wide end of the room, in a new partition wall that aligned with the wall of the stairwell, led to the new *soggiorno* (plate 33).

At just 4 feet (1.3 m) wide and 12 feet (3.6 m) long, the 1962 *ingresso* was slightly larger than the stair landing. Looking at the 1962 *ingresso* in the apartment floor plan, one might wonder whether it signifies a specific idea that motivated the floor plan of the overall apartment, which by that time had rectangular rooms arranged in symmetrical zones to either side of the entrance path (plate 34). A tradition of symmetrical plans reaches back to Renaissance masters like Bramante and Palladio, whose floor plans had formal entrance halls. Symmetrical plans were also common in Italian modern architecture of the 1930s, for instance in the designs of Piero Portaluppi, one of Zanuso's professors at the Milan Polytechnic. But that tradition corresponds not to apartments but to villas, often buildings of two or more stories. By contrast the Zanuso apartment, like many in Milan, had just one level. A small stair near the entrance led to a roof terrace that appeared in a section drawing published in 1950, but from that point onward, these spaces were excluded from published versions of the apartment.

The plan architecture of the Zanuso apartment had other distinctly modern traits as well. As noted in "Ambiente," the building had neoclassical facade details including decorated window openings, the lower level finished with rusticated stone, and a main floor analogous to the *piano nobile* of a Renaissance palazzo, with higher ceilings and balconies at the windows (figure 1.3). On the inside, from the beginning Piazza Castello, 20 resembled more an apartment building than a villa, with shops on the ground floor and four independent apartments above. While the provision of apartments in Giovanni Bossi's *primo piano* (first floor) plan suggests modern upper-middle-class housing, the plans show that domestic servants were housed in the apartment. The space was divided into rooms that were somewhat economically sized, but the distribution of these spaces created internal hierarchies, with more formal spaces placed along the street-facing sides of the plan.

The apartment layouts in the 1893 plan could plausibly have provided a guide for Zanuso, but there are noticeable differences. The bedrooms in the 1893 apartment were all the same size, but servants' quarters were at the ends of each wing, and on the courtyard side. Independent circulation was provided for the servants by corridors in Bossi's plan: one hallway next to the stairwell core served as the entrance vestibule; a second was parallel to Piazza Castello; and a third one was at right angles to the first one, parallel to Via Lanza. These hallways in three segments connected the servant's bedroom at the end of the kitchen wing to the bedrooms at the other end. This configuration, achieved in part by a vestibule whose length surpassed the width of the stairwell, provided an independent circulation path for servants.

By contrast, in the Zanuso apartment, circulation was achieved by a mixture of hallway circulation, pass-through rooms, and the stair landing. From 1958, the master bedroom was accessible only through the living room, which meant that even while the living room contained the most formal seating area, where guests were received, it was also a passed-through space. This reflected the modern middle-class lifestyle of the young family, which employed servants but in limited roles. The Via Lanza side of the apartment would have a hallway only after the final expansion and renovation, published in 1967.

After the 1962 renovations, the floor plan of the Zanuso apartment bore a general resemblance to the typical floor plan of the apartments below it, with some notable refinements. The most formal room, the *soggiorno*, in the building's corner, corresponded to the largest and presumably most formal room in the 1893 first-floor plan, and the master bedroom had been relocated to the Via Lanza side, analogous to the bedrooms on the Via Lanza side in the apartments below.

Meanwhile, the renovations to the attic introduced an increasingly regular plan geometry. The interior partitions were at right angles to one another, providing regular-shaped rooms even if the building perimeter was roughly a trapezoid and the facade that faced the Castello was curved. The *ingresso* and *studio* formed a narrow central zone between two larger areas of roughly the same size: a Piazza Castello-side zone the width of the nursery and a Via Lanza-side zone the width of the *soggiorno*, including the master bedroom and bath.

The *ingresso* in the Zanuso apartment resembles its counterpart in several of his apartment and villa designs around 1960. An *ingresso* was a space of reception and transition on the threshold of the home. Having few constraints of function, this was also a space that could assume any shape, and so it was sometimes used to absorb discrepancies in adjacent areas. The *ingresso* is a simple regular shape in plan in the apartment designed by Zanuso for his brother, Michele Zanuso, as in his own apartment.[1] By contrast, the *ingresso* in the Villa Reggiani at Jesi, for example, has an irregular shape that reflects its role as a hinge where the regular geometries of the bedrooms on the street side of the house converge with the axis of the space of repose and study on the garden side.[2]

The *ingresso*'s emergence in the 1962 floor plan, no longer a peripheral space in which one performs the functions that take place around an entrance as best one can, coincided with the full emergence of the apartment as a whole as an ostensibly intentional floor plan. The massing of the overall building at Piazza Castello, 20 closely follows the footprint, and the design is as regular as the site permits while adhering to the limitations of the building envelope that were specified by the code. For all its actual irregularities, the building is designed to appear regular in its form. The building from the ground to the eaves is a roughly cube-shaped volume. The ground-floor footprint is 22 m along Via Lanza and 20 m along Piazza Castello and the eave height is 21.85 m. The apparent cube is broken by the acute angle at the back of the lot, where the two party walls meet, and by the curved facade on Piazza Castello. But the portion of the building that borders Via Lanza is a rectangle in plan with overall proportions of 1:2 (figure 1.4).

Peripheral functions had been relegated by Bossi, the original architect of Piazza Castello, 20, to the places where the plan was least regular. The acute angle of the trapezoidal site perimeter occurs in the corner of the building, next to the kitchen, where the servant's bedroom was located (figure 1.4). Also peripheral was the courtyard, which was typical of the buildings in the curved block between Foro Buonaparte and Piazza Castello. The courtyard was nearly one quarter of the total square footage of the plan, twice as large as required by code (Regolamento Edilizio, Art. 58, p. 3); but in the context of the overall design, it was reserved for parking and other functions, rather than extending the interior living spaces.[3]

While the interior walls in the attic were aligned in increasingly orthogonal relationships over time, creating increasingly regular room shapes, the apartment's furnishings had served from the beginning, more than the walls, to differentiate and accommodate activities. This approach to designing the home was observed by Giò Ponti, who wrote in notes on the apartment as published in *Domus* in 1950 that its spaces felt "interpreted." The apartment consisted of "points of view."[4] The idea that an apartment could be divided into discrete locales defined not by walls that created functional compartments but by visible situations that arose through the juxtaposition of furniture points to a privileging of the image, with the organization and use of the space communicated visually. One might even attribute a phenomenal pastoralism, analogous to the access to nature that Zanuso had stipulated in an early published design for an "ideal house." Even a small interior space can be experienced in a series of views, like a picturesque garden.[5]

Considering the apartment in its four published versions between 1950 and 1967, one sees three general kinds of approach to the construction of rooms. The first, in 1950, entailed the accommodation of necessary functions in a single space. The furniture, in groups, signals a dining area, a place to read, and so forth. The second, published in 1958, further explored the visual aspect by introducing an abstract design into the plan through the positioning of furniture (see "Soggiorno"). The third, published in 1962, reverted to the plan, employing right angles in plan to create structured spaces within a space. (The fourth version, published in 1967, added a corridor to the rooms on the Via Lanza side, but maintained the 1962 furnishing strategy.)

The 1962 renovation marked the moment when the walls and furniture settled into an equilibrium between the first two design strategies: the walls were made orthogonal where possible, while the furniture found repose in expressive groups that situated their associated activities at orderly positions in the space. Zanuso specified the location of chairs, sofas, tables, floor coverings, and in some cases finishes in his published floor plan drawings of the apartment in 1950; he would do the same in 1958, 1962, and 1967. As further study of Zanuso's rooms will show, the presence of furniture in the floor plans reflects a transfer of the architect's projective sensibilities to the smaller scale and a consideration of everything, walls, space, and furniture, together.[6]

Zanuso's inclusion of furniture in his floor plans, which appeared hand drawn with each of the four articles on the apartment, may reflect the influence of Giò Ponti. Zanuso was similar to Ponti, among other contemporaries, in adopting an outlook in which objects as well as space and enclosures, and qualities like color and texture as well as form, all belonged to the architect as pragmatic and expressive means. Indeed, Ponti, who had graduated from the Milan Polytechnic in 1921, was a former professor and a notable supporter of Zanuso, and as editor of *Domus* regularly published Zanuso's work.[7] One example of Ponti's approach, a plan of a sitting room, shows a piano and two armchairs in the plan. The lines that indicate the movable components are few in number but carefully chosen to differentiate one chair type from another, next to the rectangle of a coffee table.[8] Plans with furniture were drawn for publication; but the depiction of furniture in plans was not a given in architecture journals at the time.

As shown on the plan of the *ingresso* (figure 2.1), by 1962 this was ostensibly a rectangular room fitted with a bookcase on one wall, but there was no actual wall behind the bookcase. Instead, the bookcase, which had two sections, was a built-in partition between the *ingresso* and the *studio*, bracketed by two solid walls that divided the *ingresso* and *studio* from the bedroom suite on one side and from the *soggiorno* on the other. Between the two sections of the bookcase was a double door made of solid wooden panels. With the doors open, the table and chairs in the *studio* were visible from the *ingresso* (plate 17). Between the bookcase and ceiling, a band of butt-jointed glass panes about one meter high formed a generous clerestory that could admit light into the fully interior *ingresso* from the *studio*'s Piazza Castello-facing windows. Glazing in the interior had been called for in the Gadda apartment below, as well; a note on Bossi's 1893 floor plan (figure 1.4) stipulates that the seven doors to the long vestibule would have glass panes.

The bookcase was the largest furniture piece in the apartment. This was not a custom, one-off partition but a product that Zanuso had developed, which was produced by Techniform, a subsidiary of Arflex, in the early 1960s (figure 2.2). Zanuso employed the product in several of his own projects. The bookcase section to the left of the doorway had two bays with six shelves each. The edges of the upper shelves on the two sides were aligned to create horizontal lines that crossed the partition's entire width, interrupted by the doorway. To the right of the doorway, the configuration of the bookcase addressed the *ingresso*'s various functions not only with bookshelves but also with tall compartments that could accommodate coats, a walking stick, and an umbrella.

The design of built-in furniture was a frequently employed tactic in the repertoire of modern architecture from the beginning, partly because the command of such objects, each somewhere between the scale of a chair and a room, could allow an architect to make maximal, precise, efficient use of space. There were some who maintained that this was the smallest object that an architect should attempt to design. The critic Reyner Banham could not make up his mind about this issue, for while he endorsed the architectural works of Marco Zanuso and other architects who turned their attention to the integration of multiple building systems, including technical apparatuses, he also argued in his 1961 essay "Design by Choice" that an architect, who was educated to design large, one-off objects built to last for fifty years or more, lacked the aesthetic sensibilities to design objects that would be produced in series or be subject to rapid obsolescence. Instead of designing furniture, Banham wrote, architects should design built-in furniture. Banham's model in this regard was Le Corbusier.[9]

Le Corbusier was widely admired in Milan, by Zanuso among others. In a 1952 article, Zanuso characterized the Swiss architect's Unité d'Habitation at Marseilles as a proof of the value of a functionalist method in the broadest sense.[10] Part of what impressed Zanuso in the Unité was its mass production component, with each apartment designed to be prefabricated and slotted into the structural frame. The commitment to mass production was a disposition that distinguished Zanuso and some of his peers from other architects in Milan. Like Walter Gropius and other Bauhaus architects—and like the socialist-minded William Morris, on whom at least two books had been published in Italy by 1963—this group grasped the utility of mass production as a mechanism for distributing the goods of design.[11]

A drawing of a "libreria" in Zanuso's archive summarizes the construction details of the Techniform bookcase (figure 2.3). A bay of the unit formed a module, each consisting of several shelves held between two vertical wooden side pieces. The shelves were

Figure 2.2 Brochure for shelving, produced by Techniform. Fondo Marco Zanuso, Archivio del Moderno, Balerna.

supported by pegs that slotted into the vertical pieces, with pre-drilled holes providing shelf height alternatives. One shelf was extendable; along its short edges were L-section brass strips that could slide over identical strips that were bolted to the vertical pieces. Two vertical pieces faced one another to form each bay. A wedge-section wooden strip with one long beveled edge was applied to the long edge of each vertical piece, which gave beveled edges to each bay. The flat sides of these edges were turned toward adjacent bays. The gap between adjacent bays was regulated by spacer blocks that, while remaining hidden, produced a shadow line between the flat sides of the vertical pieces. The shelves, which also had beveled edges, were installed so that the flat side faced up, the beveled side down. At the corners of the shelves' beveled edges, material was pared away at the joint where the shelf met the vertical support. The bookcase gives the impression of sturdy construction, like a wall, but due to the technique of beveling and chamfering both the shelves and the vertical pieces, its pieces appear to barely touch at all.

The bookcase-as-partition in the *ingresso* was short, straight, and pinned between two walls, but Zanuso had designed the bookcase to be deployed in various ways to define a space. In 1965, he would use the same shelving as a partition in the room that he designed for the exhibition *La casa abitata*, held in the Palazzo Strozzi in Florence. The bookcase was used to create two partitions that bordered a children's play area and divided it from a *soggiorno* and dining room in the large gallery (figure 2.4). In each partition, five bays of the bookcase, made of walnut, were connected to form a shallow curve. The installation also featured the chair Lambda, dining table Dinner, living room furniture Woodline, and other Zanuso designs.

The bookshelves were of particular interest to Lara Vinca Masini, a curator of the exhibition. The details that she emphasized in comments on the installation, which were published in *Domus*, included the height of the bookcases, tall enough to divide spaces without being imposing, along with their capacity to be aggregated in a straight or curved configuration; the availability of the bookcase backs as a surface for a variety of finishes, bringing color to a space and providing a backdrop for any activity, also added value.[12] It was especially important to Masini and the other organizers that this was a mass market product, because the intention of *La casa abitata* was to generate proposals that would

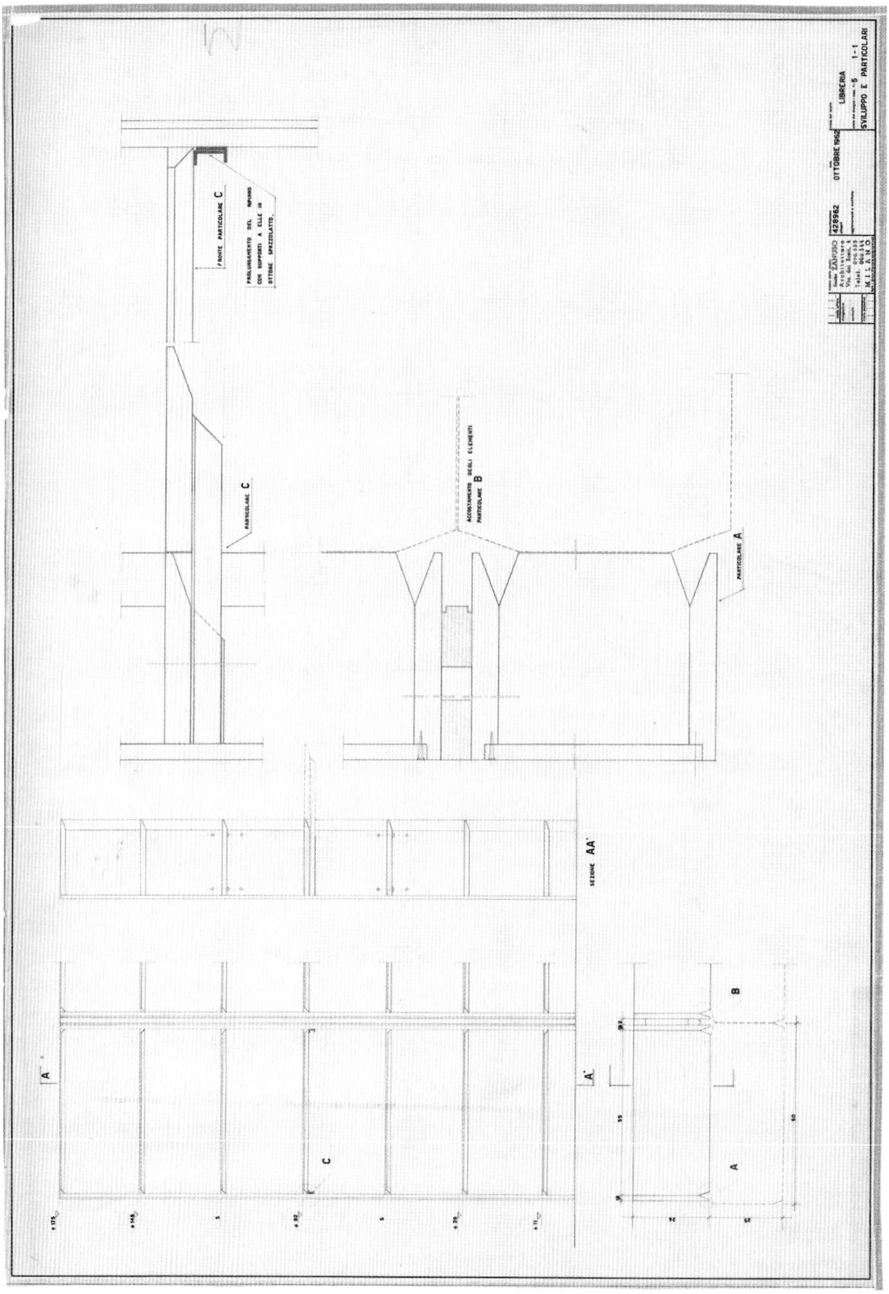

Figure 2.3 Drawing sheet of bookshelf details, 1962. Fondo Marco Zanuso, Archivio del Moderno, Balerna.

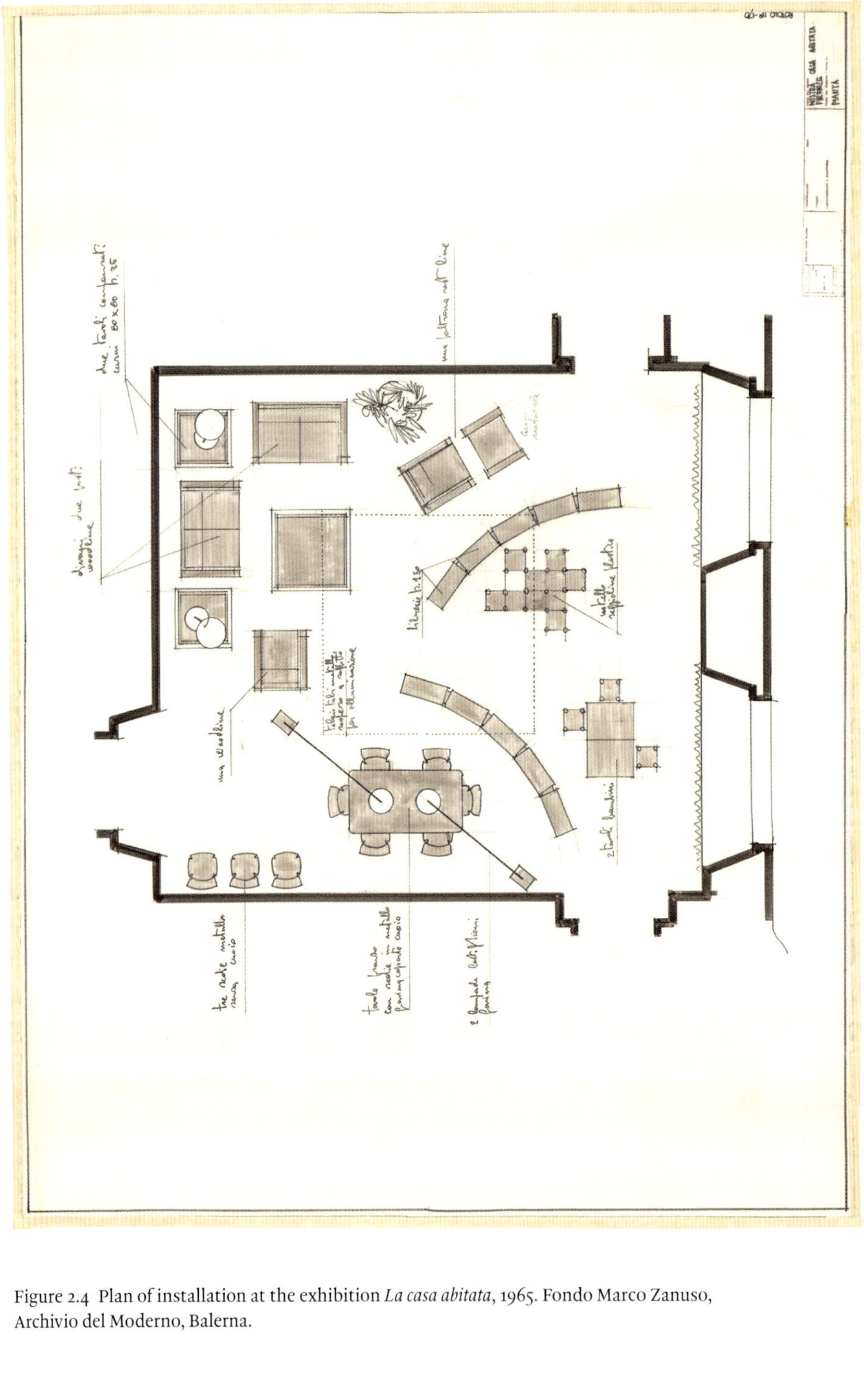

Figure 2.4 Plan of installation at the exhibition *La casa abitata*, 1965. Fondo Marco Zanuso, Archivio del Moderno, Balerna.

be accessible to consumers for whom one-off apartment designs were not affordable.

The second piece of furniture that was related to the *ingresso* in photographs of the apartment is a chair, Tripolina (plate 28). If the rectangular walls of the 1962 *ingresso* are an index of Zanuso's pursuit of normal spaces in the attic of Piazza Castello, 20, the presence of Tripolina next to the bookcase is an example of using furniture to signal and accommodate a specific function. Tripolina was a folding chair whose high, wide back gave it qualities of a *poltrona*, the large comfortable chair exemplified by the (American) Chesterfield model, associated with luxurious relaxation. But a Tripolina could fit comfortably in a corner. Its leather seat takes up little space and slouches downward, while with its collapsible wooden frame, it could be folded into a narrow column that required even less space.

While Tripolina was not one of Zanuso's designs, he and his peers designed various folding chairs in the late 1940s. The architects' interest in folding chairs was part of a broader exploration of typologies, inspired by nineteenth-century models whose names (like "campaign chair") associate them with colonial military operations, as well as by the nonfolding chairs that emerged from the Bauhaus, including designs by Marcel Breuer for chairs made of tubular metal with canvas used for seats, backs, and armrests. Zanuso designed a series of wood-and-cloth folding chairs that were exhibited at the ninth Triennale in 1951 (figure 2.5) as well as a fixed-frame iron-and-canvas chair of a similar type, including one that he submitted to a competition held by the Museum of Modern Art in 1945, made of iron and canvas from repurposed military tarpaulins. A prototype appears in photographs of the Zanuso bedroom in 1950; a similar three-seat unit was in the living room during the same period (partially visible in plate 1, bottom and plate 2, top).[13]

There are indications that the Tripolina in plate 28 may have been moved to the *ingresso* for the sake of the photograph, for in the floor plan that was published in 1967 along with the photo, the chair appears in the living room of the older girls' suite (plate 35).[14] But the way the juxtaposition of chair and bookcase signals the opportunity to sit and read would have been meaningful to Zanuso and other architects in Milan, accustomed since the war to making maximum use of limited equipment. The charm of the chair next to the bookshelf recalls Giò Ponti's remark that the Zanuso apartment

Figure 2.5 Folding chairs exhibited at the ninth Milan Triennale, 1951. TRN.IX.06.0321, photo Farabola. © Triennale Milano.

in 1950 was “tutta significante, una casa senza punti morti,” or in English, “everything meaningful, a house without dead zones.”[15] This way of thinking about furniture as generating inhabitable space could also be observed in the first issues of *Domus* in 1946, when the emphasis for Milan’s architects, seeking to assist in the reconstitution of households, was on how to make maximal use of a limited number of pieces to recreate a sense of home.

The first feature on this theme in *Domus* 205, published in January 1946, was called “Pronto soccorso” (urgent care or first aid). The architect Ernesto Nathan Rogers here made his debut as director of the journal, a position he would hold for two years, with Marco Zanuso as his assistant director. Rogers had given the journal a subtitle, “La casa dell’uomo” (The house of man). To explain the journal’s theme, Rogers offered a definition of “home.” “A house is no house if it is not warm in winter, cool in summer, peaceful in every season to receive in harmonious spaces the family,” Rogers wrote. “A house is no house if it does not include a corner to read poetry, an alcove, a bath, a kitchen. This is the house of man. And man is no man as long as he has no such house.”[16]

If a home requires a place to read poetry, a comfortable seat is essential. Accordingly, in the same issue, in “Pronto soccorso,” five architects offered suggestions for how to place and arrange old and new furniture. As the short text that introduced the five proposals described the situation: many families had furniture pieces that had been pulled from the rubble of bombings and removed for safekeeping. With the war over, they were being brought back to apartments in the city. After the salvage, the flight and the return, the editor asked, what criteria would lead from these fragments of lives to a place that would truly be a home?[17] In one proposal to serve a family of five, an architect uses floor plans and elevations to show how to accommodate the family’s needs with just a few purchases, making the most of the piece that can perform more than one function, such as a bed that doubles as a sofa and a task lamp that performs as a wall sconce when the shade is pointed upward.[18]

The act of reading, served by the Tripolina in the *ingresso* of the Zanuso apartment, is catered for not only by the chair but also by a number of details around it: the light switch behind the chair and a lamp above it, attached to the bookshelf; the books on the nearby shelves, which include a monograph on the painter Remo Brindisi and some novels, among them Charles Dickens’s *David*

Copperfield and Alberto Bevilacqua's *Questa specia d'amore*. There are multivolume reference books, too, such as a dictionary of literary works and personalities, published by Bompiani in 1959.

The photograph of the Tripolina chair and the bookcase was not focused on dramatically beautiful objects or on making the apartment look more appealing; rather it captured objects that were valued for the acts that they supported and the information they communicated about the domestic quality of the apartment as a whole and of that spot in particular. There is almost no movable furniture in photographs of the *ingresso*, but the group that appears in this space, the bookcase and chair, is a small sample of one of Zanuso's strategies of *arredamento* and a demonstration of how he integrated mass-produced objects into his designs.

From the *ingresso* in the 1962 plan, a door to the left led to a second vestibule whose two doors led to the kitchen and children's rooms. Straight ahead, through solid double doors that swung outward, was a square table and four chairs. A door to the right led to the *soggiorno*, the apartment's largest room and a natural destination for a visitor.

Plates

Alloggio in soffitta

Marco Zanuso, arch.

Le soffitte rappresentano la élite degli alloggi: l'ossatura conformista, abitudinaria, ufficiale, delle case esistenti dura dal primo fino all'ultimo piano, e cessa al piede della soffitta; in confronto alla soffitta, essa non è che una stratificazione preesistente, affondata: il livello naturale e libero è il tetto. La soffitta è la cellula aberrante e indispensabile alla vita delle vecchie case: installata sulla loro sommità, è in essa che lo spirito vecchio e il nuovo, personificati, convivono in inimitabile affiatamento.
Questo alloggio ne è un esempio.

2

Plate 1 "Alloggio in soffitta," *Domus* 244 (March 1950), 2. © Editoriale Domus S.p.A.

Mangani-Host

Eccetto il divano a tre elementi (tre poltrone Zanuso smontabili, in metallo, tela e compensato) la mensola-grammofono (sotto il trave libreria) e il camino (lastra in molera, finiture in lamiera di ottone), tutto l'arredamento del soggiorno è in mobili vecchi di casa: tavolo rotondo del 1870, poltroncine coloniali inglesi a listelli di legno, poltroncine di Chiavari 1889, poltrona a dondolo Thonet 1860; il tamburello del telefono è il porta-lavoro della nonna.
Dalla lunga finestra continua, si vede la sommità del Castello.

3

Plate 2 "Alloggio in soffitta," *Domus* 244 (March 1950), 3. © Editoriale Domus S.p.A.

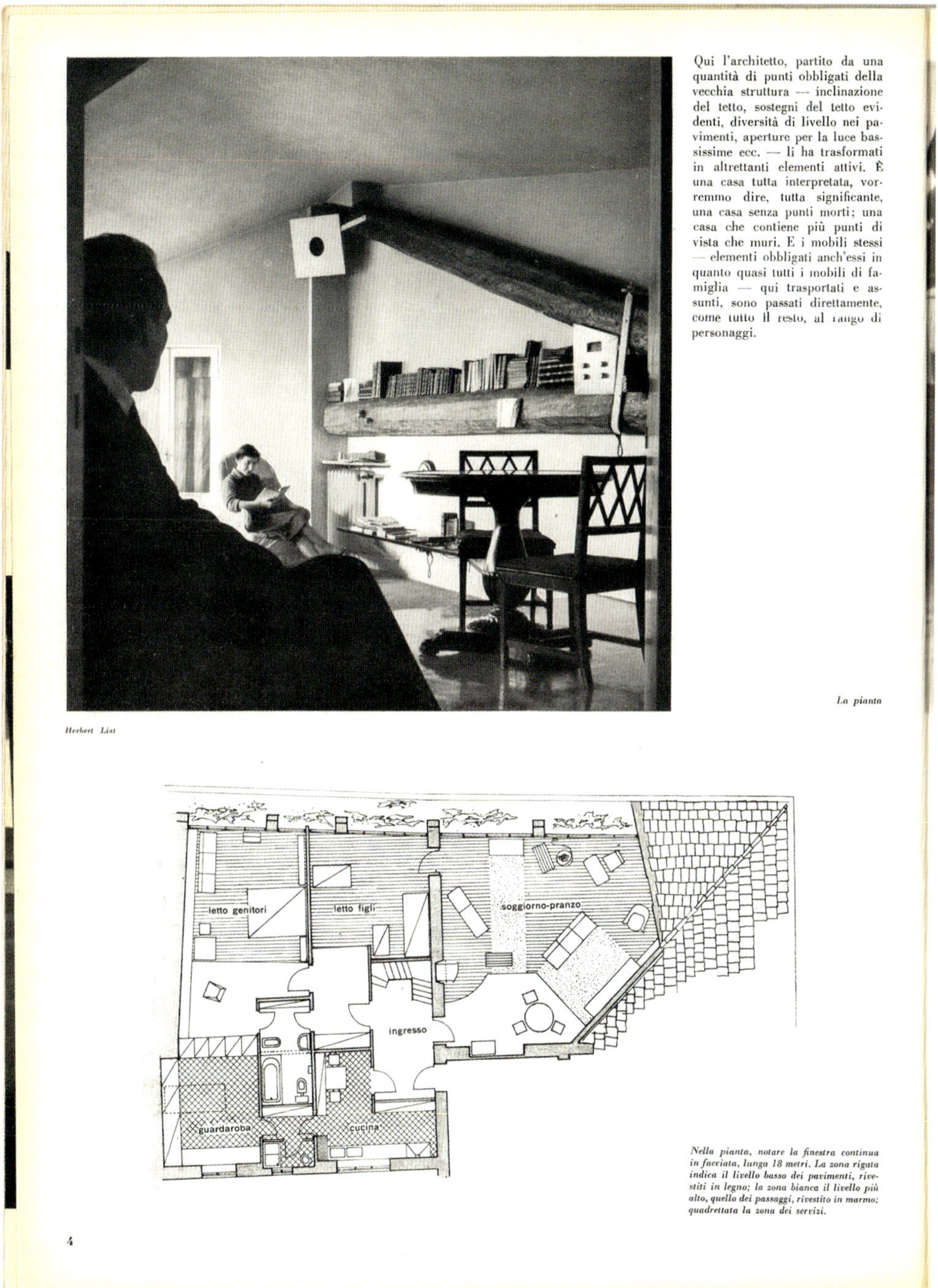

Qui l'architetto, partito da una quantità di punti obbligati della vecchia struttura — inclinazione del tetto, sostegni del tetto evidenti, diversità di livello nei pavimenti, aperture per la luce bassissime ecc. — li ha trasformati in altrettanti elementi attivi. È una casa tutta interpretata, vorremmo dire, tutta significante, una casa senza punti morti; una casa che contiene più punti di vista che muri. E i mobili stessi — elementi obbligati anch'essi in quanto quasi tutti i mobili di famiglia — qui trasportati e assunti, sono passati direttamente, come tutto il resto, al rango di personaggi.

Herbert List

La pianta

Nella pianta, notare la finestra continua in facciata, lunga 18 metri. La zona rigata indica il livello basso dei pavimenti, rivestiti in legno; la zona bianca il livello più alto, quello dei passaggi, rivestito in marmo; quadrettata la zona dei servizi.

4

Plate 3 "Alloggio in soffitta," *Domus* 244 (March 1950), 4. © Editoriale Domus S.p.A.

Mangani-Host.

Nel soggiorno e anche nella camera da letto, si osservi la differenza di livello del pavimento, dovuta a un dislivello preesistente fra la zona servizi e il soggiorno: il livello più alto segna il percorso di passaggio, pavimentato in mosaico di marmo, il livello più basso segna la zona dello stare, pavimentata in legno: il gradino fra i due livelli, specie nella stanza di soggiorno, è frequentemente utilizzato come sedile.

Nella camera da letto, un risalto del muro coperto da lunga e sottile lastra di marmo, dovuto al passaggio delle canne di scarico verso corte dell'acqua piovana, è utilizzato come mobile per libri e per toeletta. Il letto matrimoniale è un vecchio mobile di casa. La poltrona è di Zanuso.

5

Plate 4 "Alloggio in soffitta," *Domus* 244 (March 1950), 5. © Editoriale Domus S.p.A.

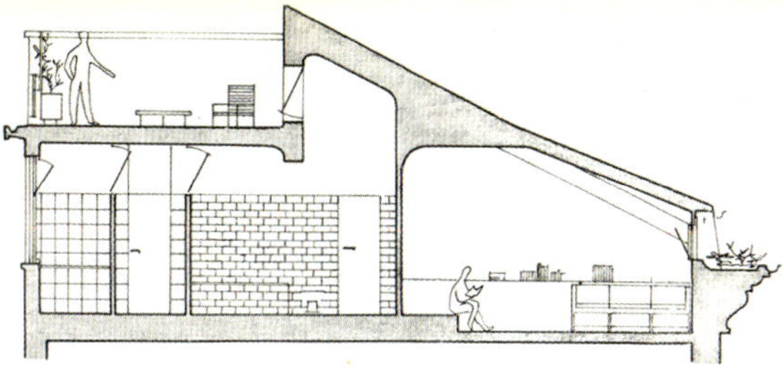

Sezione dell'alloggio: la zona di servizio è coperta con terrazza praticabile e nella differenza di quota tra questa e il colmo della falda del tetto sono ricavate due aperture: una porta nell'anticamera per accedere alla terrazza, una finestra nel bagno per la ventilazione e la luce. Queste aperture facilitano la aereazione di tutto l'alloggio, resa indispensabile dalla sua vicinanza al tetto. Sul tetto, una terrazza.

Un grande armadio passante per abiti, in lamiera verniciata, tra la camera matrimoniale, e la guardaroba; sopra, chiuso, visto dalla matrimoniale; a destra, aperto, visto dalla guardaroba. Sotto: nella stanza dei bambini.

6

Mangani-Host

Plate 5 "Alloggio in soffitta," *Domus* 244 (March 1950), 6. © Editoriale Domus S.p.A.

Plate 6 *Soggiorno*, overview looking toward Via Lanza, 1958. Photo Giorgio Casali © Fondo Giorgio Casali, IUAV Archivio Progetti, Venice.

Plate 7 *Soggiorno* corner seating, 1958. Photo Giorgio Casali © Fondo Giorgio Casali, IUAV Archivio Progetti, Venice.

Plate 8 View across *soggiorno* to *studio*, 1958. Photo Giorgio Casali © Fondo Giorgio Casali, IUAV Archivio Progetti, Venice.

Plate 9 *Soggiorno*, inner wall, 1958. Photo Giorgio Casali © Fondo Giorgio Casali, IUAV Archivio Progetti, Venice.

Plate 10 *Soggiorno* corner detail, 1958. Photo Giorgio Casali © Fondo Giorgio Casali, IUAV Archivio Progetti, Venice.

Plate 11 *Studio*, view from *soggiorno*, 1958. Photo Giorgio Casali © Fondo Giorgio Casali, IUAV Archivio Progetti, Venice.

Plate 12 *Bambine* suite, 1958. Photo Giorgio Casali © Fondo Giorgio Casali, IUAV Archivio Progetti, Venice.

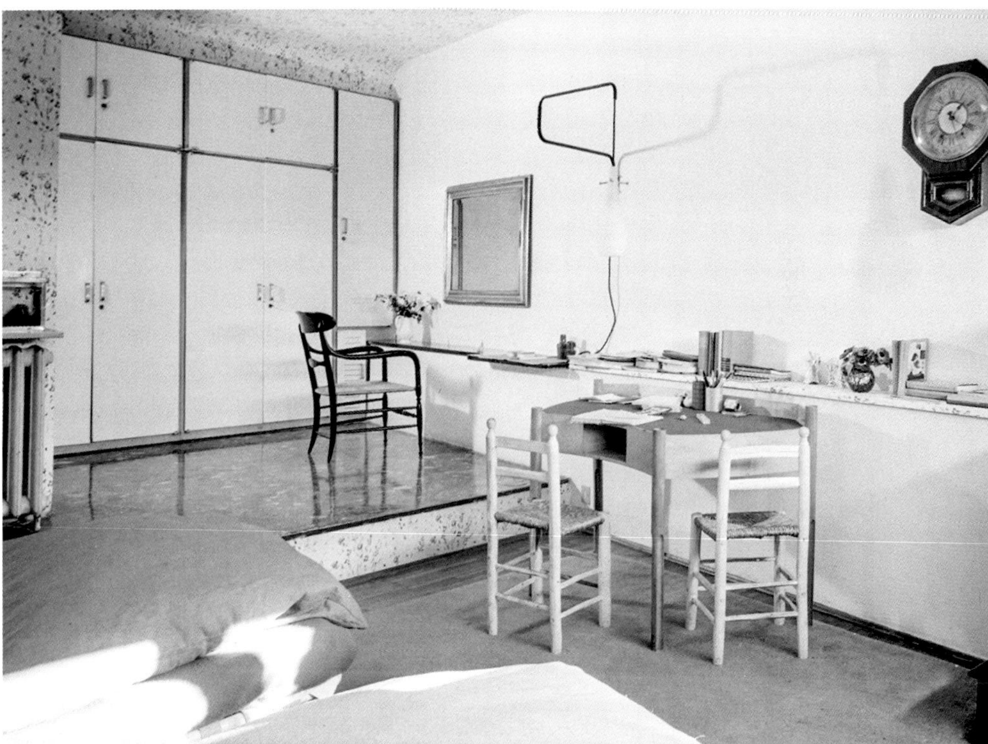

Plate 13 *Bambine* dressing area, 1958. Photo Giorgio Casali © Fondo Giorgio Casali, IUAV Archivio Progetti, Venice.

Plate 14 *Letto*, view from bedroom doorway, 1958. Photo Giorgio Casali © Fondo Giorgio Casali, IUAV Archivio Progetti, Venice.

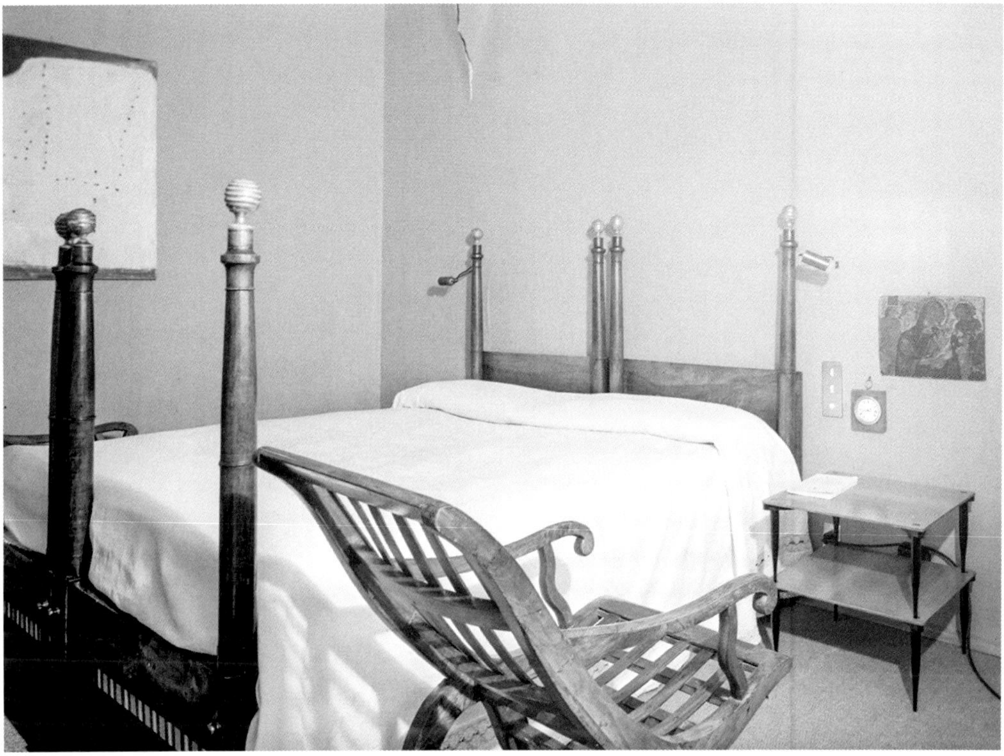

Plate 15 *Letto*, view toward corner, 1958. Lucio Fontana's *Concetto spaziale, I muri* (1957) is visible on far wall. Photo Giorgio Casali © Fondo Giorgio Casali, IUAV Archivio Progetti, Venice.

Plate 16 *Soggiorno*, view from bedroom, 1958. Photo Giorgio Casali © Fondo Giorgio Casali, IUAV Archivio Progetti, Venice.

Plate 17 *Ingresso*, 1962. Photo Ugo Mulas © Ugo Mulas Heirs. All rights reserved.

Plate 18 *Soggiorno*, inner wall, 1962. Photo Ugo Mulas © Ugo Mulas Heirs.
All rights reserved.

Plate 19 *Soggiorno*, view toward Piazza Castello, 1962. Prints by Renato Guttuso are displayed beneath the windows. Photo Ugo Mulas © Ugo Mulas Heirs. All rights reserved.

Plate 20 *Soggiorno* corner seating, 1962. Photo Ugo Mulas © Ugo Mulas Heirs.
All rights reserved.

Plate 21 *Studio*, view from *soggiorno*, 1962. Photo Ugo Mulas © Ugo Mulas Heirs.
All rights reserved.

Plate 22 *Studio*, view toward *soggiorno* doorway, 1962. Photo Ugo Mulas © Ugo Mulas Heirs. All rights reserved.

Plate 23 *Studio*, view toward Piazza Castello with table set for work. Photo Ugo Mulas
© Ugo Mulas Heirs. All rights reserved.

Plate 24 *Bambine* suite, 1962. Photo Ugo Mulas © Ugo Mulas Heirs. All rights reserved.

Plate 25 Children's bathroom, 1962. Photo Ugo Mulas © Ugo Mulas Heirs.
All rights reserved.

Plate 26 *Letto*, view from bedroom doorway, 1962. Photo Ugo Mulas © Ugo Mulas Heirs.
All rights reserved.

Plate 27 *Letto*, view toward bedroom doorway, 1962. Photo Ugo Mulas © Ugo Mulas Heirs.
All rights reserved.

Plate 28 *Ingresso*, 1967. *Estrosità nell'arredamento delle case e studi degli artisti* (Milan: Görlich, 1968), unnumbered pages. Scan provided by Fondren Library, Rice University.

Plate 29 *Studio*, view toward *soggiorno*, 1967. *Estrosità nell'arredamento delle case e studi degli artisti* (Milan: Görlich, 1968), unnumbered pages. Scan provided by Fondren Library, Rice University.

Plate 30 *Ragazze-soggiorno*, 1967. *Estrosità nell'arredamento delle case e studi degli artisti* (Milan: Görlich, 1968), unnumbered pages. Scan provided by Fondren Library, Rice University.

Plate 31 Window seat, *ragazze-soggiorno*, 1967. *Estrosità nell'arredamento delle case e studi degli artisti* (Milan: Görlich, 1968), unnumbered pages. Scan provided by Fondren Library, Rice University.

1 anticamera
2 soggiorno - pranzo
3 cucina
4 guardaroba
5 letto - bambine
6 letto

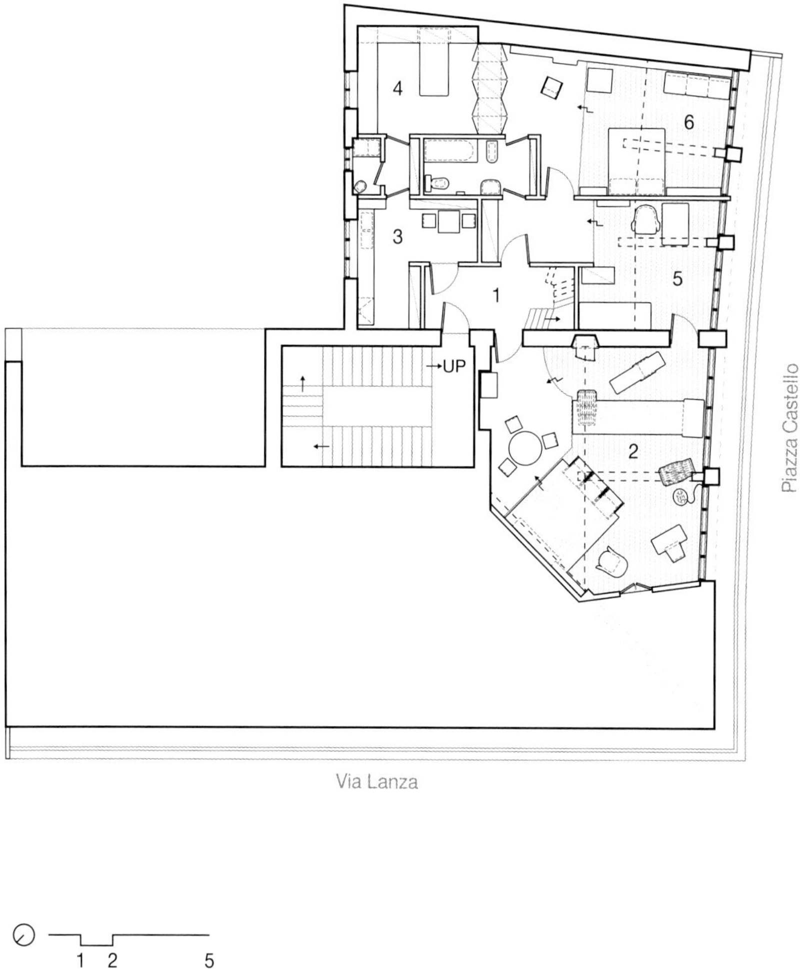

Plate 32 Floor plan of the Zanuso apartment in 1950. Redrawn from source: "Alloggio in soffitta," *Domus* 244 (March 1950), 4.

1 anticamera
2 studio
3 soggiorno - pranzo
4 cucina
5 guardaroba
6 soggiorno - bambine
7 letto - bambine
8 letto
9 letto - servizio
10 ripostiglio

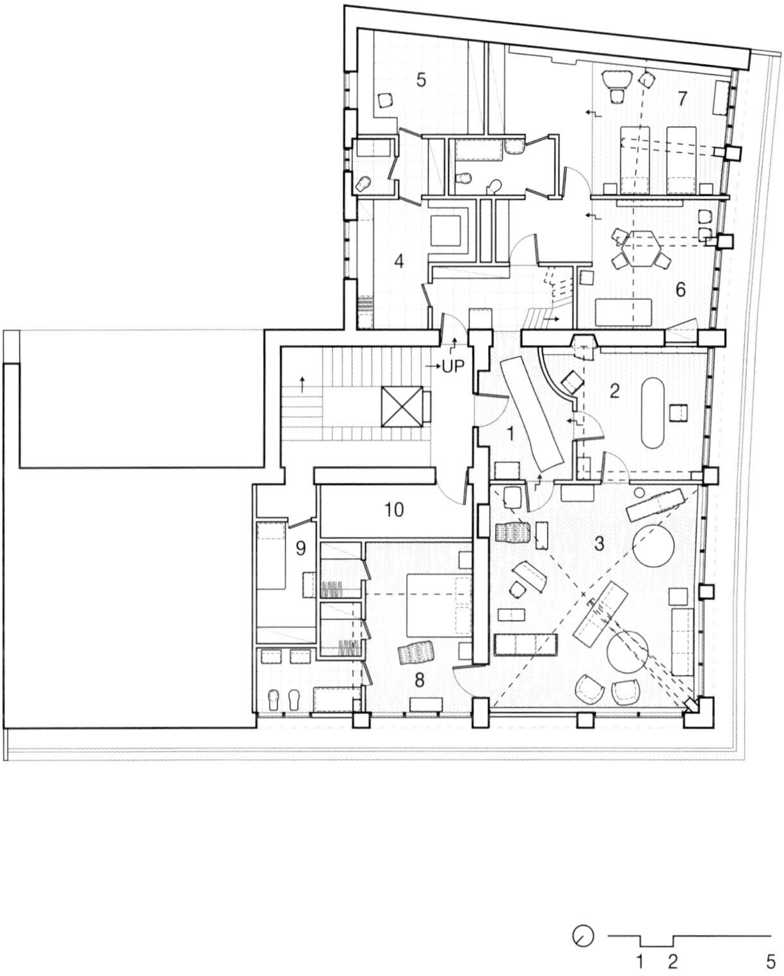

Plate 33 Floor plan of the Zanuso apartment in 1958. Redrawn from source: "Alloggio in soffitta: La casa di Marco Zanuso a Milano," *Domus* 341 (April 1958), 11.

1 ingresso
2 studio
3 soggiorno - pranzo
4 cucina
5 guardaroba
6 soggiorno - bambine
7 letto - bambine
8 letto
9 letto - servizio
10 ripostiglio

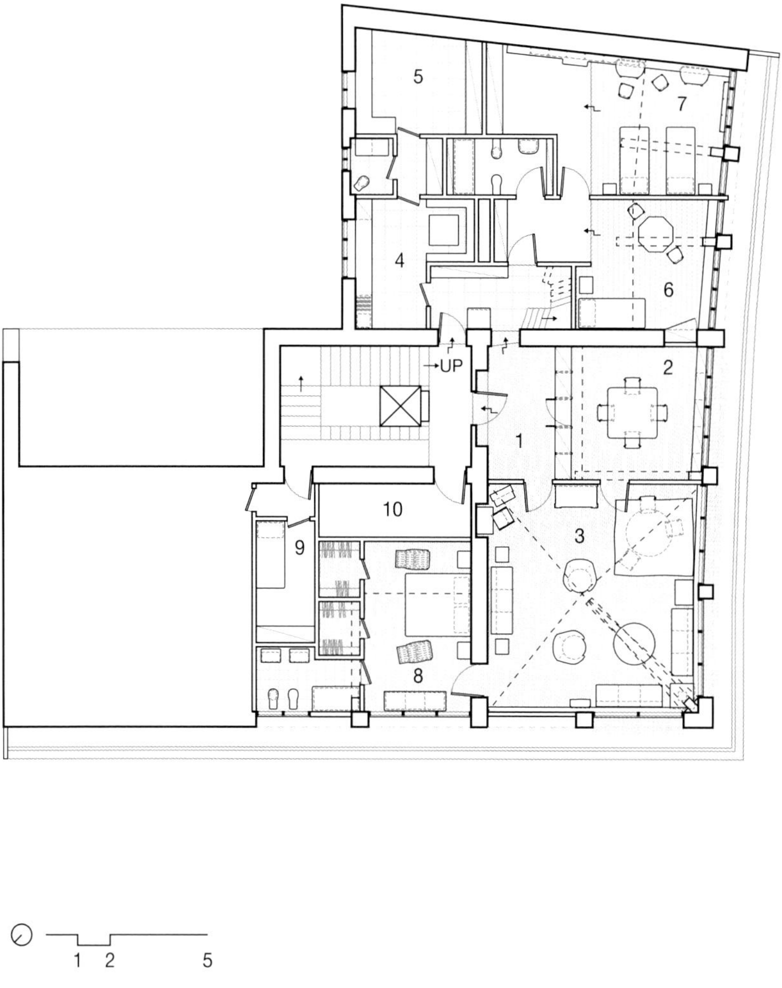

Plate 34 Floor plan of the Zanuso apartment in 1962. Redrawn from source: "Marco Zanuso: La nuova sistemazione del suo alloggio a Milano," *Abitare* 7 (1962), 12.

1 ingresso
2 studio
3 soggiorno - pranzo
4 cucina
5 guardaroba
6 soggiorno - bambine
7 letto - bambine
8 letto
9 letto - servizio
10 ragazze

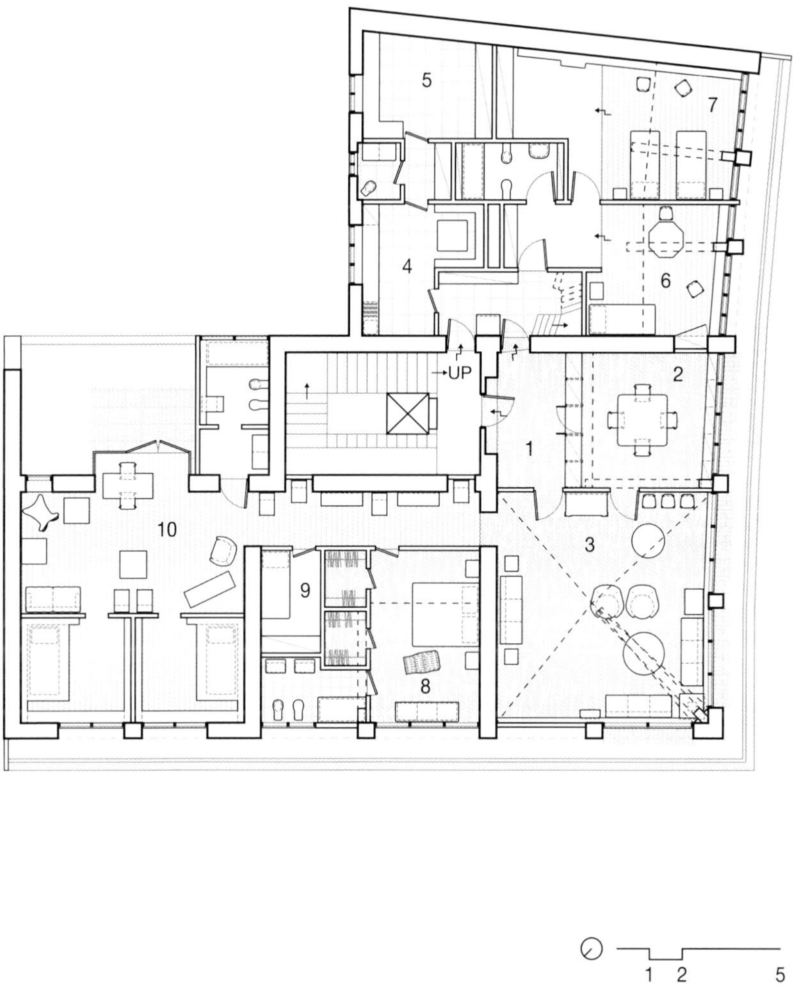

Plate 35 Floor plan of the Zanuso apartment in 1967. Redrawn from source: "Gli oggetti umani di Marco Zanuso," *Interni* (April 1967), unnumbered page.

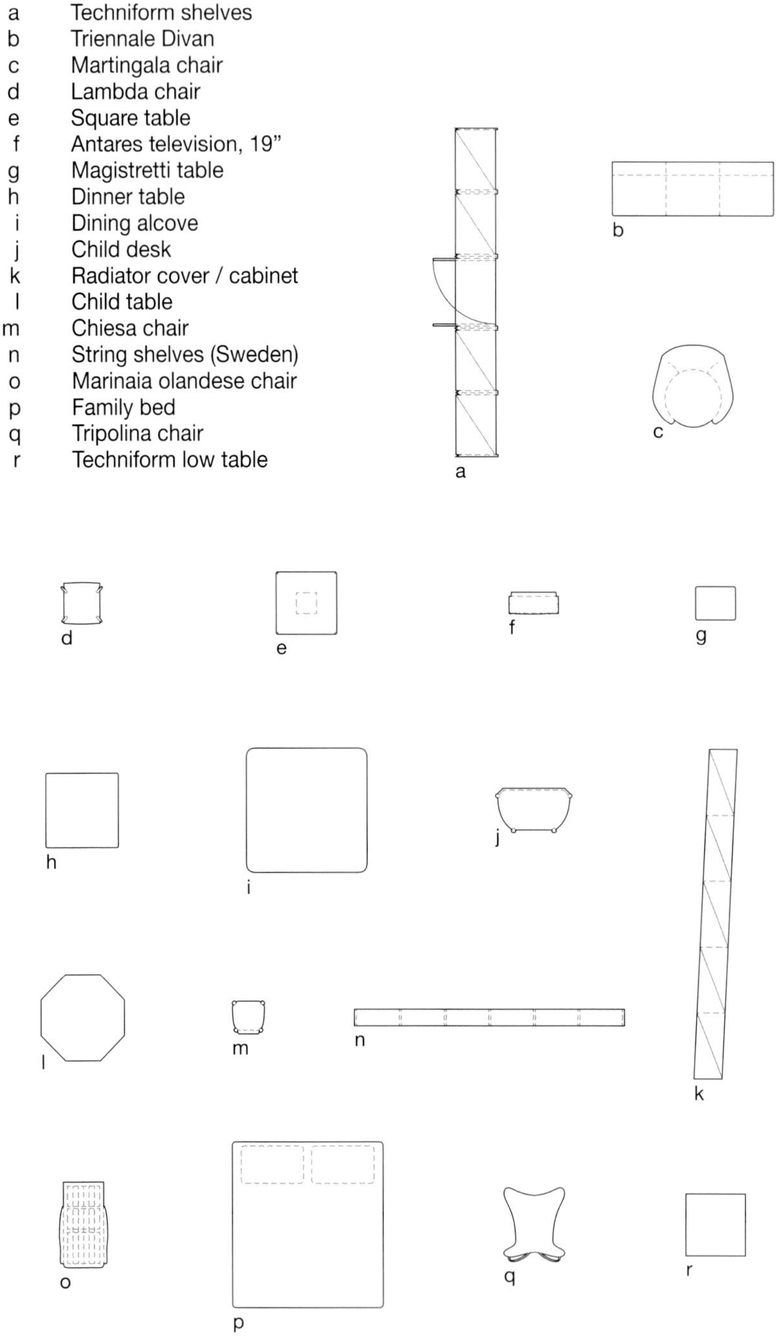

Plate 36 Key to furniture pieces in the room floor plans.

Soggiorno

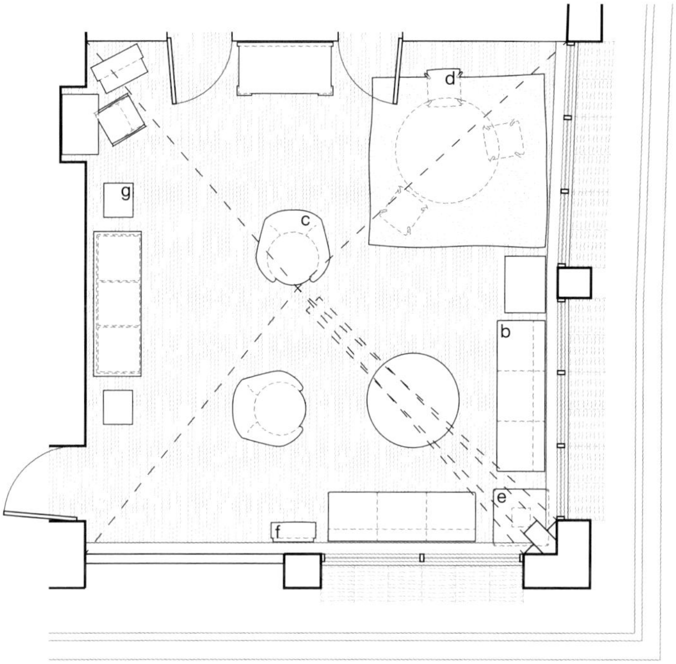

Figure 3.1 Plan of *soggiorno* in 1962.

In the Zanuso *soggiorno* in 1962, the functions of living room, dining room, and salon, traditionally each assigned to its own small room, were gathered in a single large space. As a guest you would likely come directly from the *ingresso*, leaving your coat in that vestibule and stepping into the *soggiorno* at its corner. Over to your left, near the windows that faced the Castello was a small table with chairs around it, the figure of the *pranzo*, a room for lunch indicated only by furniture. To your right, along the inner wall, were family heirlooms including an oak cabinet with decorative figurines and a pair of guitars (plate 18). This was a family with an active appreciation for sailing and sailboats; there were barometers and several artworks on the walls, including two prints by Renato Guttuso on the Piazza Castello wall as well as two large watercolor illustrations of birds on the inner wall. If you headed toward the sofas in the corner, crossing the room on a diagonal, along the way you could catch sight of a turret of the Castello Sforzesco and trees in the Parco Sempione through the band of windows beneath the sloping planes of the ceiling.

The *soggiorno* was the evident center of the home; activities such as casual dining and socializing took place there. In terms of its physical position, this room was the point in the L-shaped building plan where the two wings met. Because of its centrality, the *soggiorno* was a space whose characteristics set the tone of the project as a whole. The integration of furniture, furnishing plan, and architecture, which characterizes every room in the apartment, is evident in the alignment of furniture and architectural features that shows in the plan of this room, as illustrated in the floor plan in figure 3.1 (see also plate 36, the key to furniture pieces). How Zanuso created connections between diverse objects and spaces, crossing scales and types, is the subject of this chapter, which focuses on the living room in the Zanuso apartment and related projects.

The 1962 *soggiorno* had the benefit of the previous renovation, in which the roof timber pattern was modified to open up the attic all the way to the building's Via Lanza-side wall (compare plates 33, 34). The appropriation of this space entailed rebuilding an 8-foot-wide (2.5 m) portion of the roof surface along the edge where the roof met the parapet to create a dormer that ran the full extent of the enlarged room. The horizontal strip of windows that began on the Piazza Castello wing was extended along the parapet, turning the building's corner and continuing on the Via Lanza side. The creation of the dormer brought the height of the space up to the standard of the Regolamento (discussed in "Ambiente"), which specified a minimum of 7.5 feet (2.3 m) between floor and ceiling in inhabited attic spaces.[1] The lifting of the ceiling and removal of a wall exposed a large wood timber beam that would remain visible in the room, with a triangular opening between the beam and the surface of the lifted ceiling (compare figure 3.2).

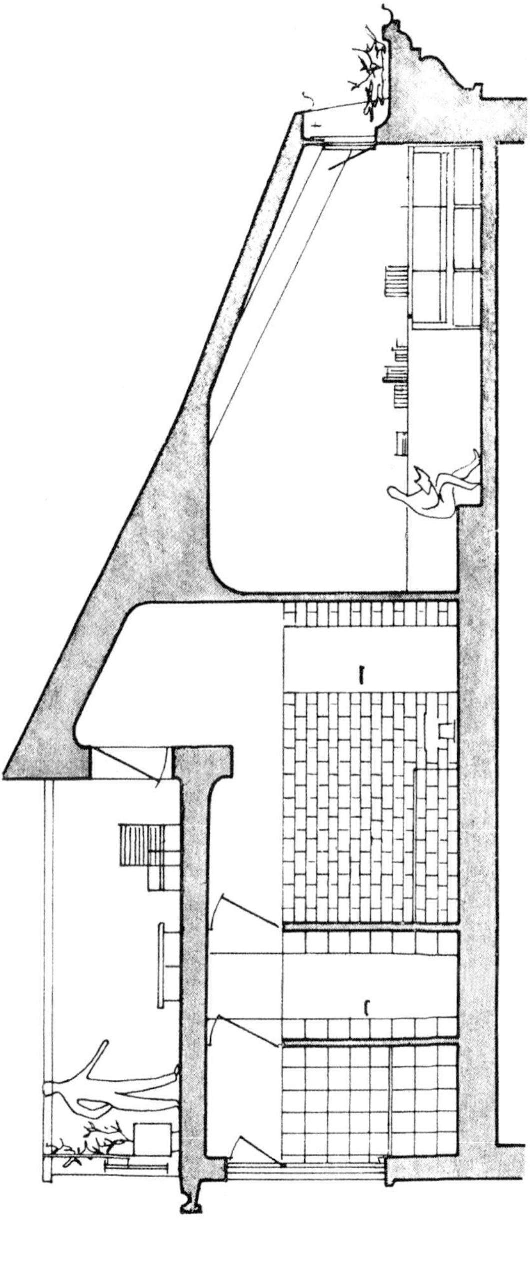

Figure 3.2 Section drawing of the Zanuso apartment. Page detail from the article "Alloggio in soffitta," *Domus* 244 (March 1950), 6.

The difference between the apartment in 1950 and in 1958 shows in the respective photographs. In 1950 the furniture looms large in the image; a photographer often had to position himself near the ground or capture the space with a piece of furniture or a person in the foreground or cut off at the edges (plate 2). The 1958 modifications to the attic, which allowed the *soggiorno* to shift into the corner of the building and increased its floor area, necessitated a change in the approach to furnishing. With the access to additional space, new possibilities of organizing the room were brought to what had initially been the small apartment of a young couple, laden with mostly inherited furniture pieces and barely accommodating their living functions while they tried to understand themselves as part of a new generation.

In the 1958 iteration, in which the *soggiorno* expanded over a floor area nearly double the initial size, the room became a three-dimensional composition of shapes and paths. In 1962, new furniture pieces were brought in and the furnishing of the room, while still relaxed, became more regimented into symmetrical and orthogonal relationships, with the furniture more closely associated with the room's walls. Some furniture pieces were substituted before the apartment was photographed one final time for publication in 1967, but the *soggiorno*'s design in the 1962 plan was essentially complete.

In 1950 you would have arrived in the apartment facing toward the bedroom and kitchen, then turned 180 degrees to enter the *soggiorno*. This room, labeled "soggiorno-pranzo" on the floor plan at that point, was pentagon-shaped (plate 32).[2] To reach it, you stepped through a doorway in the thick, possibly structural wall that was perpendicular to Piazza Castello. The wall on the right as you entered the *soggiorno* was at right angles to this thick wall, roughly parallel to the Piazza Castello facade; the walls straight ahead, toward Via Lanza, met in a shallow V. Along one of those walls were two exposed members of the roof truss that ran from the core to the building's corner; the other wall blocked the corner, but a glass door in it, behind the seated figure of Billa Zanuso, suggests that the corner was used for storage (plate 3, top).

At the threshold, you would have stood on a raised part of the floor, finished in marble and wedge-shaped in plan, in the nominal *pranzo* (dining area). The rest of the room was furnished with different kinds of seating, including two copies of a slung-back wooden chair called the *marinaia olandese* (Dutch mariner) near the telephone (plate 1). Other pieces included a three-seater version of a chair designed by Zanuso, made of canvas and wrought iron; a *chiavarina* chair, early 1900s, pulled up to a small table; a small slip-covered wooden chair, and a Thonet *chaise longue*. A chest, a side-board, and a wall-mounted cabinet were also present. In the thick wall near the entrance was a small fireplace, designed by Zanuso, which featured a brass hood (see "Studio").

When the apartment was published in *Domus* in 1950, the accompanying floor plan showed all of the furniture and even the rugs that lay on the hardwood floor (plate 3, bottom). One rect-angular carpet, an oriental pattern with a fringe, crossed from the edge of the *pranzo* platform to the Piazza Castello-side wall. Another was a solid-colored square that covered the floor between the three-seater and bookcase. Some of these pieces appear to be signifiers of conventional programs (such as reading or knitting) while others seem to respond to more general practical needs. A table and chairs call to mind a dining area and the chaise suggests repose; a cushion shown in one photograph, near the hearth, provides a comfortable seat near the fire.[3]

The short text that appeared alongside the photos and plans in *Domus*, called "Alloggio in soffitta" (Lodgings in an attic), described a few specific aspects of the plan that provide useful concepts through which to understand it. The first remark is that Zanuso has confronted "punti obbligati," immutable features of the attic structure itself, and transformed them into elements that contribute to the space of living. Those features include the attic's sloping ceiling, the visible roof-supporting structure, different levels of the floor, and the location of the few windows at a relatively low height. A second comment is that the apartment is "una casa tutto interpretata," a fully "interpreted" house.[4] One can see in the photos and plans that each object in the apartment seems to have a role or a meaning and that little space (and few things) in the room are left out of the scheme. The author notes that the antique furniture pieces are not pushed to the side but instead are admitted into the ensemble at the "rank" of personalities or protagonists.[5] The wooden Dutch mariner chairs and Thonet bentwood cane-seat chaise each have distinct, strong characteristics that merit this analogy. These last two pieces had been inherited from relatives, and while they maintained their customary functions, a lady's "work table" was given a new one: the small table with a drawer for keeping needlework in progress became a stand for the household telephone.

Looking at the plans with the accommodation of functions in mind, one counts several seating areas within the room, with more than one set of needs met by way of different groups of furniture each indicating a use or mood. There is the iron-and-canvas three-seater where one person could read in solitude or converse with others, as Marco Zanuso appears poised to do in one photo. The chair and chaise facing the fireplace offered another site for similar activities. These connections resonate with the author's remark that the apartment "contiene più punti di vista che muri" (contains more points of view than walls).[6]

Among the *punti obbligati*, circumstances that had to be dealt with, is the framework of exposed wooden timbers on one inner wall, which Zanuso turned into a bookshelf (plate 3, top). A console and speaker for a phonograph (inset in the ledge below) are also fitted into the web of the giant truss. On a second truss member, which crossed the room from the core toward Piazza Castello, an adjustable lamp resembling a desk lamp was attached to the underside with its shade turned upward to illuminate the room—a technique that had been shown in the design by Vittorio Gandolfi in "Pronto soccorso" in *Domus*, in 1946 (see "Ingresso"). With this collection of design interventions, Zanuso resisted the "obligatory" nature of this feature in the attic by turning it into a support for what he wanted to have in the space. To make a home in this apartment, the space, *punti obbligati* included, was "interpreted" by arranging and installing movable pieces, relative to a set of needs.

The idea that the Zanuso apartment, circa 1950, was "fully interpreted" suggests that there are many valid solutions to the problem of the home. If the objective was interpretation, the outcome of design research would not be an answer that was right or wrong but an iteration that fulfilled the type or failed to do so. Bearing in mind the situation in which these architects found themselves in 1945, anticipating the advent of mass production, the expertise of the architect would not consist of a mental library of ideal types; it would be a capacity to realize the type in changing circumstances, with new materials or unexpected constraints.

In any case, attention to function seems to have often been key to Zanuso's negotiation of a particular design project. The functional approach is a defining aspect of other published projects by Zanuso around 1950, and not only residential ones. When his office interior for Santoflex, a plastics company, was published in *Domus*, the author of the accompanying commentary described the project as a study in a logical approach to the issue according to exclusively modern methods and needs, not just an "abstract formal exercise on the theme of the office."[7]

All of the furniture in the Santoflex office was designed by Zanuso, and some of it was custom-built for that project. Zanuso attached a large bookshelf to the T-shaped desk, forming a "single, complete, transportable" piece. He used glass for the desk surface to multiply the number of documents that could be visible at a given moment. He used wood for both bookcase and desks. In effect, the Santoflex features architectural millwork that has been made movable—a strategy that makes sense in a context where interior space was often rental space. The bookshelf-desk resembles a small building, albeit one that was smaller than the human body, and it interacts with the mass-produced elements around it. The author notes that every seated worker has what they need close to hand, and that double-glazed windows allow isolation of different parts of the office. The architectural element and mass-produced pieces serve one another.

The problem of office design, like the problem of the home, was being interpreted. Such projects give the impression that numerous types were undergoing a process of research. But while the Santoflex office was validated by function-related reasons for the placement of objects in space and in relation to other objects, each furniture piece was also part of an abstract composition that was understood in strictly formal terms such as color, shape, and the juxtaposition of straight and curved lines, textures, and other visual qualities. In this respect, Zanuso's design for Santoflex made a distinctly aesthetic impression even though the components were mostly mass-produced pieces, including his Lady and Martingala chairs. The upholstery colors and patterns of furniture pieces, along with the visible stone and wood surfaces, contributed to the overall visual experience. One of the pieces that most evidently shapes the space, the Triennale Divan, would be a defining component of the Zanuso *soggiorno* of 1958 (figure 3.3).

When the 1958 project of the Zanuso apartment expanded the floor plan all the way to the Via Lanza side wall, the *soggiorno* absorbed the newly exposed building corner. The bookcase and speakers were gone, along with the truss they had sat on. A portion

Figure 3.3 Triennale Divan, Arflex, 1951. Fondo Marco Zanuso, Archivio del Moderno, Balerna.

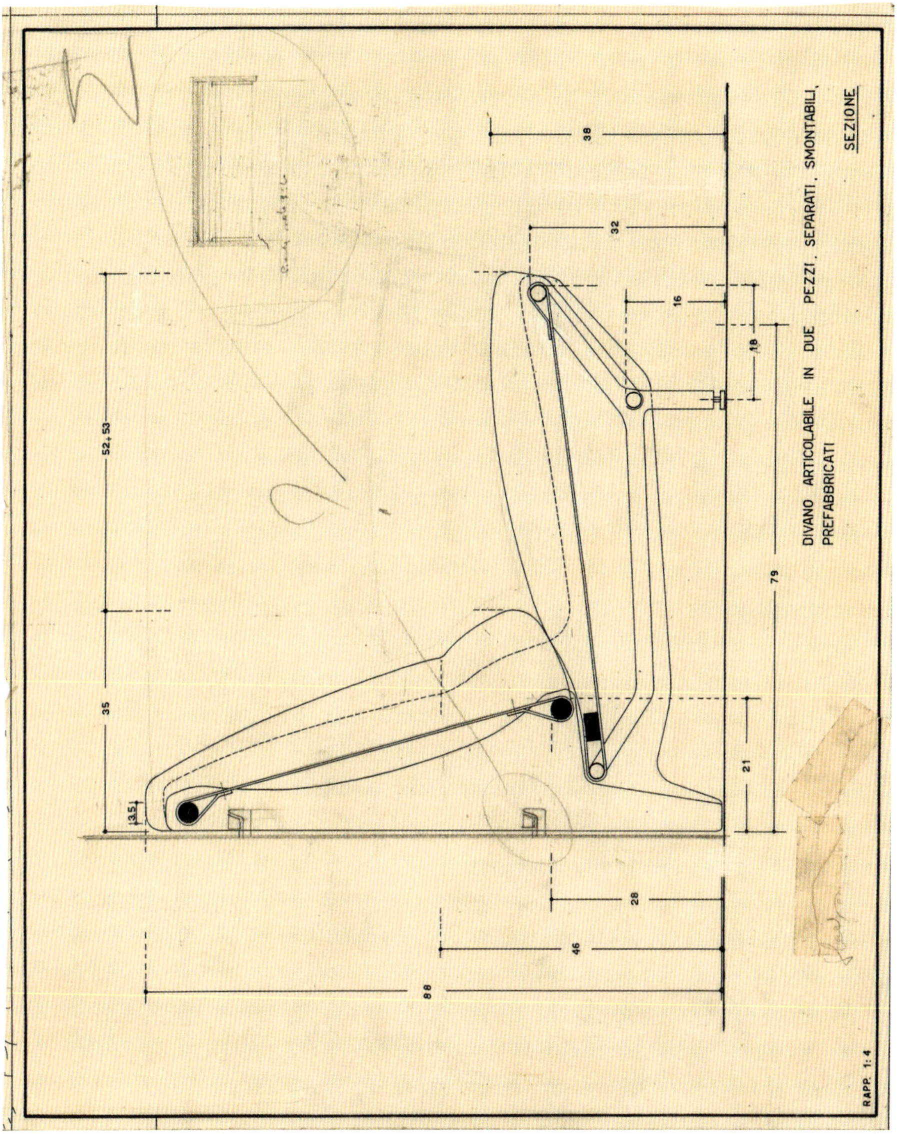

Figure 3.4 Section drawing of Triennale Divan. Fondo Marco Zanuso, Archivio del Moderno, Balerna.

of the smaller, previously occupied area was partitioned off to form the *studio*. The new *soggiorno* was approximately square and somewhat larger, about 23 feet (7 m) on a side, larger than the corresponding room in the Gadda apartment plan of 1893. As a visitor you would enter the room's eastern corner, stepping in from the *ingresso*. You would face a sofa and chairs in the opposite corner, on a diagonal path, with seating arranged to your left and right. The three-seater was placed near the door to the new master bedroom and sat on its own, facing west toward the *chiavarina* and a child's desk. One Dutch mariner chair sat near the entrance while the other was relocated to the bedroom. The *chaise longue* was near the Piazza Castello wall, a small table next to it. The floor was now all one level, covered in densely woven sisal fiber (plate 34 and figure 3.1).

The text that accompanied the plans and photos briefly summarized the changes that had come to the attic since 1950.[8] But the *soggiorno*, unoccupied this time (except for a cat in one photograph) is captured in more detail. In contrast to the early photographs in which furniture pieces loomed helpless and out of focus in the foreground, in this new set the photographer, Giorgio Casali, was able to shoot from some distance away, to capture the relationships among furniture pieces and between the furniture and the space. He could allow each piece to be seen as part of a taller, wider visual scene. Through his lens a composition of pieces emerges, a three-dimensional assemblage involving both old and new. The composition makes use of two-dimensional shapes that are part of each object and relates these to one another by means of the placement of the piece on the floor, relative to certain lines of movement or sight.

The Triennale Divan, designed by Zanuso for Arflex, was a central component of this room.[9] Zanuso's "divan" was made from a frame of welded tubular steel, strung with straps that would support its sculpted foam rubber cushions (figure 3.4). Two units of this sofa and one armchair were used to form a conversation area in the 1958 *soggiorno*, loosely grouped around a low round table in the room's far corner. The sofa's straight shape brought definition to the space, while its curved and beveled edges broke from the orthogonal geometry of the walls. These cushions were purposefully shaped to conform with the back of the sitter, taking advantage of the capacity of foam rubber to take any shape. The tapering forms of the backs and seats also minimized the bulk of the sofa, allowing views over and around the unit. These same features made it a subtle but striking presence in a room.

In contrast to a custom furniture piece that must respond to features of its context, a mass-produced furniture piece has to have an intrinsic integrity that allows it to mix with an indefinite variety of other pieces or to fit in any space. Zanuso and Arflex answered this demand by making the Triennale Divan available in a variety of upholstery fabrics—photos from around 1950 show solid colors and patterns—but it was also distinguished by its profile, determined by the edges of the frame and foam pieces. The curve in the sofa's backrest contrasts with the straight edges on other parts of the sofa itself as well as with rectilinear objects around it. By virtue of these outlines and the two-dimensional shapes it made when seen from various angles, the sofa could enter into visual relationships with other lines and shapes in the room. Together with this broader totality, it formed a configuration through which one moved en route from one part of the room to another.

The sofa had been exhibited at the Milan Triennale in 1951 in one of a series of rooms by various architects, in the *soggiorno* of the suite furnished by Zanuso, designated as "Alloggio no. 7," in a niche with an abstract painting with a faint, cloudlike figure on the wall above it (figure 3.5). The sofa, with its shaped foam rubber back and wedge-like, slightly back-tilted seat, could also be viewed as part of an assembly along with the table and chairs in other parts of the room. In Alloggio no. 7 the sofa was bracketed off from the rest of the room by its placement in the niche, where it was seen from the front with its horizontal lines most evident. By contrast, the placement of the sofa in Zanuso's apartment in 1958 put it in more direct juxtaposition with other furniture pieces and against the backdrop of walls, doors, and windows. One might say that the central sofa, which is prominent from every vantage point, contributes to the unity of the space as a coherent design.

In the photographs of the *soggiorno* that were published in 1958, Giorgio Casali responded to this aspect of the sofa. The sofa at the center of the room appears in almost all of his photographs of the room as an anchor of his compositions. In one photograph, looking toward Via Lanza from the threshold of the *studio*, the sofa is fully visible at the center in an almost isometric view with its left-back corner toward the viewer, its long back edge and short side edge pointing beyond. The view of the side reveals the bevel at the lip of the sofa's seat (plate 6). Another view, looking over the

Figure 3.5 Installation of Triennale Divan and other furniture pieces designed by Zanuso in Alloggio no. 7 at the ninth Milan Triennale, 1951. TRN.IX.06.0305, photo Aragozzini. © Triennale Milano.

sofa's back edge, shows how it was placed at an angle to the other sofa, whose back is against the Piazza Castello-side wall, and to the single Martingala chair that is placed near the Via Lanza wall. The side of the sofa seat points toward the corner, where the beam and walls converge (plate 7).

In a third view, looking over the low round table toward the open *studio* door, the sofa emerges from the lower left on a diagonal line that leads the eye into the center of the room (plate 8). The back of the sofa overlaps with the rectangular shape of the doorway. The visible floor winds around the sofa's right edges like a path leading into the room. In a photograph looking toward the internal wall, the curve of the sofa's back echoes the curved back of the Thonet chaise, a blanket draped over its back. The chaise, momentarily occupied as the photo was taken, sits in front of a niche that is put in service as a vitrine for the barometer that hangs there, centered (plate 9). Standing in different parts of the *soggiorno*, on its thresholds and against its walls, Casali was able to capture views not only of furniture but also of relationships between furniture pieces; not only of spaces but of portions of space that were shaped by interaction with the edges of furniture pieces.

At the level of overall organization, the *soggiorno* as published in 1962 reflects a few important adjustments. The two zones along the Piazza Castello side of the room remained roughly the same: a small table and chairs on the *studio* side and the seating group in the Piazza Castello / Via Lanza corner (plate 34). The plan does not indicate the new position of the telephone and its round table, which had been moved from its position on the Piazza Castello wall. In that spot instead is a single square T8 table, with wooden top and legs, designed by Vico Magistretti and produced by Azucena beginning in the early 1950s (plate 19). On the *studio*-side wall, an antique cabinet appears to have been displaced to a corner and a different cabinet put in its place between the *studio* and *ingresso* doors. Along the inner wall, groups that appear in the 1958 plan, including the Dutch mariner chairs, *chiavarina* and small desk, have been removed. The antique three-seater that had been near the master bedroom door has been replaced with a third Triennale Divan, pushed against the inner wall between the niche near the *ingresso* end, where a chair was pulled up to a small desk, and the master bedroom door (plate 18).

In the photographs of the 1962 *soggiorno*, taken by Ugo Mulas, the far corner rather than the center of the room has become the focal point. The sofa along the Piazza Castello wall remains where it was, while another sofa upholstered in a dark color sits with its back pushed against the Via Lanza wall. In the center of the square implied by these two is a low, round coffee table; across the table from each sofa is a Martingala chair. In this arrangement, roughly a square with its sides formed by two sofas and two lightweight *poltrone*, the rounded Martingalas allowed for easy movement to and from the sofas. A hanging lamp remained in place above the low round table. In the corner, beneath the beam and between the sofas, is a second low table, a Square, produced by Arflex (plate 20). As seen in the furniture plan, the three sofas in 1962 give a striking impression of a room governed more strongly by the orthogonal, for they are pushed against the walls of the roughly square room. The room has remained the same size as in 1958, but the plan appears more spacious due to the reduction in the number of furniture pieces and to their new organization.

If the 1950 project had the quality of being "interpreted," as the reviewer put it, the 1958 *soggiorno* suggested an approach that was more relaxed, as if luxuriating in the additional space that the apartment's enlargement had provided. The 1962 project retains some of these qualities; at the same time, it shows a tendency toward the adjustment of furniture positions into more formal patterns, with an emphasis on orthogonal relationships. The impact of furnishing strategy in Zanuso's *soggiorno* is not only a matter of the furniture plan and shape of walls; the furniture pieces themselves bring with them certain meanings and connotations. An object can, by means of its value as a version of a type, "stand for" a new or updated way of life, or for adaptation more broadly. The object can become a symbol of its own difference. Design as a cultural activity refers to the potential undoing and remaking of habit, and the narrative about such change. A cultural dimension of design lies in the capacity of the object to both facilitate and stand for that difference or change.

The Martingala chairs, which figured prominently in Zanuso's *soggiorno* in 1962, exemplify the various levels on which design can operate. Already present in the 1958 plan, one in the study and one in the *soggiorno*, both chairs had moved in 1962 to the *soggiorno* corner. This chair was made as a variation on the same tube steel and textile strap construction that was used in the Triennale Divan (figure 3.6). It was ostensibly a *poltrona*, hence a new version of an existing type, but it was different in meaningful ways from the classic club chair. Its differences could be interpreted relative to the moment when it was produced: it was aimed at a generation that was entering their mature years in the mid-1950s but had come of age during reconstruction, after World War II, seeking to distinguish itself from its predecessor. The chair's material attributes signaled its belonging to an age when the use of foam rubber and bent steel to make furniture was increasingly common. Its design also encouraged microadjustments in the manner of using an armchair, specifically in *who* used them. It brought all of these attributes into the spaces where it was placed. It is thus particularly evocative in the Zanuso apartment, where its juxtaposition with older furniture pieces and its placement in the furniture plan are suggestive both of a general design process and an attitude toward the social life of the home.

The resemblance between Martingala and the small slipcovered chair in the 1950 photographs (plate 3, top) is one of several indications of a design process that, far from viewing the heirlooms as obstacles to a contemporary lifestyle, took them as points of departure for new designs. The slipcovered chair offered a soft surface, while the edge of its back is a sinuous curve from the seat over the armrest and back and down the other side. The same chair is visible in a view of the children's suite (plate 5, bottom left).

The older chair can be understood as a point of departure for the interpretation of the chair type by way of a departure from the wood frame and cloth cover, putting a bent tubular steel chassis, fabric straps, and sculpted foam rubber cushions in their place. The Martingala responded to the *poltrona* type as well, for it is slightly wider, deeper, and more slung-back than the slipcovered chair. In place of a slipcover there is something more like conventional upholstery, but the fabric surface is designed to be removed and cleaned or changed, and this is expressed in a buttoned strap at the back.

Guido Canella's reading of the *soggiorno*, in a 1962 profile of Zanuso, picked up on the intimacy of the corner. Zanuso's "inviting" living room, he wrote, is a place "where a myriad of angled sofas in the shadows permit minute and intricate conversations." Such a design might still perpetuate certain "vices" of society, Canella thought, for it promotes upholstered chairs as emblems of prestige.[10] But Canella does not dwell on the ways in which the Martingala was a departure from norms of the *poltrona*. The word *poltrona* refers to a spacious armchair with high back and curved sides. This was understood to be a chair that everyone needed regardless of class. In the words of one writer, reflecting on the type in 1959, a classic *poltrona* enveloped the sitter in soft, dark leather. Modern exemplars such as Saarinen's Womb chair and Eames's lounge chair and ottoman were reinterpretations of a classic wingback armchair that might be found in an American, English, or German living room.[11]

Lady, one of Zanuso's first chairs, produced by Arflex beginning in the late 1940s, had offered the consumer the chance to purchase a designer-made chair. For the sake of serial production, Zanuso's design made deliberate, strategic use of specific materials that were unusual in Italian furniture manufacturing up to that time. Martingala, like Lady, was made of foam rubber cushions, fabric strips, and a steel chassis (figures 3.6, 3.7). In terms of dimensions and lineaments, Lady was faithful to the classic wingback with its wide seat and high back, modeled on the tall leather armchairs that were often found in smoking rooms and hotel lobbies. Martingala, too, was considered to be a *poltrona*, but its details brought a new gender reference to the familiar type. Its seat was rounder and smaller. The upholstery strap on its back resembled the belt of a coat, which resonates with the chair's low seat height that made it a convenient seat for women wearing skirts.[12]

Orthogonal and diagonal relationships organized the Zanuso *soggiorno* spatially in 1962. The approach is clearest in the plan, in which the majority of furniture pieces are drawn at right angles to one another, but the upper parts of the space were engaged as well, along with walls, floors, and furniture. Roof truss members remained exposed and visible in the children's bedroom and *studio*, but in those rooms they were parallel to nearby partition walls. By contrast, the *soggiorno* beam was a prominent feature of that room from the beginning.

A truss member that had crossed the 1950 *soggiorno* was part of the *studio* in 1958, while the truss that had held the phonograph and served as a bookcase in 1950 had been removed by that point. Meanwhile, the expansion of the space to the Via Lanza side had uncovered a previously concealed truss member. This beam passed through the upper part of the space toward the corner, descending toward the corner on the diagonal in plan (plate 33 and figure 3.1). The photographs show that this timber beam was part of the field of relationships between the movable pieces and contributes to the impression of a composition in three dimensions.

In one of Casali's photos of the corner, the beam crosses from the upper right toward the middle left edge of the image (plate 10). A second diagonal line is contributed by the lower edge of the sofa that sits by the wall; the receding lines of its seat give the photograph an effect of depth. There is even a shaft of sunlight falling on the Via Lanza-side wall to form a convenient second diagonal below the beam, nearly symmetrical with the truss member across the line indicated by the horizontal window ledge. In short, the beam, lamp, sofas, and paintings appear to occupy a single implied *xyz* continuum whose "zero" point is the corner of the floor. One can easily overlook the fact that the Piazza Castello and Via Lanza walls of the building were not actually at right angles to one another because the Piazza Castello facade was curved; the sofas at right angles and the beam above them project the appearance of regularity.

The ceiling is another fixed element that is part of the visual composition. The sloped panes that meet above the beam give the room a tent-like character. The relationships between these elements are reinforced by another intervention to the fixed surfaces as well. A painted border ran around the edges of the ceiling, consisting of a wide band painted warm gray and a narrower orange band next to it, offset a few inches toward the center.

In a room whose ceiling is not flat and whose walls do not quite form a square, the painted border, which passes above the beam without interruption, contributes to an overall sense of organization; it encourages the eye to keep moving around the space and helps to integrate the low corner and exposed beam with the rest of the room. Zanuso used a similar painting technique to emphasize the contour of ceilings in the Hotel Punta San Martino at Arenzano, which he designed with Ignazio Gardella in the early 1960s (figure 3.8).

In another project, a small flat designed by Zanuso for Roberto Olivetti in 1955 on Via Jacini, a side street not far from Piazza Castello, Zanuso made another interpretation of the home with analogous attention to all surfaces—walls, floor, and ceiling. As the surfaces of ceiling and floor visibly extend throughout the apartment, they are presented both as horizontal planes and, when seen in perspective, as backdrops for the furniture pieces, which include a few of the iconic *chiavarina* chairs from Liguria (figure 3.9). The cladding of the ceiling in tongue-and-groove wooden paneling emphasizes the contours of that plane, which is horizontal near

Figure 3.6 Martingala, cover removed to show frame and strap structure. Fondo Marco Zanuso, Archivio del Moderno, Balerna.

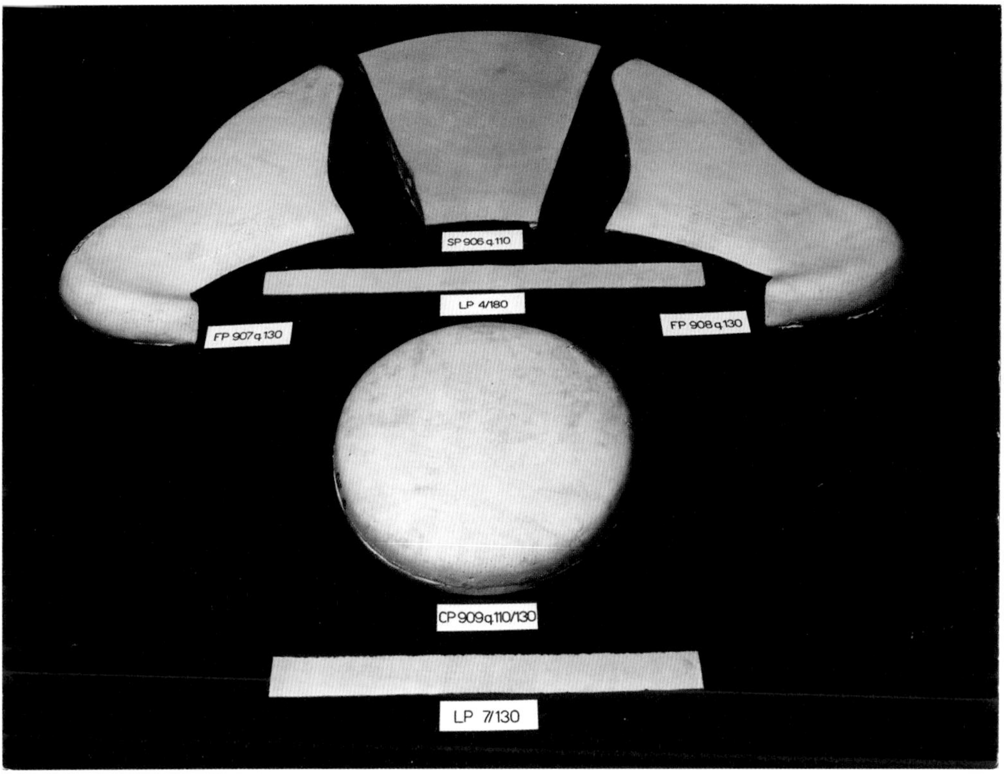

Figure 3.7 Foam pieces from Martingala in labeled photograph, undated. Fondo Marco Zanuso, Archivio del Moderno, Balerna.

Figure 3.8 Pavilion at Hotel Punta San Martino, Arenzano. © Fondo Giorgio Casali, IUAV Archivio Progetti, Venice.

Figure 3.9 Corridor of apartment on Via Jacini, Milan, 1955. © Fondo Giorgio Casali, IUAV Archivio Progetti, Venice.

the center of the building and breaks into a slope toward the balcony. An octagonal skylight near the center of the apartment, which provides a light source and an orienting feature within the suite, is an object of intermediate scale that creates a continuum between the scale of the ceiling and that of the chairs and other furniture. The edges of the ceiling around the oculus and against the white-painted walls generate a variable line drawing in two and three dimensions.

Photographs of the *soggiorno* in 1950 show a fireplace; after the 1958 renovation shifted the boundaries of the living room, the fireplace was in a small room with a character of leisure, similar to the *soggiorno*: the newly created *studio*.

Studio

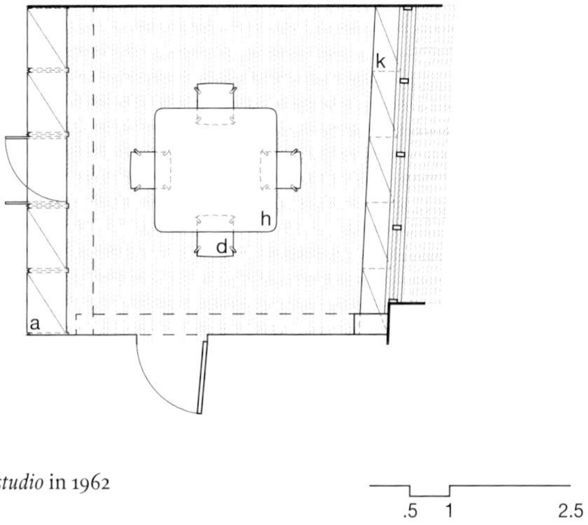

Figure 4.1 Plan of *studio* in 1962

You could see into the room called *studio* (study) from the entrance vestibule, whose double doors led to it through a partition made of bookshelves; but as a guest for lunch, you would likely look at it carefully only once settled in the corner of the *soggiorno*, sipping an aperitivo. From there, an approach to the *studio* in 1962 would reveal a table and chairs (plate 21). Stepping through the doorway toward the table, you would pass under an exposed wooden timber at the threshold, visible only from the other side of the table. With your back to the *soggiorno*, you would face a depiction of St. John the Baptist, depicted in a large framed seventeenth-century painting with his index finger raised while he turned toward you an inviting gaze. To the left of St. John was a sculptural work by Agenore Fabbri, made of plywood. Fabbri's work, in which broken shards of the composite layers seemed to explode from the center of the panel, the whole stained dark blue and purple, would suggest the theme of violence even before you learned the work's title, *Guerra*.

On the wall to the left were bookshelves facing this room, their backs to the bookshelves in the *ingresso*, and beneath the flat part of the sloping ceiling were panes of glass that let light pass through this room into the other. A patter of feet might announce the children's arrival as you sat and talked, but the sound would be muted. Perhaps you would turn toward the sun that shone through the windows. You might notice built-in casework with cabinets and square grilles, beneath the horizontal strip of window that looked out on the Sforza castle; you might marvel at how the sun and shadows on the ceiling emphasized the texture of the jute wallpaper that covered the *soggiorno* ceiling, or at the tall oil lamp by the window that someone had strung with electric wires at your host's request, whose faceted glass shaft caught the light.

Invited to sit, you would pull out your chair and notice the coolness of metal under your fingers and the friction of its rubber feet on the sisal-covered floor. Your hands might rest on the table and sense the warmth and texture of the wooden surface or the radius of the table edge. If conversation waned for a moment as your vivacious hosts caught their breaths, you could admire the place settings with crystal drinkware and blue-and-white Wedgwood plates with a pagoda pattern or, on another day, plates from Sicily where the Zanusos had relatives. If you found yourself facing the *soggiorno* your eye might wander over the objects on the wall, including a barometer and several prints depicting a board game called the *gioco dell'oca*, "game of the goose."

The *studio* in 1962 had very simple furnishings: just the table, centered in the room with four chairs around it, illuminated by a pendant light fixture, as shown in the plan in figure 4.1 (see plate 36 for a key to the furniture pieces). In his photograph of the room seen from the *soggiorno*, Mulas allowed a generous amount of blank wall to appear in the frame, giving the impression of a spaciousness that is remarkable in a room that was just 12 feet (3.6 m) wide (plate 21). This impression of compactness in furnishing and ample surrounding space is a salient effect of the interior planning in spaces designed by Zanuso around 1960, which included several projects on which he worked closely with Cini Boeri, who was responsible for residential projects in his office at the time and who would very soon establish an office of her own. In this chapter the *studio* illustrates how, in Zanuso's interiors, the impression of a lively efficiency is produced by a combination of the refinement and precision of furnishing, relative to function, and the resolution of walls in the floor plan into rooms of fairly regular geometric shapes. The principal furniture pieces in the room, the Dinner table and Lambda chair, lend themselves to the articulation of this space, especially through the characteristics that make them remarkable and autonomous design works and individuate them strongly from one another, concealing the underlying strategy of using them together.

Dinner, designed by Zanuso and produced by Arflex (1963), had wooden legs and a surface with a rounded edge. The corners of the tabletop were also rounded, which would have eased movement around the table; the tops of the legs, cross-braced by T-section steel members beneath the tabletop, were fitted into the corners and shaved flat to align with the chamfered table surface. Those legs are the defining feature of this table; they are splayed at the top, making the transition from a vertical support to a horizontal plane visible as a fluted sculptural form. This problem, how to handle the transition between a horizontal plane and its vertical support with a single piece, was one that preoccupied Zanuso at the time. He had first become interested in the transition from pillar to roof design in an architecture project, the factory for Olivetti at São Paulo, Brazil. With structural engineer Egone Cegnar, Zanuso had sought a design in which the transition was handled by a single piece. They opted for a different solution when their approach proved to be too cumbersome to construct.[1]

In the factory constructed in the mid-1960s in the Veneto for the television manufacturer Brionvega, Zanuso did achieve such a design: the production floor area was made from an array of column-roof elements, each resembling an inverted umbrella in section, with a square surface in plan that sloped to an integrated central downspout (figure 4.2).[2] The column-roof element appears as a counterpart to the leg of Dinner. The square grille in the Brionvega factory's curtain wall is another pattern that can be seen in Zanuso's designs at various scales, for instance in a radiator cover that may be observed on the Piazza Castello-side wall of the *studio* in a color photo of the room (plate 23).

The chair Lambda had originated as a study of the same problem, the joining of a pillar to a horizontal plane with the smallest number of pieces. First produced for the market by Gavina in 1964, Lambda had originated as a speculative research project

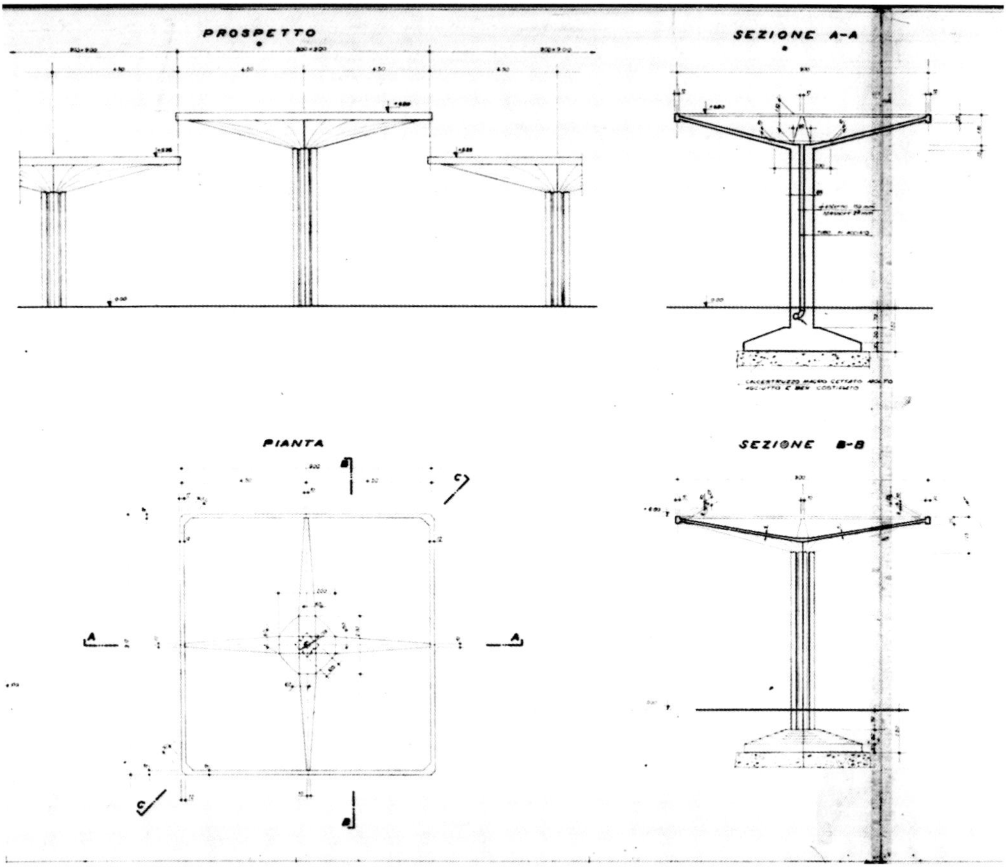

Figure 4.2 Detail of engineer Silvano Zorzi's drawing of a column-roof component (detail) for Zanuso's factory for Brionvega, Casella d'Asolo, 1964. Fondo Marco Zanuso, Archivio del Moderno, Balerna.

in the Zanuso office. Taking a recent commercial kitchen chair commission as a starting point, Zanuso and Richard Sapper, the designer who oversaw industrial design projects in the office, set out to design a chair made of metal, anticipating the availability of the material and techniques of fabrication in series, as in car bodies, and taking advantage of the stiffness and durability this material would bring to the chair's edges.[3] A close examination of the chair reveals several parts made of bent sheet metal, including a back, seat, and leg, connected by welding. There are also small saddle pieces with which two parts are joined, such as leg and seat. Subtle curves in the seat and the back, whose edges are stiffened by flanges, enable the chair to better support the sitter. In a process that spanned several years, through several rounds of prototyping and drawing they worked out a mutually compatible set of details, including legs with a U section that joined the seat in notches; a piece that reinforced the leg-to-seat transition; and another piece for the joint from seat to back, as well as the curved back component (figure 4.3). Sapper, in particular, sketched the shapes of pieces dozens of times by hand, integrating the results of prototypes that were fabricated in and near Milan (figure 4.4).[4] Some versions were tested not in steel but in vacuum-molded polystyrene, formed in wooden molds. Zanuso describes a process that ran through 40 prototypes by the time the design was offered on the market (figure 4.5).[5]

The putative influence of certain tropical plants on the design of the legs of Lambda places Zanuso and Sapper in a longer lineage of architects who made reference to the natural world in their architectural forms (figure 4.6). But Zanuso's work and his approach to the imitation of nature bear little resemblance to the revival of Milan's Liberty art nouveau style, which raised a controversy among Milanese architects in the late 1950s. In early writings referring to the natural world, the cell provided Zanuso with an important metaphor, as in his description of an ideal home in terms of a "nucleus" of a few rooms.[6] More often, his principal reference was to the inorganic world, not biology but chemistry. Among his interests referred to in a 1946 article were the structure of crystals, the rules of genetics, the many shapes of stones on beaches, and the periodic table.[7]

While Lambda made use of a lily shape, of equal interest is Zanuso's belief that a chair was, in effect, a kind of scientific problem, one small detail within a broadly scientific-realist world view.

Figure 4.3 Lambda production model, c. 1960. Photo Ugo Mulas © Ugo Mulas Heirs. All rights reserved.

Figure 4.4 Study sketches of Lambda chair details by Richard Sapper. Photo Oscar Savio. Archivio del Moderno, Fondo Marco Zanuso, Balerna.

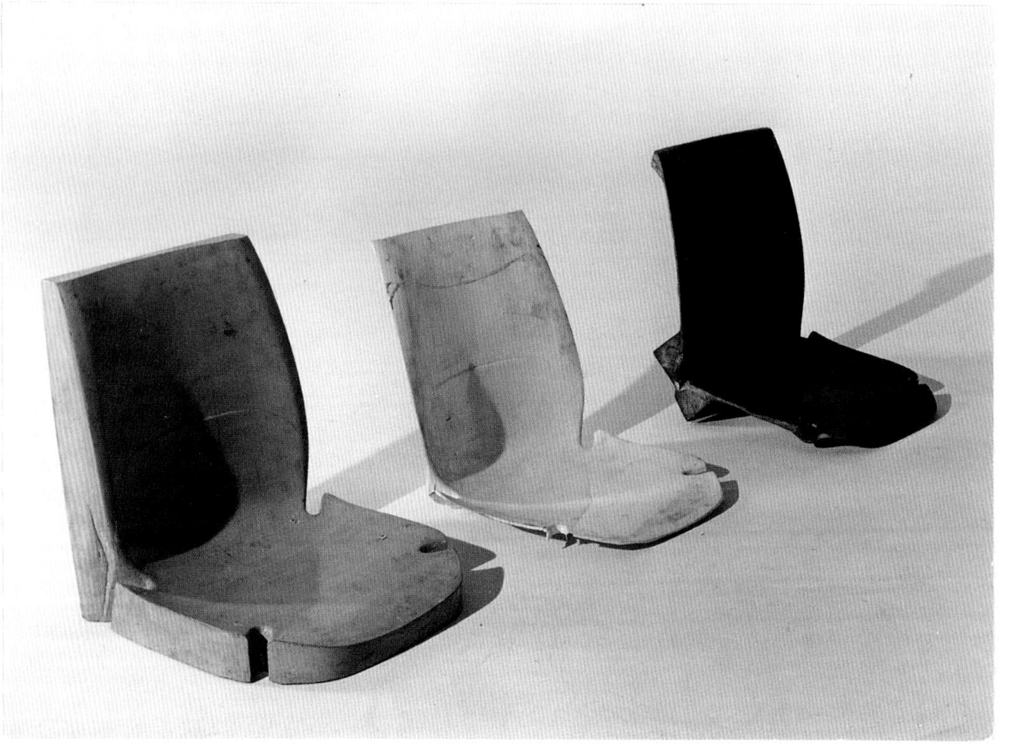

Figure 4.5 Lambda chair prototypes, c. 1959. Photo Aldo Ballo © Ballo+Ballo. All rights reserved. Archivio del Moderno, Fondo Marco Zanuso, Balerna.

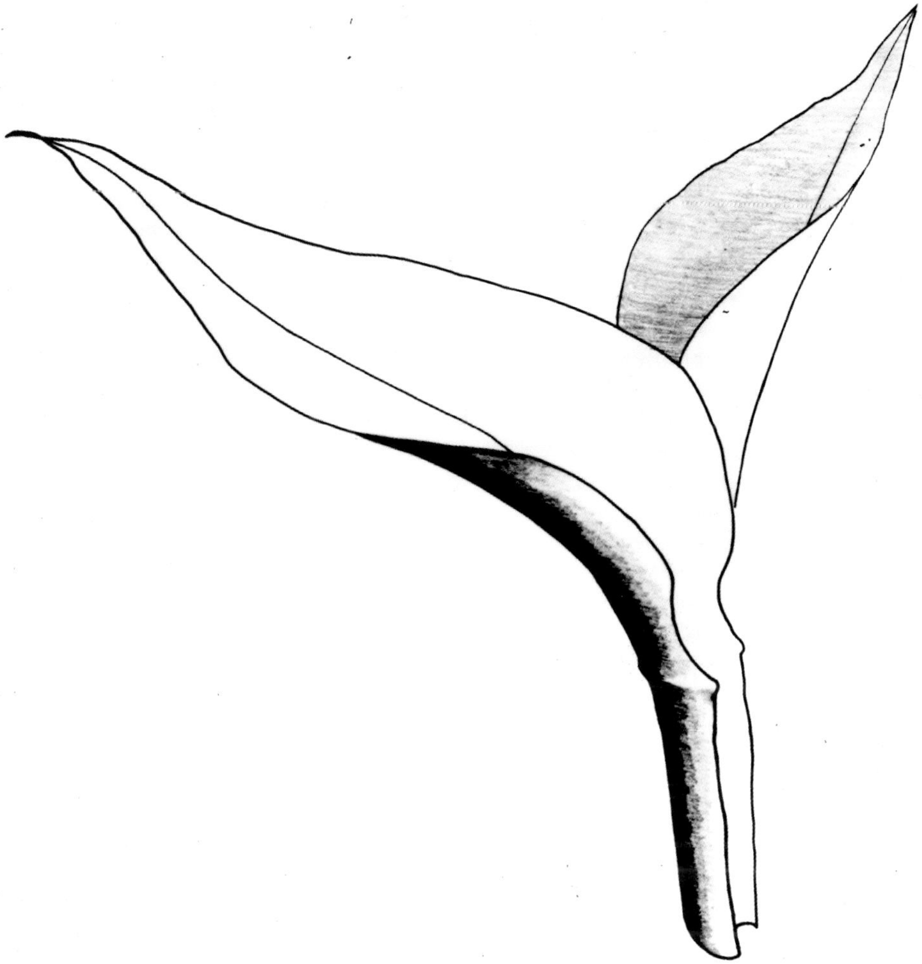

Figure 4.6 Ink drawing of calla lily. Fondo Marco Zanuso, Archivio del Moderno, Balerna.

He remarked in his essay on Lambda that "the laws of physics and mechanics are natural laws" and that "examples of the form we adopted are legion in the animal and vegetable kingdoms."[8] In his 1946 essay, Zanuso had framed design and architecture as windows of sorts onto the world of science. Seriality in an object was analogous to repetition in the biological world. The performance of materials was an expression of chemistry.[9]

It is implicit in this outlook that in objects like Lambda, the design is a mirror of truths about nature. In this sense, Lambda exemplifies Zanuso's focus on characterizing both a part of the world (the chair) and the world itself, i.e., on the creation of a living environment that is visibly of a piece with the extent of scientific knowledge. At the same time, Zanuso's was not an exclusively "scientific" project but one in which the approach to science or allusion to science coexisted with a specific cultural position in which the acts of living were material for reflection.

Zanuso's scientific-realist outlook translated into characteristics in the designs themselves that appealed to the purchaser and user of Lambda who might have similar interests. Lambda was sold in a variety of paint finishes, but it was also briefly produced in stainless steel (which proved too expensive to keep in production). A photograph by Carla De Benedetti of an apartment for a collector of ancient and modern art, published in *Domus*, shows a single Lambda placed like a statue by the door of a child's room (figure 4.7).[10] Around it are a number of objects with very different finishes, including wood-and-steel shelves and ceramic tile flooring with a twisting tape-form motif, both designed by the architects who designed this particular apartment, Franco Albini and Franca Helg. The walls are covered with fabric. A caption mentions that the Lambda and shelf units are both prototypes.[11] The gleaming steel with its linear brushed finish contrasts with the objects and finishes around it, but the dissonance was clearly seen as a positive. The photo of this room, with its mix of metal and wood, machine-made and handmade, useful object and artwork, shows how Lambda lent itself to juxtapositions of materials, time periods, genres.

In the Zanuso apartment, changes in the specification of furniture, with one dining chair replacing another, for instance, took place against the backdrop of a relatively unchanging set of functions. That these functions were constant across the apartment's lifetime is something that Zanuso observed as early as

Figure 4.7 Lambda chair prototype in apartment designed by Franco Albini and Franca Helg. *Domus* 421 (December 1964), 29. © Editoriale Domus, S.p.A. Photo Carla De Benedetti © Comune di Milano, CASVA, Archivio Carla De Benedetti.

1939. In “La casa,” an essay that he wrote while still a student, Zanuso argued that the functions of rooms in an apartment should not change. Only the manner of achieving the outcome should change over time.[12]

But the framework of function does provide a structure in which a specific model of object, such as a chair, can gain validity from its capacity to fill a particular role. The dining chair function had the same requirements in 1967 as in 1950, even as the specified dining chair changed. Chairs made of wood with a diamond lattice pattern in the back, produced in the nineteenth century and inherited from a relative, appear in photographs of the Zanuso apartment's dining area in 1950. Those chairs are also visible in 1958 photos, but they have been moved to the small lunch table in the *soggiorno*. In later photos, Lambda chairs replaced the lattice-backs in the same position. In changing the specification of the dining chair, Zanuso indicated a new motive of taste or a new set of available options, but the function remained the same.

However, the locations of some functions were not established right away; they existed for a time as furniture groupings that were perhaps more evocative than operative. The *studio* itself found a fixed position only after several years, in contrast to some spots in the apartment that were matched with specific functions from the beginning, such as the bedroom that faced Piazza Castello. The functions of household desk and dining room set both began as table and chair groupings within the living room. Their presence in the *soggiorno* in 1950 marked a moment when the arrangement of furniture contributed more than the walls did to the differentiation of domestic functions; by contrast, the dedication of a room to the working desk and dining room set brought these activities into focus as settled parts of the household.

Moreover, the *studio*, which was created as a separate space between 1950 and 1958, was initially an annex to the living room. At first the smaller space still had an air of leisure; later it became a more formal space suggestive of quiet individual work or formal dining. The study had first appeared in the 1958 renovation, when the roof structure was altered and the attic apartment expanded all the way to the building's wall on Via Lanza. In 1962 this new room was given its final, square shape by the installation of the bookshelf partition between it and the *ingresso*.

From its first appearance in 1958, the *studio* was bounded by a bearing wall that ran through all floors of the building and, in its extension toward the courtyard, also formed a side of the stairwell. The opposite wall, between the *studio* and *soggiorno*, was a lighter construction, parallel to the first one and aligned with the stairwell's other wall. This gave a definitive square shape to the *studio*, albeit with the curve of Piazza Castello registered in one wall. In the 1958 renovation, the single-step dais that had extended into the *soggiorno* from the *ingresso* and divided the raised *pranzo* or dining area from the rest of the room was extended to bring the entire *soggiorno* floor up to the same height. In 1962, the studio floor too was raised, leaving the step down only in the children's suite. The *ingresso*, *soggiorno*, and *studio* floors were now all at the same level (compare plates 33, 34).

A 1958 view through the *soggiorno* door shows the *studio* as a room with trappings of domestic comfort in traditional terms. The figure in an antique portrait painting looks back at the observer. A lattice-back side chair is visible near the doorway's right edge, while to the viewer's left is Zanuso's Martingala armchair, facing the hearth (plate 11). A pine cone is tucked in a stack of kindling and a few newspapers are standing by. The shallow fireplace, set in the thick wall of the *studio*, has a bonnet of curved brass that projects from the wall above the hearth and flue opening. Antique andirons adorned with human heads peer out from the hearth. The surface on which they sit is a masonry shelf that hovers several inches above the floor, also edged in brass. This fireplace was nearly identical to the larger one that Zanuso designed for Villa Reggiani, a single-family home constructed at Jesi in 1952.

The fireplace, desk and chair, and bookshelves are a suite of objects that were associated with the *studio* generically not just by Zanuso but in the discourse of ideas that circulated among architects in Milan. A notable early reference was a series of articles in *Domus* called the "Lessico del arredamento" (Dictionary of furnishing), published in 1943. The word *lessico* in the title makes an implicit connection between the furnishing of rooms and the parsing of phrases as one learns a language. According to one such article on the *studio* as a type, this was a room in the home with attributes of professional workplaces, though it might include the desks of various family members. The books in the home tended to collect there. If a studio in the home were to actually serve as a professional office, it would be somewhat detached from the rest of the rooms and accessed independently from the *anticamera* (entrance). For illumination, adjustable-armed lamps were preferred, since the ability to train their cone of light on the desk from some distance away allowed their cords to be kept out of harm's way.[13]

Zanuso adhered to the *Domus* lexicon to create a room that was both functional and visually indicative of an office.[14] The *studio* floor, first wood (1958) and then sisal (1962), was neutral-colored and not given to noise. This room was both close to the public space of the home and acoustically isolated by the glass panes and partition, with sounds further dampened and light filtered by curtains. In these and similar details, it was not only "furnished" but also the product of applied techniques.

In 1962, changes to the *studio* gave it a more polished appearance. The fireplace was removed, the wall covered with smooth, wide panels. The newly raised floor was covered with sisal carpet. The Martingala was moved to the *soggiorno* and the desk and chair were replaced by the Dinner and Lambda. One might wonder, given the name, whether the room was used as an architectural office. Marco Zanuso kept offices independent of his home from the early 1950s onward; he did not use his apartment for his architectural work. However, the renovation of the *studio* corresponded in time to the evolving career of another member of the household, his wife Billa Zanuso.

The prints on the *studio* walls to either side of the door to the 1962 *soggiorno* belonged to Billa Zanuso. The framed prints displayed an oval figure that resembles a row of rooms spiraling around itself (plate 22). This was not a building floor plan but a medieval board game called *gioco dell'oca*. One 1962 photograph shows the room configured as a workspace for her. Billa Zanuso's career encompassed diverse activities, from her early work in theater and radio productions to a practice as a psychoanalyst in the 1970s and 1980s. Along the way, she was a prolific writer of journalistic articles, satirical stories, and screenplays.[15] As her family grew during the 1950s she wrote in various genres, including contributions to magazines and television shows. Her most widely disseminated screenplay was "Anna," a segment of *Ieri, oggi, domani* (1963) by director Vittorio de Sica, whose theme was the superficiality of relationships in the postwar economy; the ostensible "miracle" had raised expectations only to reward individuals unequally and to leave both women and men unmoored rather than energized by new freedoms.[16] Her book on the youth of Sigmund Freud, published in 1986, was widely translated and collected.[17]

In Billa Zanuso's book *Nostra signora di Milano* (Lerici, 1963), a cross between a journal and short story collection, her subject is social class, including thinly veiled scenes from "Casa Z," perhaps based on her own home life. Her satirical style is at its peak in the sharply drawn characters. There is the young woman carefully raised to adulthood, educated and radiant but faded after a few years of marriage, the husband perpetually away on business ("Sposina"); the woman who spends years mastering English only to fall fearfully mute in the presence of a native speaker ("Ben spesi"); the men who fret over having the "right" car or job and the immaculately dressed wives who pet and comfort them like children ("A posto"); the woman haunted by the idea that by going for a walk in the sun, leaving her child in the care of a nurse, she harms the child ("Amore"). There are new homeowners who furnish with antiques but throw their living relatives' furniture away ("Bravissime"); the Milanese who work harder and longer in order to afford an endless stream of must-have appliances ("Dolce morte"); a woman who regards her face in the mirror, dresses herself in colors that clash in the trendy way, puts on nail polish and custom-dyed shoes, applies lipstick, and inexplicably crashes her motorcycle headfirst into a wall ("Divertissement de dieu").

A 1962 photograph shows various personal effects on the *studio* table, including an ashtray, Cubo, designed by Bruno Munari for Danese, 1957, and a notepad with a leather cover and shoulder strap. The typewriter, a lightweight, portable Lettera 22 by Olivetti, sits in front of the chair that faces the *soggiorno* door and the prints that framed it. In 1967 photographs, four sketches of birds (perhaps actual geese) drawn by a relative of Billa Zanuso, the writer Michele Ranchetti, appeared on the wall replacing some of the *gioco dell'oca* prints (plate 29).[18]

Around 1962, Zanuso designed *studio* rooms for several projects, each individual but, as a group, as similar to one another as family members. The *studio* in the apartment that he designed for his brother Michele Zanuso was an alcove adjacent to the living room, an irregular pentagon in plan with long shelves mounted to the wall above built-in cabinetry (figure 4.8). By contrast in the apartment for Dr. Bay, designed for a similarly upper-middle-class family, the *studio* was a square room, set in a corner carved from that apartment's *soggiorno*. The walls between the Bay living room and *studio* were full-height, but the doorway between them was exceptionally wide and spanned across a corner. Zanuso used two retractable pocket doors to create a generous visual connection between living room and office through the open corner (figure 4.9).[19] With the doors to Dr. Bay's *studio* open, the upper wall has the appearance of an angled soffit, linking the rooms visually and physically and introducing an intermediate scale between furniture and full ceiling height, mitigating the height of the space. In the view from *studio* to *soggiorno*, bookcases beside and above the doorway, washed with daylight from the *studio* windows, situate the viewer securely in the *studio* while allowing an unobstructed view of the living room. Meanwhile, in the view from the Bay *soggiorno* to the *studio*, daylight from the *studio*'s windows illuminates the smaller room like a bright box in contrast to the *soggiorno*, where shadows gather near the adjacent, windowless wall (figure 4.10).

In the Bay *studio* as in his own Zanuso made scrupulous use of his own mass-produced furniture pieces, Dinner and Lambda. The bookcases that lined the walls, including the narrow high part above the doorway, are the Eton shelves he designed for Techniform, which used the same set of details as the bookshelves in his own apartment. A second Dinner and Lambda set appeared in the Bay apartment's *pranzo*, a dedicated dining room. Dinner was also placed in the shared bedroom of the family's teenage sons, where each had his own work surface, the two tables facing each other. The tables in the sons' room were matched with Gio Ponti's Superleggera (1957), a chair that bore a general resemblance to a *chiavarina*, produced in an updated version by Cassina.[20]

These examples illustrate Zanuso's interest in exploring the possibilities of the design of room types, including his own furniture pieces in his projects. This work in the 1960s was not his first such foray; in 1945, he had written a book about kitchens. That was the year that architects Carlo Pagani and Lina Bo Bardi initiated a new publication series that built on the *lessico dell'arredamento* through a more robust format called Quaderni di Domus. The Quaderni were compendia of examples that had been published in *Domus*, often drawn from projects in Italy and abroad. Each volume featured an essay by an architect, synthesizing the collected examples. *Gli studi nella casa*, a book on the *studio* by Vittorio Gandolfi, was volume 2 in the series. Marco Zanuso's volume, no. 3, was *La cucina* (The kitchen).

Figure 4.8 *Studio*, Michele Zanuso apartment, c. 1960. Photo Ugo Mulas © Ugo Mulas Heirs. All rights reserved.

Figure 4.9 View from inside *studio*, Bay apartment, 1963. Photo Giorgio Casali © Fondo Giorgio Casali, IUAV Archivio Progetti, Venice.

Figure 4.10 View from outside *studio*, Bay apartment, 1963. Photo Giorgio Casali © Fondo Giorgio Casali, IUAV Archivio Progetti, Venice.

Cucina

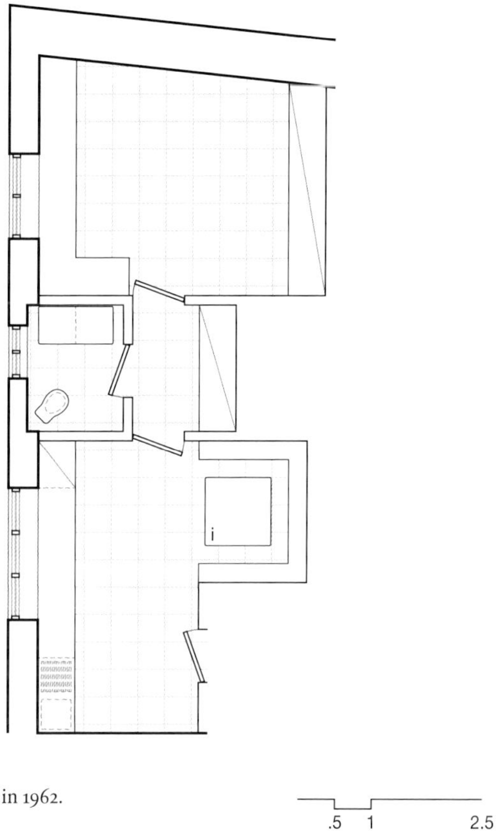

Figure 5.1 Plan of *cucina* in 1962.

After 1958, you would reach the kitchen by way of the Piazza Castello-side hallway, taking the left-hand door, which led to the kitchen and laundry. Ahead and to your left would be the stove, with its ventilation hood. At the other end of the counter were two sinks. On the wall between them a wide window faced northeast, admitting light in the morning and taking in air from the building's courtyard side. On the other side of the room, toward Piazza Castello, was a small table and seats. If your work included laundry, the machines were found in the next room, while in the last room, in the building's corner, was a place to store and care for clothes, as shown in figure 5.1.

Above the kitchen was a roof terrace, a few feet lower than the pitched roof that sloped toward Piazza Castello, which appears in a 1950 section drawing (plate 5, top and figure 3.2). The 1893 section shows no enclosed space at all between the bedroom and the building's courtyard side; the stairwell core, which would have been hidden by the kitchen in this particular view, is visible (figure 1.3). None of the available documentation indicates when the kitchen and laundry were built or whether Zanuso had any role in that stage. Nevertheless, the kitchen is a site that raises many questions about design, especially industrial design, which are essential to explain Zanuso's profile as an architect and designer. The kitchen as a functional space type was the subject of his first publications and activities after World War II, including an article and an installation at the eighth Triennale in 1947. Moreover, many of his industrial design products were destined for the kitchen.

Zanuso would design many kitchens in his architectural projects and, eventually, a mass-produced kitchen system, the ELAM E5. In the 1980s, an E5 would be installed in his own apartment, too. In the meantime, his alterations to his kitchen might more often have entailed the replacement of fixtures, such as the introduction of the Homelight refrigerator, one of Zanuso's first appliance designs, which was published in *Stile industria* in 1954 and appeared in some of his other projects around 1960 (fig 5.2).

While tables and chairs are mentioned in published documentation of the Zanuso apartment, there are no photographs of the room, and the identities of any furniture pieces that were placed there, up to 1967, are not recorded. But different types of design converge in a kitchen, including the design of mechanical equipment as well as of furniture, and the efficient use of machines and movement between stations of production is more thematic in this room than in any other. Accordingly this chapter considers Zanuso's relationship to a certain kind of mass-produced object, the appliance, as a way to better understand his concerns and his approach to kitchen design.[1] Meanwhile, the floor plans of the kitchen provide a point of departure for considering a few related ideas and projects.

Figure 5.2 Kitchen, Michele Zanuso apartment, c. 1960. Zanuso's Homelight refrigerator is visible on the left behind the island. "Cucina," *Artecasa* 18 (1961). Fondo Marco Zanuso, Archivio del Moderno, Balerna.

Furniture and industrial design are often considered together as "small objects" in contrast to architecture. While furniture can be manufactured either artisanally or industrially, furniture and industrial design were treated as different kinds of things in practice and in the literature of postwar Italian architecture culture. Zanuso sometimes designed furniture pieces for his architecture projects, a subset of which never went into wider production at all (see "Bambine"). By contrast, industrial design objects were almost always produced by machine-assisted methods, often serially in large numbers. They sometimes contained mechanical parts and entailed the assimilation of a machine to a shell-like outer casing. The priorities associated with industrial design and production were the application of techniques, the achievement of precision, and other values associated with machines. While there was a strong public interest in new designs for the home, there was also a widespread public wariness toward mechanized objects, echoed by critical voices within architecture culture. In this chapter more than the others, the object and the wider problem of the domestication of industry come to the fore.

Zanuso's first published writing on kitchen designs was an article in *Domus*, "Non dimentichiamo la cucina" (Let's not forget the kitchen); a few years later, the text was republished as the slender book *La cucina* (1945), Zanuso's entry in the Quaderni di Domus series. A compendium of photographs and plans was included, drawn from the architecture literature in the United States, Germany, Great Britain, and Scandinavia. In his comments, Zanuso wrote about the interdependence of efficient circulation, storage and visual access, the regulation of temperature, and whether or not to provide a place to sit and stay in kitchens. He also reported in detail the findings of recent studies of the optimal distances between pieces of equipment, the crossing of paths, the work surface, the furniture, and other parameters. As scholars have noted, Zanuso referred to concepts drawn from a preexisting literature on kitchens produced by Italian architects in the 1930s.[2] He noted that architects had made strides in the problem of organizing kitchens and that appliances were becoming more technically advanced and affordable. He predicted (correctly) that the new appliances would become more affordable and widely available. Italian households at every income level would soon be able to prioritize the smooth functioning of their kitchens. He included excerpts from a time-and-motion study done by the industrial engineering department of New York University to bolster his explanation of the minute spatial planning that a modern kitchen would demand.[3]

One indication of Zanuso's personal concerns about kitchen design is his remark in *La cucina* that in many Italian households, especially less well-off homes, the kitchen was the only place where the whole family could gather and relax; other rooms were too small. As long as the kitchen was relied on for that purpose, the scope for its design as a place to efficiently prepare food was limited.[4] This insight about the close association between the kitchen as a space of production and as a place to gather is registered in the one distinct renovation to the kitchen that is documented in the four floor plans of the Zanuso apartment renovations: the moving of its door. In 1950, one entered the kitchen through a door opposite the entrance to the apartment. One found oneself facing shelves or cabinets and a small table and chairs. It took another 90-degree turn to enter the main kitchen space, where the stove was set in a niche further to the left. After the 1958 renovation, one turned in the hallway to enter the kitchen facing the stove. Turning right to face toward the laundry, one had the work counter on the left and a 5-foot-wide (1.5 m) alcove on the right (compare plates 32, 33). Now the small table and chairs were no longer in the circulation path nor in the cooking area. This second configuration, with the table in its alcove, was still in place in the apartment's last published drawings, in 1967.

If one compares Zanuso's observations on the kitchen to ideas expressed by Giuseppe Pagano, elaborated for example in Pagano's 1942 article "Civiltà industriale" (Industrial civility), in some respects Zanuso seems to respond to the considerations about industry, in the sense of mechanization, that Pagano introduced into the discourse. In his article, Pagano expressed misgivings about the industrial realm, which he described as "too recent" to have been assimilated to culture and be truly civilized. He was hopeful that the seeming detachment of cultural practices such as engineering and poetry from one another would be resolved, to the point that the products of the building production industry would be as compelling in spiritual terms as works of architecture. "There exists around us a civility of the machine," Pagano wrote, "which exerts a decisive fascination on the more sensitive temperaments and those less bound to ancient conventions. Around us full of confused appeals to a civility of tomorrow exists a supranational reality called industry, with its laws, its pride, its maledictions and blessings."[5] But in order to fully experience this new order, a nation had to confront it and own it. Pagano called for "a new faith" that would look toward how society could improve and would naturally avail itself of new and potent means and discover a "civility of the machine."[6]

Pagano had turned his attention to industry as curator of the first exhibition of industrial products at the Milan Triennale, in 1940, titled an "international exhibition of serial production," dedicated to the ways that producers were paying attention to the aesthetics of the mass-produced object.[7] While part of the display featured products by various producers, including FIAT, Olivetti, and Pirelli, an opening section gave a general introduction to the idea of the series, including a display of natural structures—animal, vegetable, and mineral—with cellular or crystalline organization. Pagano's emphasis on bringing emotions together with industry, involving "faith" and "civility," had a tone of exhortation, like a manifesto. Zanuso and Paolo Chessa's comments in their article "Il modulo," an essay on the theme of prefabrication published in *Domus* in 1946 (also mentioned in "Studio"), were a remarkable echo of Pagano's invitation to imagine continuity between the found natural world and the manufactured artificial one.

Pagano applied his ideas about civility not only to mass-produced mechanical objects but also to the functional domestic environment. In notes to the *Tecnica d'abitazione* (Technique of living) exhibition at the sixth Triennale (1936), he addressed analogous issues on the topic of interiors and furniture in a way that amounts to an appeal for the modernization of the home. The importance of living in a home that met the spiritual needs of the moment was paramount for Pagano. The home was not only where one carried out basic routines of survival; it was also a place for the "spiritually elevated" contemplative moments that define one's character. He argued that each period undergoes an adjustment in which the house reaches a distinctive form, adapted by its occupants. The house was a project in which an architect could achieve "coherence" among all factors of life; as such, it was an index of civilization.[8]

Zanuso's relocation of the kitchen door in 1958 resolved the problem of how to reconcile the social aspect of mealtime with the imperatives of preparing food. The adjustment of the plan was small, concerning informal dining, but the practical uncoupling of the productive space from the sitting area had freed it to be optimized for production without compromising the kitchen's social function. This is the epitome of the kind of adjustment that Pagano described.

Zanuso had tested ideas about efficiency and organization in the kitchen in his design for Villa Scotti (1946–1947), the renovation of a small structure on the edge of Lago Maggiore into a house, designed in collaboration with Giovanni Albricci. The Scotti kitchen was a carefully planned room for cooking, with a double sink, two stoves, built-in cabinets, and a semidetached working surface with drawers opening in two directions and a niche for a rolling pin. An elevation drawing of one wall showed cabinets for linens, tableware, dishes, pots and pans, temporary storage of ingredients, and metal bins below the counter for fruits and vegetables. The plan gives the impression that the use of every utensil has been thought through, that each one has its place. But while there was space for two cooks to move around the room, there was no communal table; any social gathering would have taken place in the adjacent dining room (figure 5.3).[9]

Not long afterward, at the eighth Triennale exhibition in 1947, Zanuso exhibited a concept for a small apartment: a galley kitchen with parallel counters, one of which doubled as an armoire for the adjacent living/dining room. The armoire, open at counter level, allowed for the illumination of both spaces and the passing of dishes in one direction or the other (figure 5.4). Zanuso would not employ a pass-through cabinet in the kitchen of his own apartment, but he did build an armoire that could be opened either from the small room labeled "guardaroba" (wardrobe) or from the master bedroom (plate 5, bottom right).

In other work on the problem of the kitchen, Zanuso took on the problem of cost in his domestic kitchen designs. The apartment he designed for his brother Michele Zanuso and family around 1960, mentioned above, used wall material covered with patterned tile and incorporated open shelving as an alternative to the more common approach of custom-built cabinets. An article in *Artecasa*, a popular home furnishing magazine, promoted the design as an appealing solution from both a design and cost perspective.[10] Apart from demonstrating the variety of means for achieving a designed space, the Michele Zanuso kitchen also highlights an advantage in Zanuso's work at different scales: the ability to specify ceramic tiles that he himself had designed was a decisive factor in validating the wall-based approach as an alternative that did not compromise on

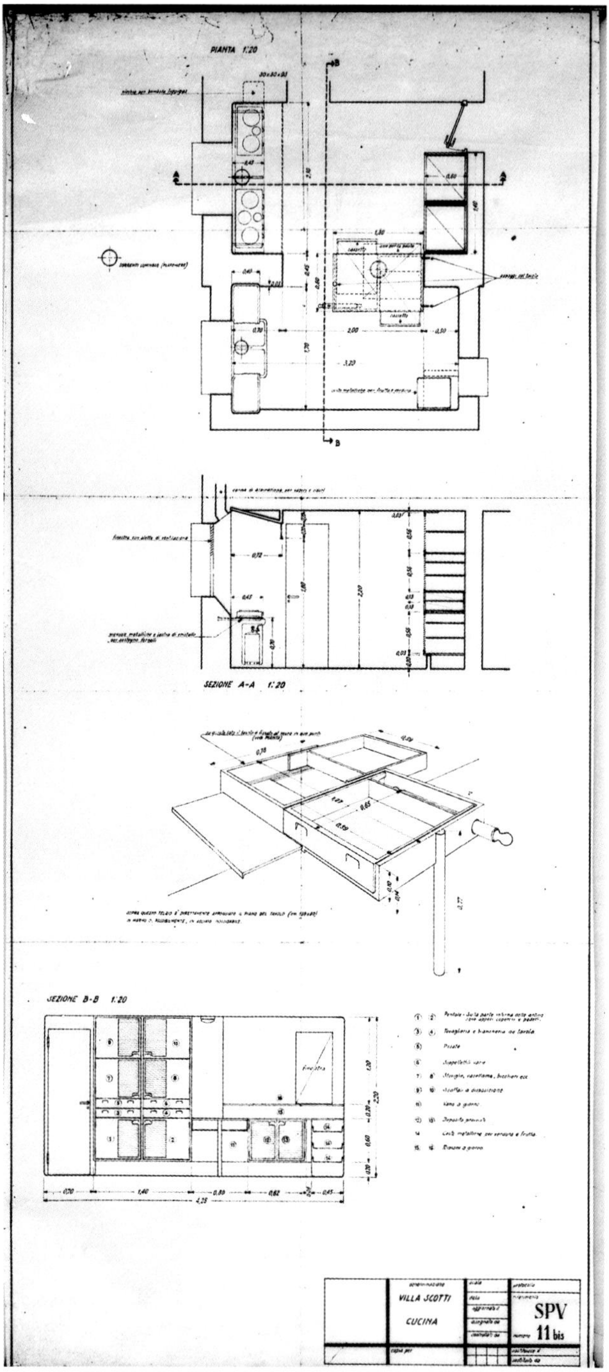

Figure 5.3 Plan drawing of kitchen (detail), Villa Scotti, Premeno, by Zanuso with Giovanni Albricci. Fondo Marco Zanuso, Archivio del Moderno, Balerna.

Figure 5.4 Kitchen installation at eighth Milan Triennale, 1947. © Triennale Milano.

aesthetics. By that time, Zanuso had at his disposal several of his own wall tile designs produced by Ceramiche d'Italia (CEDIT) for finishing the walls and integrating them into the space.

Zanuso's focus on finding the location of every tool, surface, and piece of equipment that would best support the use of the kitchen was put into action in a design method that sometimes entailed an interview with his client in order to establish the best distribution of things.[11] Such a conversation produced a diagram, implicit or literal, that could be built out in any number of ways. The optimization of a floor plan was part of Zanuso's method that was incorporated into both architectural kitchen designs and the serially produced system that he had begun to develop by 1960.

Zanuso applied the same meticulous planning to the most extreme examples of serially produced kitchens to emerge from his office, those for entirely prefabricated structures. The first of these was the Emergency Capsule (1972), the "environment" Zanuso designed with Richard Sapper for the exhibition *Italy: The New Domestic Landscape*, held at the Museum of Modern Art in New York. Intended to be a complete residential unit that could be collapsed and fitted into a shipping container chassis that would serve as the unit's structure when assembled, the Emergency Capsule could be transported by ship, airplane, truck, or helicopter to a suitable site for installation by a small team equipped only with conventional hand tools. The Emergency Capsule kitchen was outfitted with a stool and work surface around which cabinets were arrayed, resembling a miniature topological equivalent of the Frankfurt Kitchen designed by Margarete Schütte-Lihotzky, one of the examples Zanuso had featured in *La cucina*.[12]

In a more conventional project, beginning in the 1960s Zanuso designed a number of kitchen fittings for production by the company ELAM, led by Ezio Longhi, a young entrepreneur who had taken over his family's cabinetry company In Moda. A lightweight plastic dining chair and table were produced, Minisit (1970), as well as a wardrobe cabinetry system for other parts of the home, E6.[13] The largest and most prominent of Zanuso's ELAM designs was E5, a kitchen with coordinated cabinets, countertops, and shelving in various finishes. Architectural details such as the dimensions and profiles of cabinet doors and other components were worked out in advance and implemented in production based on a customized selection for each project. Zanuso made use of E5 in a number of apartment projects, including the apartment for Dr. Bay (1963), where the extensive use of materials with a mirror-like finish mitigated the kitchen's interior location and limited square footage.[14]

Through the ELAM kitchen system, Zanuso achieved a degree of prefabrication for domestic architecture. A high mark of this objective was the installation of an E5 kitchen in an apartment building on Via Adelaide Coari in Milan (initially named for nearby Via Paolo Solaroli), one of two condominium projects that were designed by Zanuso and built using the FEAL VAR-3 system, which included a curtain wall of aluminum, steel, and glass installed on steel-framed volumes.[15] These two architecture projects, built in 1965, near the end of the period of most intense optimism and anticipation among a group of Milan's architects who sought to promote prefabrication, made the most extensive use of ready-made components and finishes of any of Zanuso's projects at the time (figure 5.5). With the conjunction of the prefabricated kitchen and partly prefabricated building, Zanuso demonstrated how the architect-designer's work could be fitted together to form all or part of a living space.

In addition to his many architectural designs for kitchens and parts of kitchens, Zanuso devoted attention to the aesthetics of the mass-produced objects in his industrial design projects, many of which were kitchen appliances. These designs often give the impression of a single overarching design move, such as a mechanism or trait that defines the whole. A knife sharpener produced by Necchi (1963) presents itself as a smooth cylinder of colored ABS plastic, concealing the machine. The grinding surface sits beneath and beside a slot for the knife, which is cut away on one side allowing the grinding mechanism to be seen and accessed from more than one angle, meeting the requirements of different kinds of knives. The defining mechanism in other objects is not directly visible but nonetheless defines the design.

The weighing platform on the kitchen scale designed by Zanuso for Terraillon appears to hover over the bottom of the scale; the connection between the two parts is hidden (figure 5.6). This tendency to hide the mechanism is pervasive among Zanuso's designs for more elaborate and mechanically complex appliances, often designed with considerable involvement by Richard Sapper, the principal collaborator on design in the Zanuso office for several years beginning in the 1950s.

Homelight, a refrigerator, can be glimpsed in the background of the Michele Zanuso apartment, mentioned above. This project

Figure 5.5 E5 kitchen, ELAM, installed in an apartment in Via Solaroli building. Photo Publifoto. Archivio del Moderno, Fondo Marco Zanuso, Balerna.

Figure 5.6 Terraillon kitchen scale. Fondo Marco Zanuso, Archivio del Moderno, Balerna.

involved function-enhancing refinements to a preexisting model, a tall rectangular block with rounded corners and edges, with dedicated compartments for fruit and meat, racks for bottles, and a separate freezer compartment. The fruit bin was differentiated from the meat bin by a change in materials, plastic in the first case and enameled steel in the second. A tray above the meat bin collected the condensation caused by defrosting. Bottle racks were placed on the door, taking advantage of the bottles' relative slenderness. The freezer's small size relative to the refrigerator was linked to the tendency of Italian households not to store frozen food. These details were singled out by the author of the short review of Homelight in *Stile industria*, who described Zanuso's design as an instance of what "design" means in the context of industrial production. "Modern design" means that the artist approaches the work in the spirit of research and imagination, not just with a narrow view of technology and the requirements of its production. The designer's role is to characterize the object's form while arranging its parts for the user's best advantage.[16]

Functionalism was the goal, but there was more to Homelight than efficiency alone. A central feature was the circular handle, a ring of brass set in a plastic-lined impression on the surface in order to protect the enamel. While the management of different foods and temperatures was achieved through design decisions based on research into function, the handle established a visual connection with the user so that these thoughtful details could be discovered. On the left side was a tab, behind which the handle joined the hinge on the latch mechanism. On the right side, the user would find that a portion of the circle curved forward and inward.

This was an object that confronted the user with idiosyncrasy, by extension an object that could be perceived as challenging at first encounter, but the circle is a distinctive shape and the subtraction of part of its figure would draw attention to the place where the hand should be put to pull the door open.[17] In notes in the tenth Triennale catalog that included Homelight, Zanuso pointed out that the handle worked equally well for left- and right-handed users.[18]

Another approach that distinguished Zanuso's industrial design projects, exemplified in the kitchen appliance, was an encasing cover that would appeal to the eye and hand and conceal the machine while meeting practical needs of the mechanism inside, such as ventilation. An example is the *macinacaffè* (coffee grinder) designed for Subalpina in the early 1960s. The unit's overall shape included a cylindrical shaft and above it an apple-shaped rounded upper part. The cylinder contained the motor, while the rounded part widened to accommodate the blade, which sat in a steel bowl, and the coffee beans. In Zanuso's design, one of many developed with Richard Sapper, the curved shape of the lid, which was made of a clear plastic material, had an interior shape that redirected coffee bean fragments toward the blade (figure 5.7).[19]

The superimposition of circles that is explicit in the drawing of the *macinacaffè* is also a point of method behind the smallest and least complex object among all of Zanuso's designs, the kitchen tile SZ1, designed in 1954 in collaboration with Alberto Scarzella in the Zanuso office and produced by Ceramiche di Lurago d'Elba (figure 5.8).[20] The long shape of the tile, a composite of alternating convex and concave lines that come together in acute angles, appears irregular at first glance but was actually derived from a regular triangular grid.[21] SZ1 was a consumer product available to anyone, and the underlying geometry made the tile a vehicle for personal expression; it could be arranged in numerous patterns and configurations, including rows, rosettes, and swirling forms. The use of more than one color expanded the possible expressions of the tile into additional figure-ground patterns (figure 5.9).[22]

For the same company that produced the SZ1 tile, Zanuso also designed a factory building, constructed in Palermo, Sicily. The tile and building demonstrate two different approaches to seriality, albeit in designs at vastly different scales. The main work floor of the factory, a covered area, was created by the construction and repetition of longitudinal bays. Each bay was made of a double row of columns topped by long beams with flared flanges running their full length. Roof joists were thin slabs of concrete propped on their edges, resting on the flanges and topped by roof slabs. Light was admitted by long skylights between the roof slabs and beams and under the roof joists in the end facades.[23]

The defining conceit of the object in this case is this concrete assembly; the building was produced largely through multiplication of these few components. The building, designed by Zanuso with the structural engineer Luigi Antonietti, has the appearance of a technical object, for profiles drawn from structural engineering are visible, including the V-shaped beam with its stiffening

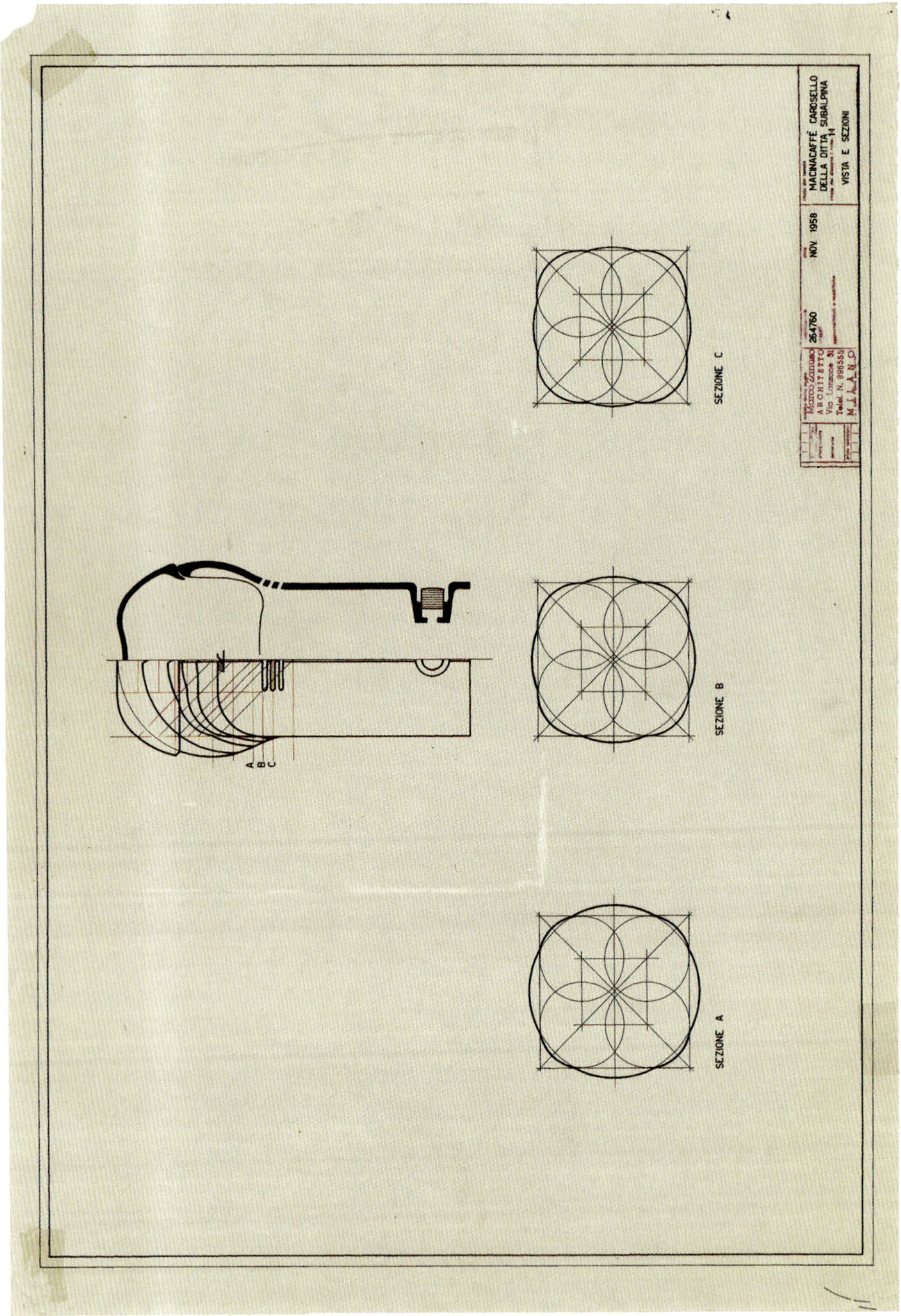

Figure 5.7 Drawing of Carosello coffee grinder, 1958. Fondo Marco Zanuso, Archivio del Moderno, Balerna.

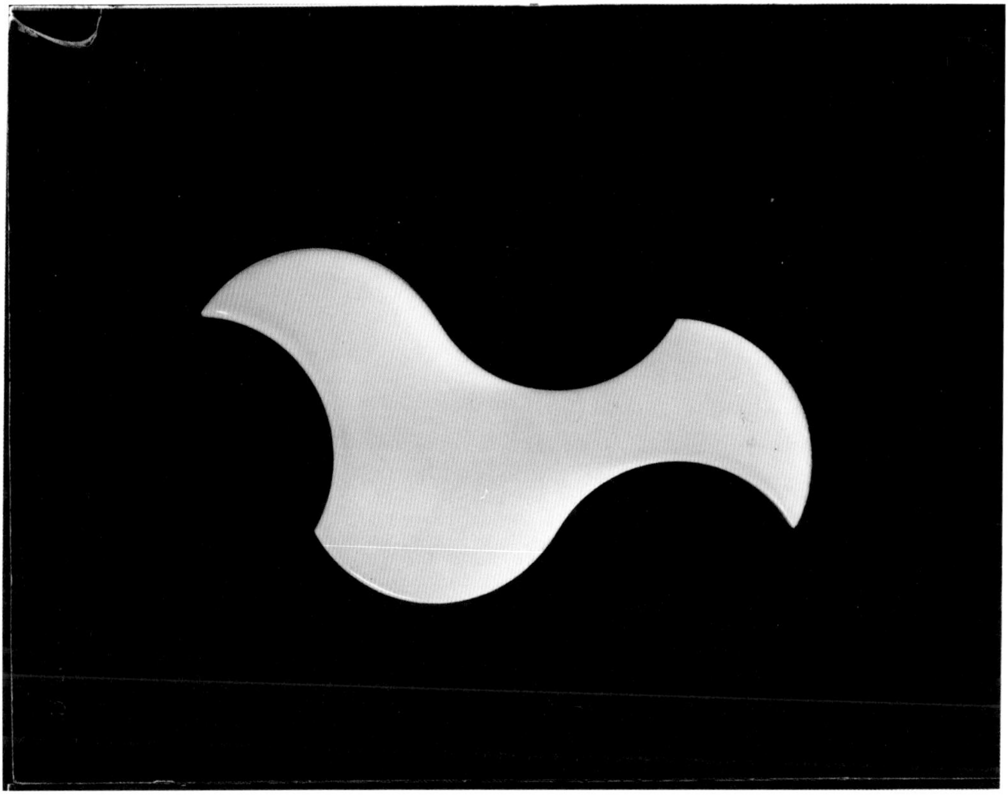

Figure 5.8 Studio photograph of SZ1 tile, CEDIT Palermo, 1954. Photo © Ballo+Ballo. Civico Archivio Fotografico, Comune di Milano.

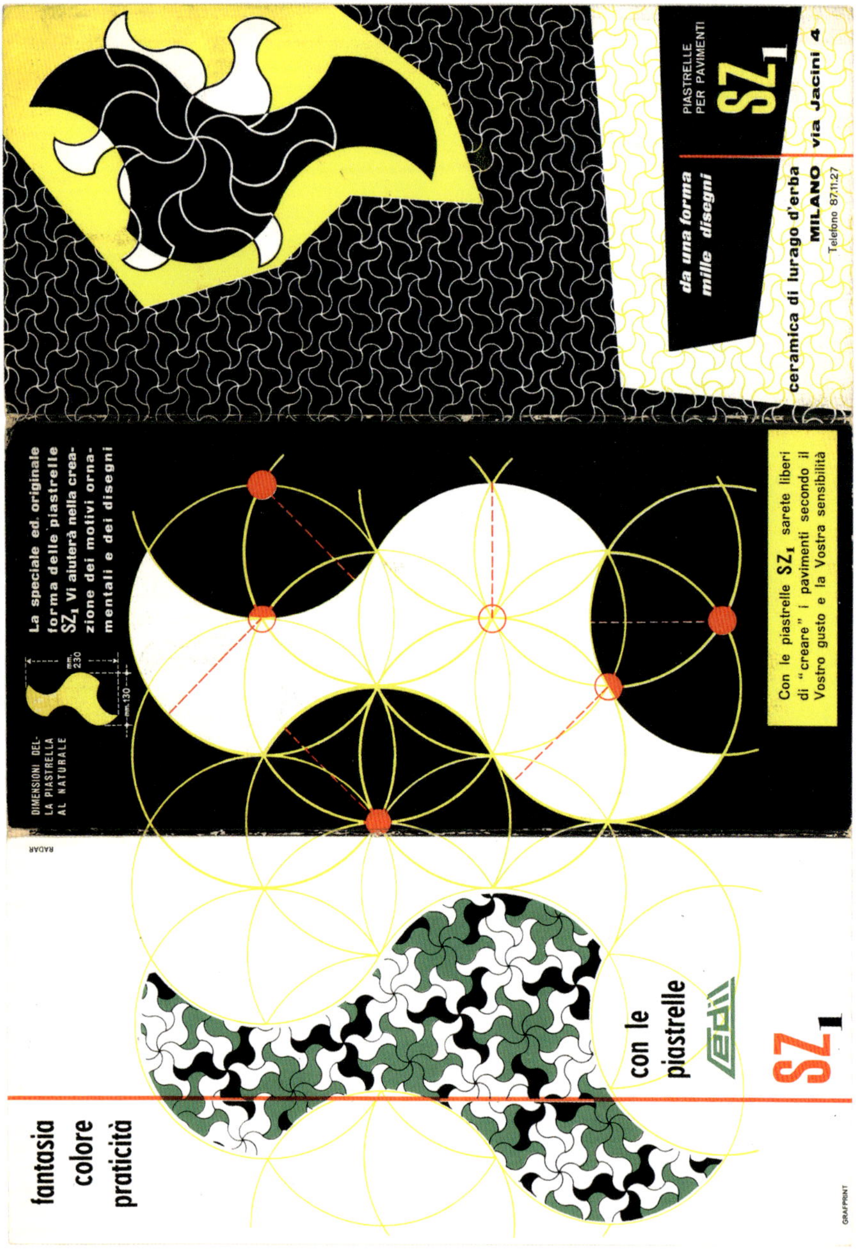

Figure 5.9 Brochure for SZ1 tile, CEDIT Palermo. Fondo Marco Zanuso, Archivio del Moderno, Balerna.

flanges and the columns that are cross-shaped in section and flare slightly from bottom to top to ensure their stability. The repetition of parts, too, is a signature of engineering structures. Other details suggest an architectural sensibility; for instance, the boomerang-shaped joists, which taper toward their ends, are gently rounded. The clarity of the joints gives the building an ostensible lightness that expresses the concern of the architect to enable the viewer to understand how the building is put together. The joists that leave the observer with an impression of a boomerang shape actually sit on small vertical feet. The material seems pared away to a minimum. The grid of columns is not set on the same spacing across the whole project.

The employee housing that Zanuso designed for the same campus in Palermo, constructed next to the factory, was also characterized by the aggregation of nearly identical units. The repetition of the house volumes, with their asymmetrical pitched roofs and elegant offset from one to the next, is not drawn from the realm of industry. The conceit of repetition, which is so suggestive of the industrial, is also a longstanding trope in architecture. On closer inspection, the factory, too, is more complex than appears at first glance. Between factory, tile, and house the differences are not hard and fast but subtle and complicated. While they at first appear to be objects from different worlds, a further consideration reveals qualities common to all of them.

In summer 1955, Zanuso oversaw the exhibition of a subset of the objects that had been exhibited in Milan the previous year, at the tenth Triennale. Sponsored by the Italian Cultural Institute and called *Selected Examples of Italian Industrial Design*, the exhibition was held at the Design Council gallery in Belgrave Square in London. The catalog, under a red cover featuring a white image of a FIAT car body, was designed by Germano Facetti, a young Italian graphic designer living in London, and featured over 30 miscellaneous objects including handbags, fabric, and ceramics as well as adding machines, motors, and an automobile's speedometer console (figure 5.10).[24]

Collectively these objects referred to industrial manufacturing in Italy in general, or at least in the region of Lombardy around Milan. Individually each object was an expression of a piece of the reality of contemporary industry. Zanuso advocated for industrial design to become a phenomenon in which consumers formed an intentional society that would exert its influence by linking its

Figure 5.10 *Selected Examples of Italian Industrial Design*, 1955. Exhibition catalog cover designed by Germano Facetti. © Italian Cultural Institute, London.

values to the economic demand that would shape the economy. Exhibitions like the tenth Triennale would introduce the consumer to goods with this end in mind. In published remarks on the exhibition, Zanuso noted that the public response had been impressive, and this struck him as an ideal outcome. Design should not be directed from on high, at the level of the state; a robust economy could only develop with the input of the public along with producers, artists, and designers.[25] The "mass" phenomenon that Zanuso anticipated entailed producers coming together with designers to remake the world together, one product at a time. When this anticipated outcome did not happen, Zanuso continued to appeal to producers to work with designers.[26]

The design and refinement of the Zanuso apartment between 1949 and 1967 and the design of numerous objects for mass production during the same period were undertaken in that moment of optimism in which Zanuso and other designers sought to position themselves as agents of a historical change in the economy and everyday surroundings. Zanuso's small objects show a sensibility marked by an alertness to small differences that would yield affordances and advantages of various kinds and to how regular geometric shapes, associated with the requirements of machines and their parts, could also serve to engage the user through the visual and tactile senses.

The wide window above the kitchen sink in the Zanuso apartment may have predated Zanuso's arrival, but he showed a distinct sensitivity to lighting in his apartment and engaged a wall of the terrace, above the kitchen, to provide illumination to an adjacent space in the apartment, the children's bathroom. It was the children (who had a suite of rooms to themselves on the Piazza Castello side of the house, labeled on the floor plans as "Bambine") who ate their meals at the small table and chairs in the kitchen.

Bambine

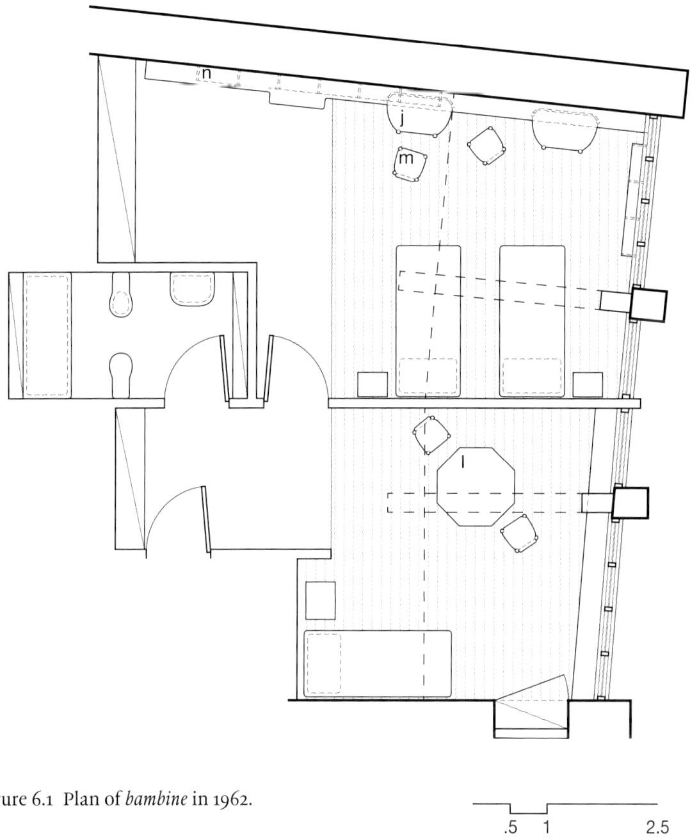

Figure 6.1 Plan of *bambine* in 1962.

You would reach the children's bedroom by walking parallel to Piazza Castello, leaving the *ingresso* behind you and crossing the hall that led to the kitchen, to the left. The next room, which opened on your right toward the windows, had a bed, a small table, and chairs. This room, which was opposite the children's bathroom on the left and washed with afternoon light from the southwest-facing Piazza Castello-side windows, was the original nursery and the bedroom of the youngest child, who was still very young in 1962. A few more steps led through a second door and into the more spacious bedroom at the end of the building on the Piazza Castello side. These two rooms and bathroom comprised the children's suite, marked "Bambine" on the plans and illustrated in figure 6.1 (see plate 36 for a key to furniture pieces).

In 1950, the Zanusos' two older daughters occupied the first of the two rooms. Labeled "letto figli" (children's bedroom) on the plan, that middle room, with a crib and caretaker's bed, had to be passed through to get to the adults' bedroom. The sole photograph of the *letto figli* shows a half-length curtain hung from a visible rail to screen the part of the room that served as circulation to the bedroom or bathroom (plate 5, bottom left). Doors to the bathroom and adults' bedroom are visible behind the open curtain. A major renovation took place in 1958, following the birth of the Zanusos' third daughter. Additional space was carved out under the roof and a new bedroom was created for the adults (see "Letto"), leaving the old bedroom to the two older daughters. Once the end bedroom was transferred to the children, it was the one that was included in published accounts of the home.

Before you and to your left, as you stood in the doorway to this room, was a marble-floored dressing area. The wall to the left side had a built-in armoire with a grid of painted doors. If the cabinet doors were open, you might see the daylight from the windows in the *guardaroba*, the room next to the laundry room on the courtyard side, from which the cabinets could also be opened. You could see Castello Sforzesco through the horizontal band of windows that illuminated the room from your right, across an area whose wooden floor, a step down from where you stood, was covered with a low-pile carpet (plate 12).

On the wall straight ahead, a single shelf crossed the room from the cabinet end, where it served as a dressing table, to the window end, where it held an assortment of objects. The shelf maintained a consistent datum across the room. In the raised part of the room, near the wardrobe, it was a slab of marble, part of which jutted out a few centimeters more than the rest to form a small desk-like surface about half a meter wide, with rounded corners (plate 13). With a mirror on the wall in front of it, the wide part of the shelf formed an abstract but functional vanity table. In a photograph from 1950 (when this same space had served as the parents' bedroom), this ledge is laid out with hairbrushes (plate 4, bottom).

In front of the ledge in 1962 were two desks. The labeling of the room as "Bambine" in the published plans reaffirmed the use of that particular space as a bedroom, now for the older children. The desk that had been in the *soggiorno* was relocated to the children's room. With the study function absorbed into the room—their version of *studio*—the *bambine* was a part of the home in which functions were indicated by furniture more than by walls. From another point of view, *bambine* was an extensively served suite, with many details analogous to the accommodation of adults adapted to the scale of children. With these details in mind, this chapter explores how the *bambine*, as a mirror and extension of Zanuso's experiments in the design of schools and their furniture during the late 1950s, illustrates his concern with modernity in the sense of accommodation and services, achieved through design.

A 1962 photograph of the view toward the corner and windows (plate 24) shows a well-appointed room. The ceiling was decorated with wallpaper whose printed pattern resembled sprays of flowers, extending down to the windows on the Piazza Castello side. At the other end of the room the wallpaper followed a curved transition from ceiling to wall just above the built-in armoire and covered the portion of the adjacent wall near the bedroom door. The wallpaper also covered the riser of the step by the dressing area and was wrapped around a portion of the shelf on the wall.

In a photograph of the same part of the room taken in 1958 (plate 12), sunlight cast on the ceiling's surface from a low angle suggests a photo taken in the afternoon. Zanuso's two older daughters, then aged eleven and thirteen, are present. One, seated at a desk facing the wall, applies her attention to an open book while the other, also reading, perches on an antique chest beneath the windows. A portable record player sits on the chest while a globe on a stand sits on the shelf, in front of a framed painting. Beneath the shelf is a kneeler for saying prayers, with a built-in cabinet; on the shelf are two vases with cut flowers, a small sculpture of a child, a few books, paper figurines.

The photograph speaks of more than just an inventory of objects or the shape of a space. The occupants' comfort, their capacity to sit and occupy themselves, is supported by services of various kinds, and clues to several of these are present. The woman in the foreground, her back to the camera, may have been

Billa Zanuso or possibly a "signorina," a young woman employed seasonally to teach the children English or another foreign language.[1] To have live-in domestic service workers was conventional in upper-middle-class households in Milan at the time. For some women, domestic staff were as much a source of unease as they were a necessity.[2] Arrangements could vary and domestic workers might be part-time rather than living in the apartment. The Zanuso apartment had a small, fully interior room that opened off of the stairwell on the Via Lanza side, labeled "letto servizio," a servant's bedroom, in the 1958 apartment floor plan. This room was still present in the same position in 1967, accessed from an interior hallway that led to the master bedroom and older daughters' suite.

A service of another kind that appears in images of the bedroom is the step in the room between the dressing area and the rest of the room. This corresponds to a level change between the kitchen and bathroom area on the building's courtyard side and the bedroom on the Piazza Castello side.[3] The level change, which at 12 inches (0.3 m) is slightly taller than a normal stair, had been present in the attic apartment before the Zanuso family arrived. But for an "ideal house," unbuilt but published in 1942, Zanuso had designed a single-family home in which a floor level change between service and living spaces, about 2.5 ft (0.75 m), provided for the distribution of utilities. The step in the apartment, too, may have facilitated the extension of wiring and pipes for the radiators, one of which is visible in a view of the raised part of the room (plate 13), but it likely owed something to the fact that the kitchen area had been built over the roof of the original building while the rest of the apartment was an attic from the beginning.

In the Piazza Castello apartment, Zanuso was able to develop the floor plan in a condition of relative openness in which spaces could be freely reconfigured, but first he had to contend with the constraints of the sloping ceilings and large timbers that initially divided the space. The change in floor level in the apartment was another such constraint. The step, which, as a section drawing shows, was sometimes treated as a convenient place to sit, is visible in the living room and bedroom in 1950 photos but was eliminated by 1962 in all of the rooms except the children's suite.

The bedroom's single operable window is a sign of another kind of service. Notes on the apartment published in 1950 explain that Zanuso had two openings cut in one wall of the roof terrace, above the kitchen. One was a door that could be reached by climbing the small stair in the entrance hallway, while the other was an operable clerestory window in the children's bathroom. These were part of a passive ventilation scheme that drew air through the bedroom door, into the bathroom and hallway, upward and out through the openings around the roof terrace. The terrace and clerestory were not photographed for publication, but they appear in the published section drawing (figure 3.2). A handle for opening and closing the window is visible on one wall in a 1962 photograph of the children's bathroom (plate 25).

There are many objects in the room, too, that "serve." The attic roof posed a problem for lighting, especially in rooms that had only one exterior wall. At some point between the building's construction in 1893 and the photo shoot in the Zanuso apartment in 1949, the roof had been built up near the street facades. As the sloping roof plane descended from the ridge, the lower part was tilted up to sit at an angle to the supporting timber member beneath it, raising the ceiling height on the inside at its low edge near the wall and opening a gap of several inches between timber member and ceiling. Windows were installed in a horizontal band across the apartment's Piazza Castello-side walls from the edge of the facade wall to the surface of the ceiling. The light could be shut out by integrated window shades.

Among the visible small light fixtures, the lamp that illuminates the desk, designer unknown, was made of bent tubular metal; it is cantilevered from the wall but hangs like a pendant lamp (plates 12, 13, 24).[4] A hinge between the lamp's two curved arms gives it a generous articulability within its radius, while the hinge mechanism allows it to sweep around to light the desk at one time of day and the dressing area at another. Other lights in the room include the wall-mounted lamp above each nightstand, beside the parallel twin beds. The beds, made up with pillows and duvets with their heads against the wall, utilized a novel foam rubber mattress, newly in production by Pirelli and other companies. While these beds do not appear to be foldable, they resemble folding bed designs by Zanuso, exhibited at the Milan Triennale in 1951, with thin mattresses on fabric straps affixed to bent tubular steel frames.[5]

In the children's bedroom as in other rooms in the apartment, contemporary designs and family heirlooms alike were put to use. On the wall not far from the swing-arm lamp was a wall-mounted clock with a visible pendulum. Beyond the lamp a *chiavarina* armchair made of jointed wood pieces with a woven cane seat sat next to the vanity in the dressing area (plate 13). Relatives of Marco and Billa Zanuso had given them this chair, which appears in the earliest photographs of the apartment.[6] In contrast to the slender-limbed *chiavarina*, the chair that Zanuso's older daughter sits on in the photograph mentioned above (plate 12), with one leg tucked into the chair's legs, was a common inexpensive chair called a *chiesa*; it could often be found assembled in rows in the naves of churches. The *chiesa* stood on two seat-height, square-sectioned legs at the front and two round-sectioned legs that rose the full height at the back, capped by small wooden spheres. The back was formed by two flat pieces and the legs were braced by dowels below the seat, which was roughly square in plan and made of woven straw.

The photograph in which the children are shown gives the impression of a moment of quiet productivity that has been achieved by bringing together various kinds of services into a harmony that seems improbable given the apparently difficult condition of the attic, with its sloping ceiling and visible roof timber. That the apartment was proof that this could be achieved was always a subtext of its publication in journals, where Zanuso's apartment in an attic could be offered as an example of a common situation in postwar Milan, where affordable housing options were scarce. The presence of timbers and beams in domestic spaces was also a situation that confronted tenants and their architects.

Another point of subtext, never fully explicit in Ponti's commentaries about the apartment in *Domus*, is that the harmony in question is not a matter of a consistent formal signature with crisp, neat geometries and specific shapes characterizing everything in the room. Photos of the Zanuso children's bedroom illustrate how the solution has been achieved not only by the careful selection of each furniture piece, including the negotiation of antiques like the wooden chest, but also by the strategic placement of light fixtures, accommodation of heating and cooling, and, riding on the room's previous life as the master bedroom, the design of the built-in armoire, which provides storage space without protruding into the room.

The coherence produced by these design management gestures is a quality experienced in practice, not a visual formal consistency; in this respect, its impact was transportable beyond the precincts of an upper-middle-class household like Zanuso's on

Piazza Castello and into other contexts. The child-size desk that appears in the photographs is a notable expression of that aspect of Zanuso's architecture practice, his regard for the object that attained a general usefulness that could apply to different kinds of situations, and by extension to different kinds of people. While this desk was developed for a particular architecture project, its details, worked out for the needs of children in a group home, addressed a situation that was characteristic for children. It was resolved to a level of detail that speaks to an intimate knowledge of the child's experience. During the same years, Zanuso developed a new design for the standard desks of Milan's school system, culminating in a prototype that was exhibited at the Palazzo Reale in Milan.[7]

During the 1950s, Zanuso conducted extensive typological investigations of furniture for children, working with the young architect Cini Boeri, who worked in his office at the time and was also a mother with small children.[8] Only a few of their designs would be produced for a wide audience, but the reach of these designs, including this desk and other furniture for the same project, had an impact beyond the project for which they were commissioned, amplified by their dissemination in exhibitions and circulation in architecture journals and popular magazines.

The institution for which the child's desk was designed, called Le Carline, was a philanthropic project of a type that was not uncommon in the 1950s, years still suffused with memories of World War II and marked by wartime losses and trauma. These projects were often driven by charismatic, philanthropic individuals, and the community of architects was often involved.[9] Le Carline was a home for orphaned girls, commissioned by Anna Bonomi Bolchini, a philanthropist and businesswoman, owner of a real estate company known for its work on the Pirelli tower in 1959.[10] Le Carline, named for Carlo Bonomi, Anna Bonomi Bolchini's adoptive parent, entailed the renovation of a 30-year-old building to accommodate 80 children and teenagers, aged five to twenty. Zanuso, working with Boeri, added an extension to the existing villa, creating a new entrance and adding a living room, offices, and a chapel, arrayed around a hexagonal courtyard. For the chapel's faceted ceiling and walls, Bonomi commissioned artworks by Lucio Fontana.[11]

Zanuso and Boeri divided the resident population into two age groups and developed different accommodation types for each.

Those five to fourteen years old were assigned to rooms of six to eight beds, each with personal storage space. By gathering four beds around a shared, low-profile armoire, they created a type that tactfully avoided reference to hospital wards.[12] Zanuso would exhibit a similar scheme in the exhibition *Colore e forma nella casa d'oggi* (Color and form in the house of today) at Villa Olmo in 1957. In comments about the show as a whole in the exhibition catalog, Bruno Zevi praised the scheme's grouping of low-profile furniture in the center of the room, which, by leaving the room's perimeter free for circulation, highlighted and activated the room as a space (figure 6.2).[13]

The desk used in the Zanuso apartment was designed for the older girls' wing at Istituto Le Carline, where each teenager had her own room with a desk, chair, and bed. Zanuso's design took as a premise that while children would benefit from furniture adapted to their smaller bodies, their routine actions and needs could be met by design in ways analogous to the accommodation of adults. Each teenager was to have her own chair and desk with a place for pencils, books, everything, as well as the small bed and night table (figure 6.3).[14]

The form of the desk, approximately trapezoid in plan with subtly curved sides, was wider at the far edge and narrower toward the sitter. The desk's far edge was flat, the better to fit against a wall or another desk, but the front, facing the sitter, was concave, assisting her in reaching every part of the desk surface, while the sides were convex, allowing for ease of movement around the unit. On the front was an open compartment with a drawer to each side where books and implements could be stored. At the back edge of the desk, which is pushed against the wall in both the Zanuso apartment and the Le Carline dorm room, the rim rises several centimeters above the surface. Drawings of the exhibition version show operable compartments on both sides, right and left, where things could be stowed, while the center was deeper. The legs of the desk, round in section like large dowels and tapered at the top and bottom, sat on slenderer feet that give the desk an appearance of light weight (figure 6.4).

For the exhibition of the desk at an exhibition called *Mostra del mobile singolo* (Exhibition of single furniture pieces) in 1957, a matching chair design was produced, featuring a wooden frame with cloth or leather sling seats. In addition there were two tables. One, a very simple model designed to fit into a corner, can be seen

Figure 6.2 Young girls' dormitory room, Istituto Le Carline, Milan, 1959. Photo Giorgio Casali © Fondo Giorgio Casali, IUAV Archivio Progetti, Venice.

Figure 6.3 Teenage girl's dormitory room, Istituto Le Carline, Milan, 1959. Photo Giorgio Casali © Fondo Giorgio Casali, IUAV Archivio Progetti, Venice.

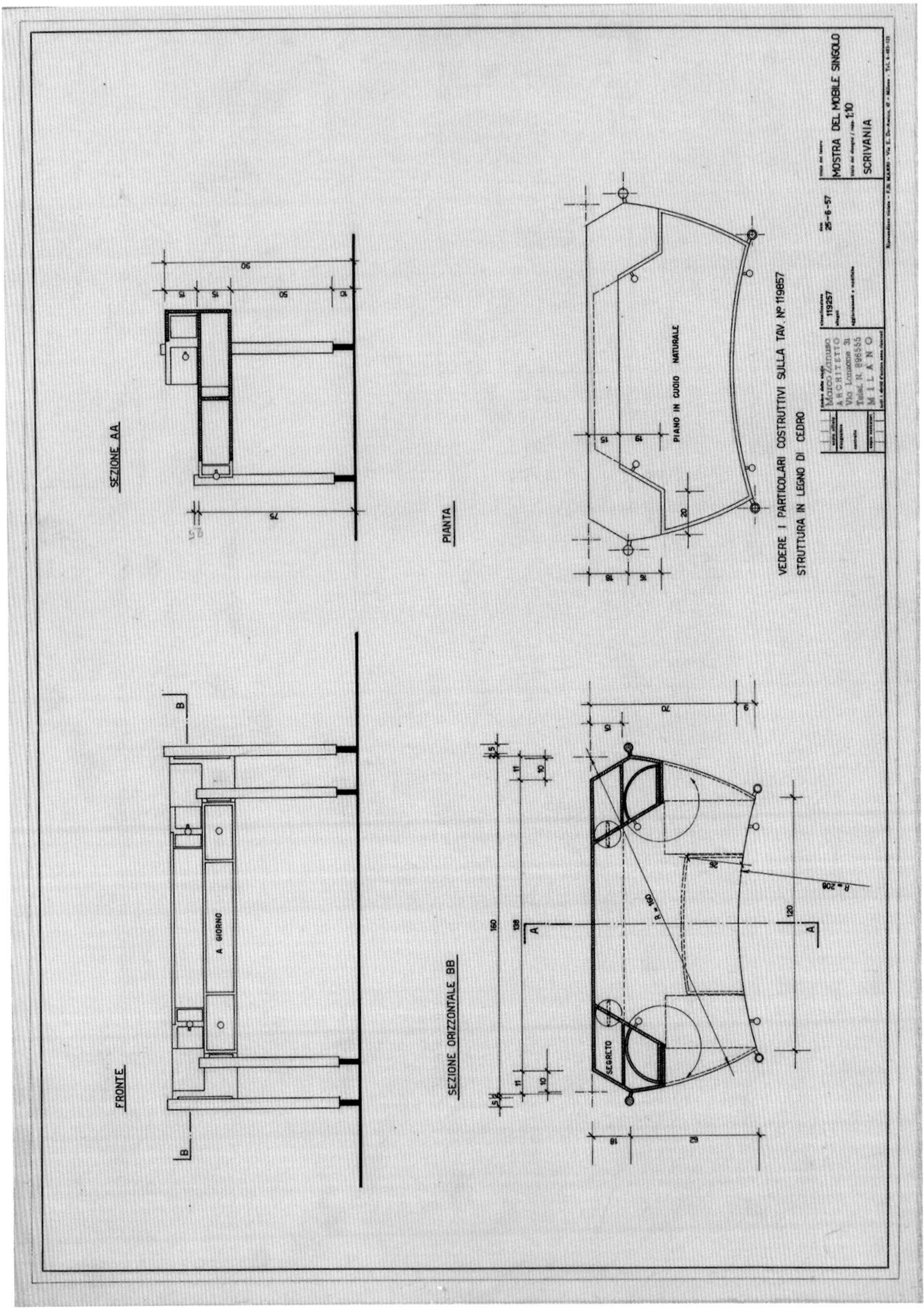

Figure 6.4 Drawing of child's desk for *Mostra del mobile singolo*, 1957. Fondo Marco Zanuso, Archivio del Moderno, Balerna.

in the photograph of the younger children's dorm room, in the corner. Another was designed to sit next to the desk. In plan it was a circle missing a portion defined by an oblique angle, resembling a pie with a large slice removed from it. It was to sit on three legs, and the upper part of each leg was hollowed out to create a pencil holder. On a drawing it is labeled as a "service table" (figure 6.5).

Although the Le Carline desk was designed for a specific institution, it had qualities in common with designs for the market. As a desk for a dormitory, it was produced in numerous copies; it was also general enough in its details and emphatic enough about catering to the user to stand on its own in a range of rooms, just as a market product would have had to be. These designs were scaled for children, but they point to design strategies that recur across Zanuso's oeuvre: the use of simple geometric shapes such as the circle, the softening and rounding of edges, the economical use of material, shaving and tapering of elements where possible, creating space and reducing weight. Another aspect evident here is the relation of these objects to one another. Between the desk and the "service table" next to it is a kind of family resemblance, the leg of one resembling the other, the curve of one figuring as an exaggerated version of the other, the legs of both adorned with dark, slender feet. The desk fulfills the essential function, the service table is an accessory to it: in Zanuso's imaginary, one object is sometimes the point of departure for another.

A photograph of a classroom in Le Carline shows tables in two rows along with a copy of the Zanuso desk, flanked by small blackboards at the front of the room. Each table has a peg on its side where a school bag can be hung, a further elaboration of a design in support of a certain function, in service of the pupil. The provision of a service table where personal possessions can be stored, as in the *Mostra del mobile singolo* design, is analogous to the peg: it is an elaboration of form that arises from knowledge of the object's use. The accessory table that was designed to sit next to the Zanuso desk was not a simple reproduction of the style of the desk in a smaller format; it was there to meet the need of the user—even a child—for a place to put things. The two resemble one another in part as a result of the aesthetic and material analogy or commonality of parts.

On the walls near the desks in another room that was furnished with rows of the desk (figure 6.6) are shelves from the String system which was designed by Nisse and Kajsa Strinning,

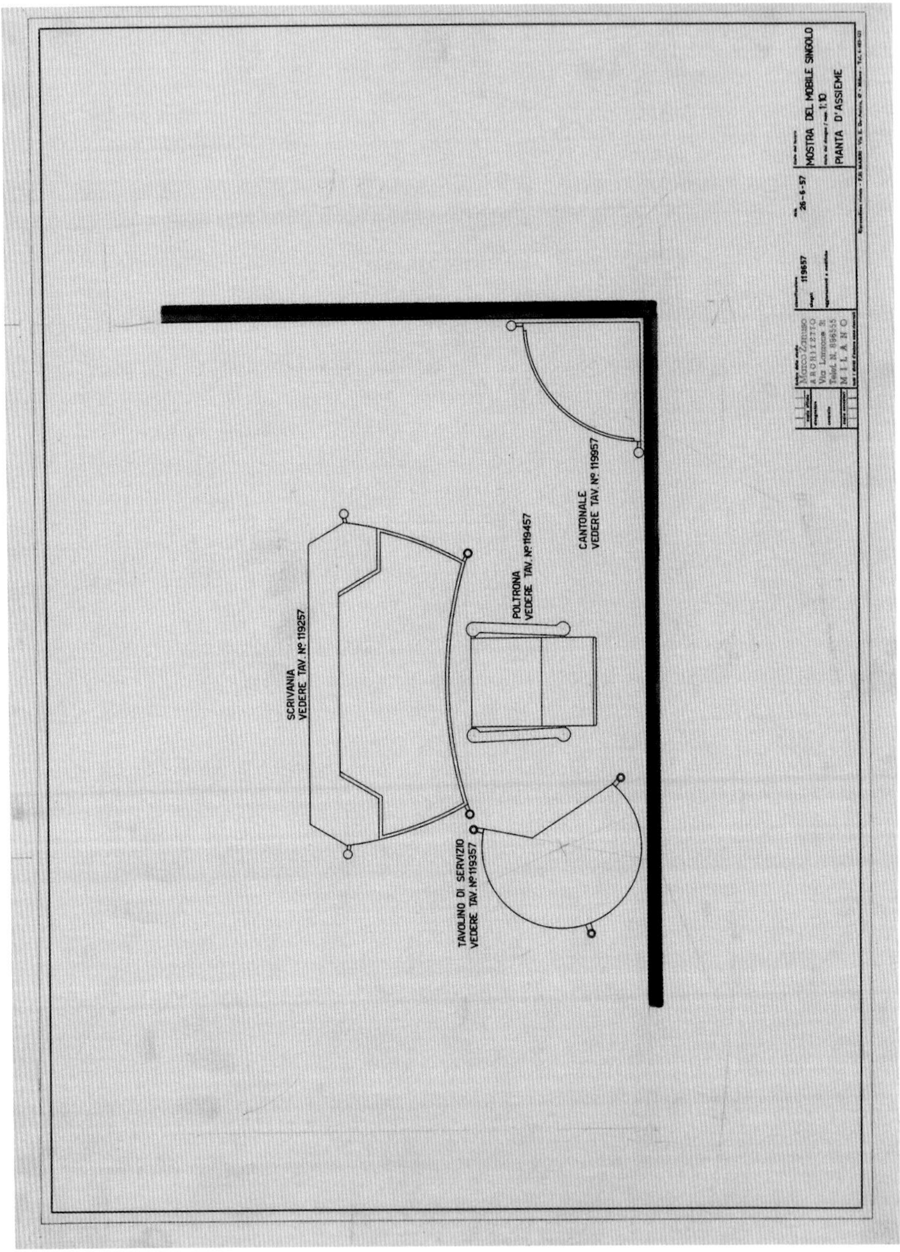

Figure 6.5 Drawing of desk and accessories for *Mostra del mobile singolo*, 1957. Fondo Marco Zanuso, Archivio del Moderno, Balerna.

Figure 6.6 Classroom, Istituto Le Carline, Milan, 1959. Photo Giorgio Casali © Fondo Giorgio Casali, IUAV Archivio Progetti, Venice.

produced in Sweden and awarded a prize at the 1954 Milan Triennale. Zanuso installed these, too, in his 1962 *bambine* suite. His use of these shelves and desk in his own children's bedroom highlights the laboratory aspect of his apartment, suggesting that it served to test and verify ideas that were destined for the wider world. The visual shaping of space by application of wallpaper to the wall, breaking the monotony of what would otherwise be an unadorned box, is another technique that Zanuso used in his children's room and in the Le Carline dorm room.

For another of Zanuso's architecture projects, the Asilo Nido at Gubbio (1959), the architects designed chairs and tables for preschool-aged children.[15] The building served a small community in the mountains near Perugia, and the furniture has a rustic appearance not unlike the *chiesa* chair in the Zanuso bedroom: chairs with four legs, the two taller ones connected by curved slats that formed the back, each topped by a ball. The low tables and seating establish a child-scale datum within the tall classroom spaces (figure 6.7). In the Gubbio Asilo Nido classrooms, as in the Le Carline dorm room and his own children's bedroom, Zanuso engaged the ceiling by decorating it; but in the Asilo Nido, the shaping of interior space would take an even more pronounced form and participate in a yet more complex approach to the coordination of form, space, furniture, and fittings to calibrate the architecture to the needs of its smallest occupants.

Zanuso composed the Asilo Nido's floor plan from seven overlapping squares, each of which would accommodate a different program, arranged in a V. The main entrance led into a flat-roofed area in the crook of the plan, where children hung their smocks by a hexagonal interior patio whose glass walls let light into the heart of the building. On one side of this patio were two classrooms and a dining room; on the other side were offices.

The squares in the plans translated into an assembly of six one-story volumes, each with a pyramid-shaped roof (figure 6.8). The walls of these volumes were the same height all around the building, 7.2 feet (2.2 m). Above, each volume had its own pyramid-shaped roof. The size of each roof was determined by the size of the room, and the positions of the different-sized rooms could be seen from the outside. Once acquainted with the building, even a child could easily comprehend how it was configured. In any case, each room opened directly onto the yard; the children could move freely between the classroom and the outdoor setting without traversing hallways or other circulation spaces. This ease of navigation reflected a priority for the school, whose governing educational program emphasized independence and assigned the children tasks through which they had the experience of supporting their small community.[16]

The clarity of the project extended to the relationship between the shapes of the volumes as they appeared from outside and the rooms as they appeared inside. Zanuso painted minimal decorations on the classroom ceilings, each of which resembled the underside of a pyramidal tent. In one room a triangle of a contrasting color was painted near the top of each roof plane, deliberately misaligned slightly to the ceiling's symmetrical creases. Four identical spherical pendant lamps hung in the space, heightening the experience of three-dimensional depth. The child-sized furniture below established the stratum of space in which the smock-clad children carried out their work and play tasks.

While the furniture for the Asilo Nido at Gubbio was part of Zanuso and Boeri's extensive work on children's furniture in the late 1960s, the architecture reflects Zanuso's approach to architectural form as seen in his factory buildings of the 1950s. In the reception of the building around 1960, one critic in particular, Carlo Ludovico Ragghianti, saw the Asilo Nido as a work of architecture very much of its time, suffused with sensibilities formed in the context of industrial production. Ragghianti, whose remarks on the Asilo Nido were published in the art journal *Sele Arte* as notes to a pictorial survey of Italian art on the cusp of the 1960s, argued that the moment in Italian art could only be understood by examining all types of artistic production.[17] His essay was a polemic against art critics who failed to question conventional categories and instead insisted on looking at painting and sculpture only, rarely at architecture, hardly ever at industrial design, graphic design, or photography. Instead, Ragghianti explained, his survey "documents a quantity of works of art of every kind, beyond any division or conventional hierarchy, because it wishes to help to overcome many prejudicial positions of taste, and indicate a more comprehensive attitude towards the value of present-day art."[18]

To demonstrate his point and to disabuse his fellow critics of any conventional distinctions between different kinds of objects, Ragghianti gathered different kinds of work, including paintings and sculpture but also furniture, lighting, ceramics,

Figure 6.7 Classroom, Asilo Nido, Gubbio, 1959. Photo Giorgio Casali © Fondo Giorgio Casali, IUAV Archivio Progetti, Venice.

Figure 6.8 Asilo Nido, Gubbio, 1960. Photo Giorgio Casali © Fondo Giorgio Casali, IUAV Archivio Progetti, Venice.

mass-produced objects and accessories, architecture, and designs for urban residential quarters and cities. He called attention to the "aesthetic quality" that all the objects had in common. The repetition of forms, one theme that is hard to miss, is evident in sculptures by Bruno Munari and Enzo Mari, as well as in Cubo, an ashtray designed by Munari and produced by Danese (which can be seen in photos of the *studio* and *ragazze-soggiorno* in the Zanuso apartment). On another page, Ragghianti placed a chair and the La Rinascente building in Rome, both by Franco Albini; the flaring of beam elements at the joints is a visible trait of both chair and building.[19] Ragghianti placed Zanuso's work just after Munari's and included the factory for Olivetti in Brazil along with the Asilo Nido; the two structures made evident use of a repeated module.[20]

In a number of apartment designs during the same period, Zanuso elaborated on the use of design techniques that are apparent in Le Carline and dramatically on display in the Asilo Nido at Gubbio, including the design of furniture with dimensions suited to the height, reach, and functional needs of child users; the placement of lighting fixtures with an eye to function and to enhancement of the space; and the use of wallpaper or paint on interior walls to relieve the eye and animate the space.

The freedom expressed in the Asilo Nido in the design of the shape of the room and its high ceilings was not often available in apartments in Milan, but some apartment projects went well beyond the mere decoration of preexisting spaces. The apartment designed by Zanuso for his brother Michele Zanuso and family featured a spacious two-room play area for the children, with built-in shelves rising to counter height, a built-in armoire, and child-sized furniture (figure 6.9). The hexagonal table designed by Zanuso and Boeri for the Le Carline dining room made an appearance in the project, with *chiesa* chairs around it, in addition to an antique desk.

In addition to repeating the furnishing solutions in some one-off pieces in other projects, Zanuso provided images to dozens of magazine articles on various aspects of homemaking. An example is an article in *Amica* (September 1962) which featured two children's rooms by Zanuso and Boeri, one of which was from the Michele Zanuso apartment. The desk and bed from the teenager's room at Le Carline appeared in a similar article, described as "the room of a young girl." In this way, publications extended the reach of the Zanuso apartment and other architecture projects, even if the buildings and pieces involved were produced in limited numbers.

Figure 6.9 Children's room, Michele Zanuso apartment, 1962. Photo Ugo Mulas © Ugo Mulas Heirs. All rights reserved.

In 1962 the room labeled *bambine* sustained a number of functions, from sleeping to dressing, studying, and relaxing. When that room had been the adult bedroom, beginning in the late 1940s, the functions were fewer. That simplicity of functions, suggested by furnishing with just a bed, table, and chairs, was maintained when the adult bedroom, the *letto*, was moved to the building's Via Lanza side.

Letto

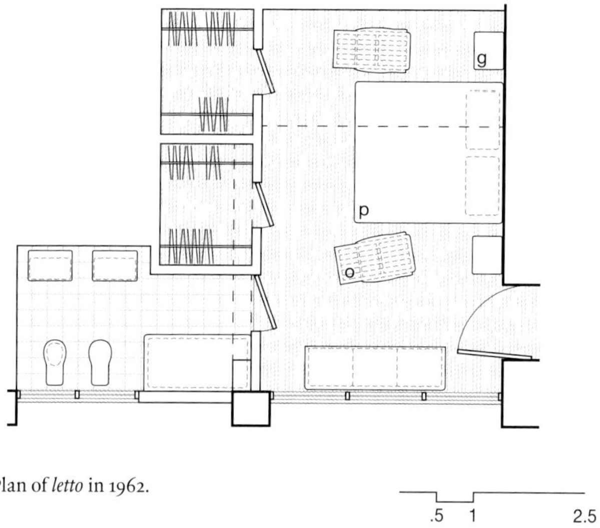

Figure 7.1 Plan of *letto* in 1962.

In this most private space of the apartment, you would find yourself among furnishings and adjacent rooms focused on just a few tasks: sleeping, dressing, and bathing. The bathroom door would be straight ahead as you entered, with two closets to the right of it. The three-seat bench on your left would pass almost unnoticed beneath the window and the sloped ceiling's low edge. In 1958 your eye might have lingered on the standing lamp in the corner, with the rounded cone of its sculpted shade turned up or down (plate 14), or on the three doors (bathroom, closet, and closet) whose sloping top edges made them seem taller and acknowledged the ceiling's slanted plane even while making it less noticeable by integrating it with the wall. A photograph of this view in 1962, looking toward that wall, shows all three doors open and a bouquet of flowers half-visible on the nightstand next to where the photographer stood. A robe hangs from a hook on the bathroom door, a rack of ties hangs on one closet door (plate 26).

To the right as you stood in the doorway was the bed, actually a pair of antique beds bound together, with brass balls topping the legs that continued up the sides of the wooden headboard. To either side of the bed from 1958 onward was a small nightstand made of two stacked wooden tables with pointed legs, designed by Vico Magistretti, produced by Azucena beginning in the late 1940s and known as T8. Two wall-mounted lamps, one on each side of the bed, resemble the 31 by Gino Sarfatti (1950). Each is a cylindrical tube concealing a small lightbulb, anchored to the bedpost by a single straight rod that is jointed at either end, providing a limited adjustment of the cylinder's direction. The position of these lamps suggests that they were reading lights, but the way the light fixtures are pointed toward the wall in one image, not toward the bed, recalls how task lamps were often put in service as ambient lights as well, according to the frugal advice of architects writing on furnishing in the first issues of *Domus* after World War II.[1]

The bedroom was created by the renovation recorded in 1958 and remained essentially unchanged until 1967, including its relationship to the living room, with which it shared a door in 1962, as shown in the floor plan in figure 7.1. The 1958 renovation had tilted up another part of the roof, near the corner of the building and along the Via Lanza side, pulling the ceiling away from the diagonal timber beams that supported it to bring the ceiling height up to code near the windows at the bottom of the slope. Timber beams would remain exposed and visible in the bedroom suite, as they did in the children's room, *studio*, and *soggiorno*. The beam in the bedroom, about 5 feet (1.5 m) from the floor at its low end, is visible just beyond the bathroom and closet doors (plate 26).

The furniture in the bedroom had been brought over from its previous location, on the Piazza Castello side of the building, and reinstalled in more or less the same relationships: a double bed, two chairs, side tables. The two closets and their mirrors speak of a place where one got dressed, but this room appears not to have been used for more than sleeping or reading; nor was sleeping, served here by antique beds, a subject of investigation. A more fruitful point of departure might be dreaming. When Zanuso described his "ideal" house, illustrated in drawings and a model and published in *Domus* in 1942, during the war, the bedroom was characterized in terms of sanctuary.[2]

Zanuso's imagined house, ideally located on the periphery of the city, would be a place where the family could grow, with an aesthetic continuity among all of its objects and surfaces. While it would be well lighted, it would sit on a plot with walls in spaces that were carefully delimited. It would offer a place to gather but also a place to work and think alone.[3] Zanuso's house design had what he called a "nucleus": a rectangle with 3:1 proportions that formed a continuous space for the domestic functions. Over time, it could be extended by building further into the landscape. The bedroom in the ideal house, along with an adjacent bathroom, was placed at one end of the rectangle; the piano and dining table were at the other end.

The master bedroom in the Zanuso apartment, the *letto*, was similarly at one end of the apartment in 1962. Its position on Via Lanza was likely quieter than on the side facing Piazza Castello, where there was a streetcar. The qualities of this room invite consideration of how it served as a space to gather one's thoughts while reading or falling asleep: to rest, broadly speaking. In this respect the few items that decorated the room bring up an important set of facts about Zanuso's practice: his relationship to art and artists.

Artworks adorned the bedroom walls in 1962 along with a clock and barometer, reminders of Zanuso's passion for sailing. Above the nightstand nearest the door, on the *soggiorno*-side wall, was a framed drawing, print, or painting, probably by Renato Guttuso, of whose work the family owned several examples around 1960 (plate 27). Other works by Guttuso in photographs of the apartment in 1962 included two drawings of heads that hung beneath the windows on the living room's Piazza Castello wall, as noted above (plate 19). Casali's 1958 photograph of the bedroom shows a small work, a painted wood panel, in the same location above the nightstand (plate 16). It is clear from the continual presence of paintings and drawings in the bedroom, as in the *soggiorno*, *studio*, and the children's bedroom, that Zanuso believed in living spaces in which one was surrounded by art, presumably to partake of the mental state of contemplation.

On the wall opposite the windows was a single large work, *Concetto spaziale, I muri*, 1957, by Lucio Fontana (plate 15, left).[4] The media of this particular work, described in a catalogue raisonnée as "pastels and holes," are characteristic of Fontana's *Concetto spaziale* series of punctured and sliced canvases. Zanuso and Fontana were friends and occasional collaborators. The stylistic range in the work of Fontana, who often pursued diverse series of explorations in parallel around the time when the work on Zanuso's wall was created, is demonstrated in the contrast between *Concetto spaziale* and the decorations he created for the ceiling of the chapel in Zanuso's building for Le Carline, the home for orphaned girls. There, Fontana contributed a round altarpiece and a series of bas-relief medallions in a classical mode recalling Renaissance-era relief sculpture, addressing the theme of the Via Crucis (way of the cross). A pattern of curved abstract motifs, inscribed in white-on-gray plaster in the chapel's ceiling, were also part of Fontana's contribution to the Le Carline project (see "Bambine").[5]

The presence in Zanuso's bedroom of Fontana's canvas, which refers us to the acquaintance between the architect and the artist, invites us to consider the wider set of Zanuso's collaborations with artists in the early 1950s. In the objects that he created in these collaborations, the way his own stipulation of form makes way for the interventions of others demonstrates a rigorous restraint of architectural form. Accommodation, in this sense, is an aspect of method that is implicit not only in Zanuso's buildings but also in some of his simplest objects.

A photograph of the master bedroom in 1950 is instructive as a reminder of the range of ways in which Zanuso used objects to accommodate functional needs (plate 4, bottom). Reflected in the mirror above the marble shelf in the original *letto* is the opposite wall with a chair near the edge of the bed, with a shelf attached to the wall to function as a nightstand. With the shelf, an object has been made to serve a role that is fulfilled by its very general characteristics (such as flatness and simplicity of attachment to the wall). By contrast in the chair, the design is elaborated through extensive manipulation of materials. The chair is essentially a canvas sling suspended from a freestanding steel frame, but that schema is just a point of departure in the design toward an ultimate form in which the shape and relationship of pieces of the frame, as in the arms of the chair, are determined by its relationship to the seated human body that is accounted for in the design but is, of course, physically separate from it. The chair, more than the shelf, is shaped by the presence of something independent of itself. Zanuso would approach accommodation in both of these ways in the design of his apartment on Piazza Castello.

To a greater or lesser extent, Zanuso's designs in collaboration with artists made way for independent entities in proximity, not only the human occupants that the objects served but also other forms, designed by other authors, in and around the physical structure. Zanuso demonstrated a comparable openness to incorporating the formal products of other imaginations in building and object designs where the mechanical or technical apparatus, rather than the artwork (or in some cases along with the artwork), was a determining factor. The Fontana painting in the Zanuso bedroom is related to a series of buildings, exhibits, and storefronts completed by Zanuso during the 1950s that illustrate his contact with the discourse on art and its public that was centered in a group of Milan's artists.

An early collaboration between Zanuso and Fontana, the decoration of an office building on Via Senato, was Zanuso's first large-scale realization of a building with an artist's intervention, a concept he had tested in a model that was exhibited at the ninth Triennale, showing an apartment building with mural inserts at every floor by the artist Corrado Cagli. Meanwhile Lucio Fontana, with architect Vito Latis, would demonstrate this paradigm in another project built in Milan in 1951–1952.[6]

Designed by Zanuso with architect Roberto Menghi for an American ex-military businessman seeking to establish roots in Milan, and constructed at the corner of Via Senato and Via Sant'Andrea in 1946–1947, the building was L-shaped and six stories high, with a roof terrace.[7] A driveway from Via Sant'Andrea led to a courtyard with parking, one half-level below street level, while, from Via Senato, a visitor would pass through a full-height atrium and up a half-flight of steps to enter. The building was constructed from a concrete structure of floor slabs and columns finished with a cladding of polished granite, with elongated round-cornered openings cut into it around the windows.

Fontana designed handles for the double doors in the atrium, each a unique nebulous curling form reminiscent of a seashell (figure 7.2). These were made from a red clay material by the ceramics firm Gabbianelli, finished with a blue-and-white glaze. Fontana also contributed ceramic panels in the facade beneath the windows. Each window was set in a rectangular opening with rounded corners in the granite facing. Fontana's glazed ceramic panels, raked by hand in horizontal lines, sat below the windows within these openings. On the front facade by the entrance, behind the

Figure 7.2 Door handles by Lucio Fontana, office building at Via Senato, 5, Milan, in 2008.

tall glass curtain wall of the atrium, Fontana's ceramic relief panels covered the exposed edge of each floor plate, forming a multistory, multipart mural.

The suite of Fontana's decorative interventions here is distinctly neoclassical, and indeed the building itself, with its overall rectangular prism shape and its windows organized in grid patterns on each elevation, gravitates toward the physiognomy of a Renaissance palazzo in certain respects, though it might be compared more proximally to an urban American office building from the early twentieth century. At any rate, descriptions of the building tend to move quickly from allusions to the past to a consideration of the building's modern features. A critical assessment that appeared in the *Architectural Review*, for instance, reads like a catalog of modern building, including the walls of "polished pink Baveno granite," the "continuous glazed panel of 120 metres" that "rises above the main entrance to the full height of the building," and the "three-foot aluminium grille round its base" that "gives the surprising effect that the building is floating clear of the ground."[8] The building also had its own generator, water and fuel tanks, and machine shop.[9]

Fontana's work for the apartment building at Via Senato, during a period when he was creating artworks for more than one new building in Milan, was an early manifestation of a trend in which a number of artists created works for new buildings, interior and exterior.[10] Many of the artists and architects involved exhibited their work in the group exhibitions of the time, such as the eighth and ninth Milan Triennale in 1947 and 1951, respectively.

Zanuso's activities with artists coincided with the artists' pursuit of involvement with industrial production, adopting in their way an attitude that Zanuso and a few other architects had embraced already in the mid-1940s. While Fontana is the most widely known among Zanuso's artists, the projects Zanuso realized with the painter Gianni Dova were more closely associated with Zanuso's modernist, rationalist leanings and with the ideas about the potential collaboration between architect and painter that Zanuso espoused around 1950.

These ideas were explained by Zanuso in "Architettura e pittura" (1952), one of his few speculative theoretical writings. An important premise for him was that abstract art allowed the artist and architect to work in aesthetically compatible interventions in the spatial continuum.[11] Moreover the architect working with rationalist norms in mind, producing buildings that were effectively monochrome and validated by geometrical precision, lost nothing by leaving the decoration of surfaces to the artist.

Zanuso's built experiment with these ideas, concurrent with the publication of "Architettura e pittura," was the apartment building on Viale Gorizia.[12] The building featured a mural by Gianni Dova that resembled a net of multicolored braided diagonal lines covering the building's entire front facade (figure 7.3). Dova's intervention was both more comprehensive and less conventional than Fontana's had been in the Via Senato building. The cords of color in the mural seem to pass behind one another, imposing in some places a pictorial depth upon the facade's undulating orthogonal bays. The medium of Dova's mural was a surface finish material called Fulget, produced in a gamut of colors. This connection between the art world and building finish product exemplifies the interest of artists in new building products that supported their participation in architectural projects. Architects were being encouraged to take an interest in these new means as well; a notable advocate of Zanuso and Dova's building and of the possibilities of Fulget was the architect Giò Ponti, editor of *Domus*. In a short article published in March 1952, Ponti took pains to elicit curiosity in his architect reader about Fulget's vivid color and "natural beauty" along with its low cost and resistance to damage, emphasizing its suitability for architectural works. The piece was illustrated with a close-up view of the finish material on the adjacent page, showing a surface finish in which a fine-grained gravel was pressed onto the surface and overlaid with a colored binding material.[13]

The way Gianni Dova's mural took over the full extent of the front facade of Zanuso's apartment building on Viale Gorizia, realizing its own pictorial space to the scale of the building, is somewhat awkward as the building appears today, seen in between its conventional neighbors. But in the series of Zanuso's designs, this building made an indisputable break from the template that had constrained his previous proposals. The relationship between the mural and the building is quite different from the art's relationship to the architecture in Zanuso's unbuilt scheme with Cagli's balcony panels or in the Via Senato building, which accommodates Lucio Fontana's contributions as shadow-like echoes of the architectural motifs (windows, floor plans).

In the editorial essay of the issue of *Domus* where the building on Viale Gorizia was published, Ponti wrote on the distinction

Figure 7.3 Apartment building on Viale Gorizia, Milan, 1952. Photo Giorgio Casali © Fondo Giorgio Casali, IUAV Archivio Progetti, Venice.

between the *architettura d'arte* (architecture of art) that determined the rapport between the disciplines in advance, according to convention, and the *arte architettonica* (architectonic art) that embraced a broader set of possibilities. His example of the latter was a windmill in Rotterdam, illustrated in an adjacent photograph.[14] The abandonment of the neoclassical paradigm that Ponti expresses hope for is self-evident in the Viale Gorizia building, which appears on the following two pages, captured in photographs by Giorgio Casali. Ponti presented Zanuso's building as a work of architecture proper as distinct from other buildings in Milan whose architecture was "dedicated" only to a conventional architectural language of allusion and rhetoric. Ponti proposes that the "walls" of the streets should be dedicated instead to the artists of the day, and he introduces Zanuso's building as a fearless test of the concept, with his facade dedicated to Dova.[15]

Part of what drew Ponti to projects like this one was their bold use of color. In an essay published in 1952 in *Edilizia Moderna*, he made playful but provocative remarks about common misconceptions. The people who dress in gray and speak of "tradition," he said, forget that the masterpieces on which tradition was based were products of a social life characterized by holidays and festivals, by people who never dressed in gray pants. Homes, too, were colorful. Ponti describes how he uses color in his own work and remarks that color can be experienced not only in juxtaposition but also in sequence, by a visitor moving through a space.[16]

Zanuso's attitude to color in 1942 was more moderate than Ponti's, but an interest in color is suggested by his frequent collaboration with artists. In his writing about domestic architecture, Zanuso had mentioned color as a source of stimulation and proposed a color scheme in which the quieter parts of the house would be monochrome while "the table where one eats, the sofa, the armchairs, the raised carpeted area where one reads, or converses, or rests, are arranged in the brighter, more ample, more richly detailed, more colored zone."[17] Still ambivalent in 1951, Zanuso expressed reservations about an architect's capacity to work in color. The new volumes of modern architecture were "almost always white or monochrome," the better to clearly show their "capacities of expression and weight." Color is "held at a distance," for it "could disturb an equilibrium that architecture, as yet in its evolutionary phase, can still not control."[18]

An interior by Zanuso from around the same time that included works by artists and engaged with color in a provocative way was a showroom interior for the Società del Linoleum, a distributor of rubber flooring materials, constructed in downtown Milan with an adjoining small reading room where architects could meet informally and catch up on reading journals and which occasionally welcomed special visitors, as when an exhibition of photographs by Lucien Hervé was held there in 1953.[19]

The circular decorations on the reading room floor, echoed in the plan shapes of the desk and curved metal stair leading to the mezzanine, were a moment of vivid interaction between furniture pieces, including a circular desk designed by Zanuso, and the floors and walls. In both the reading room and showroom, artists Gianni Dova and Mario Ballocco made graphic, brightly colored compositions using the company's product line. Integrated into the walls, these obviated the need for racks or shelves and activated the space itself, which in the case of the showroom allowed the space to remain uncluttered. In this project Zanuso, wary of using color, made an experiment on that theme with the painters, and for publication the graphic designer Albe Steiner, contributing the color. Steiner's collage cover design, bringing back color that was suppressed in the black-and-white photographs, also demonstrates how the painters' interventions, each with a certain constructivist geometric rigor, could lend themselves to integration into the two-dimensional space of the journal page (figure 7.4). The painter Ballocco in particular would pursue a consultant practice focused on that theme, launch another journal devoted to color, and teach color theory at the Milan Polytechnic.[20]

The linoleum showroom, first published in *Edilizia Moderna* and *Rivista Pirelli* in Milan, was also mentioned by the architect Paul Damaz in his book on the "synthesis of the arts" in European architecture. The preface to Damaz's book, written by Le Corbusier, underscores its connection to a discourse that had emerged in the mid-1940s in discussions of projects like Ronchamp and the UNESCO building, examining architecture's relationships to other arts, led by Le Corbusier and Josep Lluis Sert at meetings of CIAM, the International Congress on Modern Architecture.[21]

More indicative of the discussion that was happening among *artists* in Milan, as distinct from the architects, were remarks about the project written by Gillo Dorfles, who in an essay on the

Figure 7.4 Società del Linoleum showroom, Milan, pictured in graphic studies by Albe Steiner for the front (left) and back (right) covers of *Edilizia Moderna* 48 (1952). Archivio Albe e Lica Steiner, Archivi Storici e Attività Museali, ACL, Politecnico di Milano.

linoleum showroom speculated about the artists' use of color, shape, and texture as two-dimensional means to invite and influence the movement of visitors across the space. This "functional art" seemed to Dorfles to promise an expanded role for the artist in the industrial age. Specifically, the architecture, which dominated, carried out "delicate" technical tasks to construct the space as a working showroom and support for the art, while the artists "Dova and Ballocco have drawn on completely personal themes and were able to liberally construct their artistic inventions, adapting them to the atmosphere and the 'style' of the place in collaboration with the architect."[22] That characterization agreed with the perspective of Mario Ballocco, one of the artists who contributed to the showroom.

Ballocco, as editor of the journal *AZ* beginning in 1949, had cultivated a discourse around the future of the artist in the post-World War II industrial era, marked by the emergence of new materials, especially synthetic surface materials in a wide range of colors, that were poised to turn any surface into an artist's canvas. "Color is a vital necessity," he wrote in one editorial. "It is impossible to imagine life without color. . . . It is only in the work dreamed by man that color ends up monotonous and heavy."[23] Channeling ideas of interwar modern movements for the postwar decades and echoing sentiments of concrete art, Ballocco predicted that the functions of objects would be preserved while through "concrete" strategies, expressed in geometrically rigorous forms, the objects would be renewed and transformed.[24] Along similar lines, contributor Bruno Munari expressed the hope that artists who could find sites for their art in everyday spaces might bridge the divide between the artist and the general public.[25]

In the last few issues of its run (1949–1952), the journal *AZ*, which had started as a conventional arts magazine and published on a variety of art forms, including music, poetry, and architecture as well as painting and sculpture, turned to the theme of the artist's relationship to industry. The final issue doubled as the catalog for an exhibition at the Fiera Campionaria of 1952 on "industrial aesthetics." Marco Zanuso's chair Lady, produced by Arflex, was among the exhibits along with a scooter, a rifle, and a sewing pattern but also rolls of rubber and linoleum finish material and similar raw materials.

While the discourse on the synthesis of the arts in architecture was focused narrowly on buildings and mainly on certain paradigms of the "integration" of the arts, including the mural and the statue in front of the building, by contrast the discourse in AZ, which amplified the artists' purview and imagination, looked to superimposed spatial relationships, to building materials, and to mass production as generative starting points.[26]

Zanuso's immersion in problems related to mass production, including small objects with an eye to the building scale and attending to means and materials as well as to the forms of objects, defined his practice in the 1950s and 1960s. In most of his projects the surface finishes, design of furniture, and other elements were far less coordinated than they were in the linoleum showroom. Zanuso was an advocate of the coming together of many creators in a single work, but not of the *Gesamtkunstwerk* concept in which different parts of a space had to resemble one another. Nevertheless, his association with this group of artists and his work in specific collaborations highlights other aspects of his work.

One is the way that he entered into these projects with the outlook of one member of a multiperspective project team and tended to conceive objects in which the architecture leads from among the other components rather than imposing an order from above. A project that illustrates Zanuso's capacity to think and act as a designer in parallel and tandem with other forms of design is the showroom for Arteluce, the company of lighting designer Gino Sarfatti. The reading lamps attached to the bed and the standing lamp in the corner of Zanuso's bedroom are possibly Sarfatti's 31B (1950) and a variant of 1003 (1946), respectively.[27] Images of fixtures arrayed in the showroom demonstrate how Sarfatti had added a cultural value to the technical assembly of the bulb, wires, and stands through an engagement with a shape vocabulary that was familiar from abstract painting (figure 7.5). The lampshades, with their rounded or angular conical shapes, might have been drawn from any number of abstract paintings; one thinks of the Spanish painter Joan Miró. These sit on straight metal rods and stand on legs or disc-shaped platforms. Zanuso's design created a setting for these pieces, without ostentation, introducing a disc-shaped soffit on the ceiling and a ribbon-like strip of wall that wound through the showroom and shaped the display area while remaining independent of the actual architectural walls, discreetly screening the display space from the administrative spaces in the shop (figure 7.6).

What is most vital in Zanuso's work with artists, as an indicator of his architecture and design sensibility around 1952, is the centrality of attention paid to the optimal function of things and spaces relative to their use. For the painters Ballocco and Munari, a functional aspect in an object shaped by the artist could ensure its presence in everyday life. Similarly, Zanuso and other architect practitioners of rationalism firmly believed that their modern buildings and objects would validate themselves to a public facing stylistic choices by virtue of the modern object's ease and effectiveness in use.

As noted above, Zanuso's objects often have a kind of functional diagram or scheme. This is almost never literal or explicit, but in descriptions of the project it emerges as part of the method. The Zanuso apartment on Piazza Castello is a project in which this aspect of his method is most explicit and documented. The essay by Eugenio Gentili Tedeschi that introduced the Zanuso family apartment when it was published in *Abitare* in 1962 offers indispensable insight into this process and stance. Gentili Tedeschi begins by noting that the architect in the attic had bearing walls and sloped ceiling surfaces to contend with, along with the possession of a number of inherited pieces, as we have seen. Nevertheless, Gentili Tedeschi discerned a kind of precision in the design. "The way of living is completely defined," he wrote. The result was "completely relaxed and articulate"; "almost nothing is left to do but locate the individual objects in corresponding pigeonholes that are predisposed to contain them."[28]

There can be "pigeonholes" for furniture pieces corresponding to the family members' activities only in an overall armature of functions and locations. Zanuso's approach was what he called a "maieutics" (Socratic interrogation) to arrive at a list of needs and to develop the plan. The minute examination of habits served to characterize the home in terms of an inventory of practical requirements. No written documentation exists of such a process behind the apartment at Piazza Castello, 20, except for the plan; but Gentili Tedeschi enumerates a set of requirements including "sitting, going to bed, reading, studying, gathering for conversation, and so on," as tasks or activities to which Zanuso had matched each furniture piece.[29] Rather than proceed from conventional assumptions about certain types of pieces—for instance, valuing pieces of one style over another—Zanuso relied on an inventory in which the

Figure 7.5 Lighting display, Arteluce showroom, Milan, 1951. Photo Giorgio Casali © Fondo Giorgio Casali, IUAV Archivio Progetti, Venice.

Figure 7.6 Rear view of lighting display, Arteluce showroom, Milan, 1951. Photo Giorgio Casali © Fondo Giorgio Casali, IUAV Archivio Progetti, Venice.

"utility" of each object was defined first and foremost in terms of its capacity for practical use.

The process of identifying requirements ensures that new ways of doing things are accounted for. As an example of changes in furnishing that follow from a change in use, Gentili Tedeschi mentions the tendency to use lighter-weight, more frequently changed linens, which allow for shallower, more numerous storage cabinets in contrast to the massive armoires of times past. Another example is change in women's clothing, such as the abandonment of corsets that allows women to sit more comfortably in low chairs.

Gentili Tedeschi outlines a process, attributed to Zanuso, in which a list of such use cases is drawn up and the objects are compared, taking into account a range of different kinds of value, including the value that new materials or techniques bring to certain objects. Subjective considerations can be taken into account as well when choosing which pieces to keep and where they might be used. One might choose to keep an object for purely sentimental value in one instance and for fully utilitarian reasons in another. The resulting plan emphasizes the coordination of needs on one hand with satisfactory pieces on the other. Zanuso's use of the criterion of satisfying tasks in the apartment to place pieces produces a number of diverse solutions and is "indifferent to the character of the objects employed time after time," Gentili Tedeschi notes.[30] Zanuso's approach was also independent (at least in principle) of generic or received formulas for furnishing rooms. The *soggiorno*'s corner with its sofas and chairs, for instance, was not a recapitulation of the *salotto* of times past; it was a configuration of modern seating that promoted the informal conversations that distinguished the present day.[31]

In remarks on antiquarianism in another article, the transcript of a conversation that was staged by *Abitare* on the value of antiques and collectibles, Zanuso expanded on his view of how to contend with old and new furniture. Older pieces might have personal sentimental value or may express an identification with family history; but one should not suppose that it would be possible to turn back the clock, given that the pace of life and ways of doing things had changed. Luckily, as Gentili Tedeschi observes in his discussion of the Zanuso home, some older pieces can still serve in their old roles, while others may be employed in new ways.[32]

This last point is exemplified in the chair in the Zanuso bedroom that was referred to as a "marinaia olandese" (Dutch mariner) in a penciled note scrawled on the back of a photograph in the Zanuso archive. In photographs from 1958 a pair of these slung-back, slat-backed wooden armchairs had moved to the bedroom, one on each side of the bed. These were among the furniture pieces that the Zanusos had inherited from relatives; one is visible in the earliest photographs of the apartment, in 1949 and 1950. Although it was not a new design, nor made of industrial materials, the chair had a value in the apartment that was fully independent of its style or character, derived instead from its capacity for an assigned role.

The *marinaia olandese* sat without conflict among other older pieces in the bedroom, including the twin beds with brass ball ornaments, the three-seat bench along the Via Lanza-side wall, and the barometer on the wall between the bathroom and closet doors (which also appears in early photos). Positioned right next to the bed, its back turned toward the foot of the bed leaving ample space between it and nightstand for getting in and out of bed, the Dutch mariner provided a temporary resting place for clothes. This gave it a task to fulfill in the overall functional scheme, drawn by Zanuso on plans of the room. This chair placement, one example of Zanuso's approach to *arredamento* (furnishing), shows how in the apartment a comprehensive design could confer a sense of adequacy, suitability, and contemporaneity on any component.

Marco Zanuso's designs for architecture and interiors near the start of his practice in the mid-1940s accommodated artworks. The series just reviewed illustrates different schemes of their inclusion, from the systematic array of inserts in the facade seen in the office building on Via Senato to the "overlay" approach on Viale Gorizia to the shops featuring artists' compositions and lamps in the spatial framework of the architecture. A common thread that links all of the projects is that the architecture serves in the design as a syntactical chassis in which the independent interventions or objects made by others may be freely placed. In the showrooms in particular, as in the Zanuso family apartment, the framework is constituted not only by a physical support but also by the architect's rigorous study of the distribution of functions in space.

The renovation that created the *letto*, recorded in the 1958 plans and photographs of the Zanuso apartment, entailed the extension of the raised part of the roof all the way to the Via Lanza side of Piazza Castello, 20. In 1962, this giant dormer, which was required to bring the ceiling height up to code under the low end of the sloped roof, stopped at the far end of the servant bedroom, just beyond the master bedroom suite. A major change took place in 1967, however, when the bedroom door was moved to a new hallway, parallel to the stairwell. The hallway was created to serve a new bedroom suite, the *ragazze*.

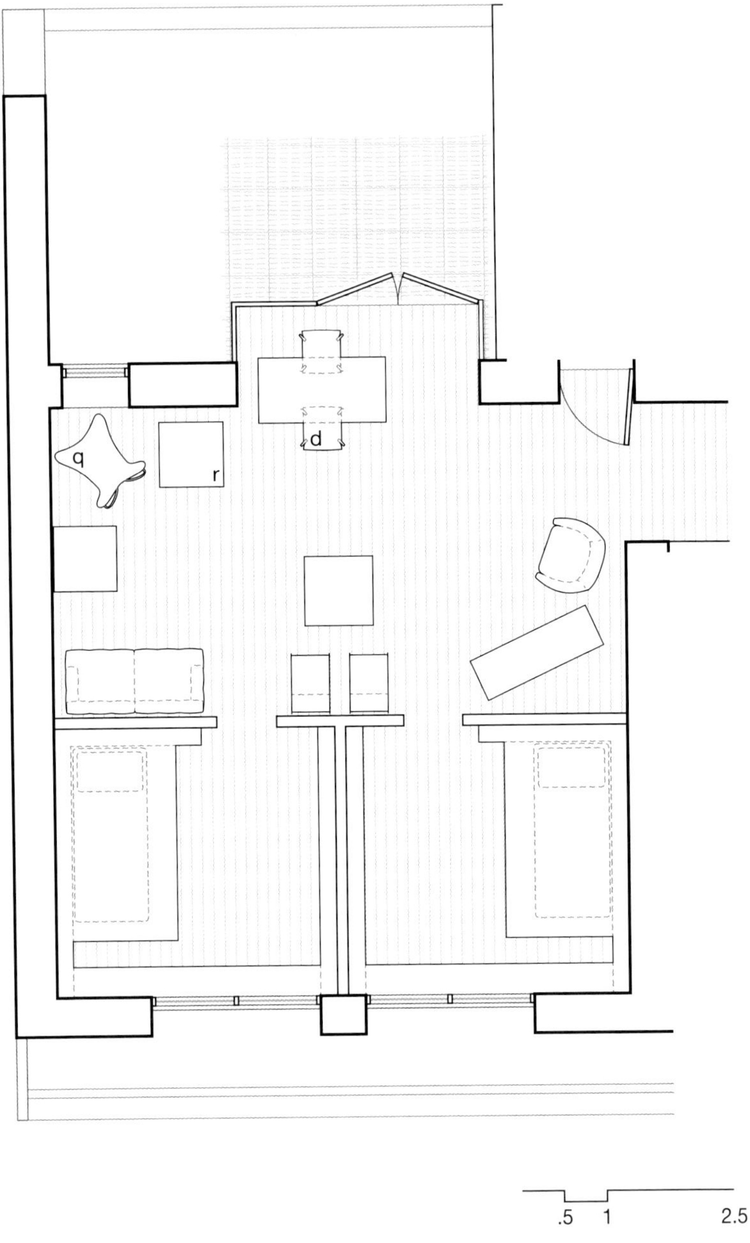

Figure 8.1 Plan of *ragazze* in 1967.

Ragazze

From the *ingresso*, you would turn right to cross the corner of the *soggiorno*, where someone sitting on the sofa might look up from their book or paper to greet you. Walking down the hallway past the new door to the master bedroom, you would arrive at the small living room in the suite that was shared by Zanuso's older daughters, who were college-age in 1967. Through a door to the right were a kitchenette and bathroom, the bathroom window opening onto the building's courtyard. To the right as one crossed the room's doorless threshold, beneath a soffit was a niche that held a working table made of a cloth-covered board on red trestles, with two Lambda chairs. In the courtyard-side wall of the niche were double doors that opened onto a terrace, as shown in the floor plan in figure 8.1.

A window at the far end of this same wall, near the corner of the room, was set in a second, smaller niche, furnished with a seat cushion and providing a resting place, in one photograph, for a guitar and balalaika (plate 31). Through the window, behind the instruments, the terrace is visible in the same photo. The courtyard-side railing had against it a layer of fencing made of lightweight reed material lashed together, such as one might find at the seaside. This reed material, which can also be glimpsed outside the walls of the apartment living room in some photographs, served to screen the windows of the suite and to filter the lower part of the view into an abstract pattern. A similar material covered the trellis over the terrace near the doors to shade it, a configuration that recalls by analogy the more expansive trellis in the open-air dining room of the house that Zanuso designed for his brother, Michele Zanuso, at Arzachena, Sardinia in the early 1960s (figure 8.2).

By 1962, when the apartment floor plan had acquired the *ingresso* and fulfilled the promise of nearly square and rectangular rooms, some of the artifacts of the attic had been eliminated from the plan, if not from the section, where the ceiling planes still sloped down toward the outer walls. In 1967, with the conversion of the remaining attic into livable space, the Zanuso apartment reached another milestone: it finally occupied the full footprint of the building at Piazza Castello, 20, from the party wall on Piazza Castello, around the corner, to the party wall on Via Lanza (plate 35).

From the beginning, the building had been more nearly rectangular in the part that bordered Via Lanza, which, unlike Piazza Castello, was not curved. The distortion of the trapezoidal site was more pronounced on the ground level than on upper levels, where the courtyard, which contained the least orthogonal corner, was outdoors and experienced only visually. The Via Lanza wing of the apartment was divided into three sections separated by thick walls. Each section was roughly a square, equal in size: the *soggiorno* at the intersection of the two wings; the master bedroom suite plus servant's bedroom in the middle; and after 1967 the new suite at the end, with the daughters' *soggiorno* and two bedrooms together forming a square shape in the plan.

Photos of the bedrooms were not published; little more is known about them than what appears in plan: each provided privacy and each had a bed and cabinet, a window, shelves. This chapter focuses on the small *soggiorno*, which recapitulates the approach that was used in other rooms: groups of furniture in a generously proportioned space signal and situate activities such as reading, studying, or socializing. This *soggiorno* was formed by some of Zanuso's furniture and industrial design products that had gone into production in the mid-1960s. A radio perched on the desk in one photo is one of Zanuso and Sapper's designs for media and communications instruments in the late 1960s. Meanwhile, the sofa Square, present in a two-seater format, alludes to other projects in which Zanuso had used that piece and the furniture

Figure 8.2 Shaded dining area, vacation home at Arzachena, Sardegna, c. 1962. Fondo Marco Zanuso, Archivio del Moderno, Balerna.

system to which it belonged. The *ragazze* suite, though simply furnished, alludes in its details to the manner of *arredamento* that had reached maturity through Zanuso's apartment and design projects of the early 1960s.

The radio is TS 502, designed by Zanuso with Sapper for Brionvega (figure 8.3). This portable, battery-operated radio had a number of characteristics that were common to many of Zanuso and Sapper's designs. The unit made use of simple regular geometrical form, in this case a rectangular block, square in section. It had a smooth plastic outer housing that covered a chassis block with attached components. A discreet grille allowed the unit to remain cool. An antenna could be extended up from the top as well, or slid almost completely into the unit when not in use. All of the corners and edges of the rectangular block were softened by a rounded edge for a comfortable grip. The plastic housing was available in a variety of colors; the unit on the table in the *ragazze-soggiorno* was black. A double strip of metal around the unit at the center protected the edge of the housing and concealed a latch and hinge: the unit opened to reveal controls on one side and a speaker on the other. When closed, it was easily portable. A handle, inset in the top surface, could slide up for ease of carrying.

There was not a single television in photographs of the Zanuso apartment published in *Domus* in 1950 or 1958, in *Abitare* in 1962, or in *Interni* in 1967; but an unpublished photograph of the *soggiorno*, taken in 1962, shows a television attached to the Via Lanza-side wall (plate 20). Zanuso and Sapper's written description of the Doney 14" for Brionvega, 1962, the first transistorized television to be produced in Europe, demonstrates that they had thoroughly familiarized themselves with this highly technical object. They made sense of its complexity with metaphors drawn from architecture and everyday life. Zanuso and Sapper described their process with Doney 14" as one in which they were compelled to elaborate the design around the signal "path." "The design of a television of the conventional type generally begins with the setting up of the circuit," they wrote, "i.e., with the definition of the path that the electronic signal has to travel from its capture by the antenna to its conversion into light on the electroluminescent surface of the cathode ray tube."[1] The project entailed finding a place for each component, mindful of required separations, adjacencies, and tolerances.

Figure 8.3 TS 502 radio, by Zanuso with Richard Sapper for Brionvega, 1963. Photo Giorgio Casali © Fondo Giorgio Casali, IUAV Archivio Progetti, Venice.

The television in the Zanuso living room in 1962, likely Brionvega's Antares 19″, did not have a rounded shape like Doney or the TS 502 radio; but its corners were chamfered for ease of handling. The status of the television in the interior is ambiguous. The placement of the box-shaped unit on a bracket attached to the wall anticipates the common placement of televisions in rooms today, when flat-screened units are hung like framed canvases. More typical in photographed interiors that feature Zanuso's television sets is a position on a shelf off to the side, like the dark shape at the left edge of one photograph of the study, which resembles Zanuso and Sapper's 1969 Black (plate 29). The electronic device, with its exterior designed with a level of attention one might give to a piece of sculpture, was treated as one small object among others, passively on display.

Among objects on the nearby coffee table is the model 275 table lamp that Zanuso designed for Oluce, produced from 1963 onward (plate 30). One of two examples in the room, it is a design that Zanuso often used in multiples. A feature of the 275 that facilitated the integration of the lamp into furniture plans was its proportions: its height and width were roughly the same dimension. With its shade a circle in plan, the lamp was effectively inscribed in an abstract cube. As a consequence, it was visually compatible in a discreet way with square tables and other objects with the same geometry, including the model of sofa, called Square, that appeared in the same room. Meanwhile the spherical shape of the lampshade, flattened at the top and extended into a cylinder on the bottom, created a wide, low profile, lightened, however, by the open space between shade and base, which was emphasized by the arm, a strip of metal that rotated on a pin, offset from the center of the circular base, connecting the base and shade.

Zanuso's designs for industrial design products like the radio and television were usually not prominent in photographs of his own apartment. By contrast, the studio of Achille Castiglioni, which in the 1960s moved to an address not far from the Zanuso apartment, also on Piazza Castello, was clearly the domain of an object designer, being visibly full of small objects, gadgets, and toys.[2] The furniture pieces in Zanuso's *ragazze-soggiorno*, most of which were designed by Zanuso himself, were mass-produced products, just as the appliances were. The pieces in this suite may at first glance appear to be a random assortment, but these items were designed to be deployed together to shape spaces in the home. The Square sofa system in particular, instantiated in a two-seater against one wall, demonstrates Zanuso's reconciliation of mass production with the architectural aims of furnishing.

Square was produced by Techniform, a subsidiary of Arflex in the 1960s, previously introduced here as the producer of the bookshelf-partition in the *ingresso*. This was a broad, deep, slightly reclined sofa with plush foam rubber cushions. Its name reflects the soft rectangular forms of its cushions, armrests, and overall outlines. Square sat on stout metal legs and could be configured with wide wooden feet or with casters for ease of movement. It was available not only in a two-seat but also in three-seat and one-seat formats. The nearby coffee table and side table in the *ragazze-soggiorno* were also produced by Techniform; though they were not part of the same system, they appear to have been roughly the same size and were placed in an analogous position to their Square system counterparts. A Square system table did appear in the corner of the main *soggiorno*, between the two sofas. There, as in the *ragazze-soggiorno*, the table filled the open angle between two seating units that were next to each other and at right angles to one another (see plates 20, 34, and the *soggiorno* floor plan).

The pages of *Domus* show that such furniture, designed for combining into square plans, was produced by more than one company; MIM of Rome was another example.[3] But while journals often featured these pieces in isolated groupings, or in a way that emphasized the stand-alone chair, sofa, or table, Zanuso's work was the rare example that was presented as a contributor to an actual architectural design. Zanuso often used this furniture system in the living rooms he designed around 1960, in the same way that he continued to use the Triennale Divan produced by Arflex for some projects, as well as in his own living room: for instance, in the living room of a vacation home at Arenzano on the Ligurian coast (figure 8.4).[4]

The architectural potential of Square is demonstrated in a number of projects. The system is applied extensively in the apartment for Dr. Bay, 1963.[5] The Bay apartment occupied the 18th floor of a tall residential building, situated on an axis between the city center and central train station. The outer walls of the apartment, which took up an entire floor, were a truncated diamond shape in plan, with flat ends and a beveled shape on the two long sides. Within this frame the apartment was laid out among interior walls that were varied and, while not organized on a regular

Figure 8.4 Triennale Divan in a vacation home at Arenzano, 1962. Photo Giorgio Casali © Fondo Giorgio Casali, IUAV Archivio Progetti, Venice.

grid, were insistently orthogonal to one another. Already discussed above was the *studio*, a small room with pocket doors that opened and closed on a corner to allow for either overlapping or discrete spaces.

The wide *soggiorno* in the apartment designed for Dr. Bay, next to the *studio*, had not one but three alcoves of seating, each a small open square in plan. In these areas, each anchored by a rug, the multiple units are similar, creating an impression of visual homogeneity that reveals complexity through variation. Each conversation nook is made up of different combinations of the seating: two two-seaters and one *poltrona*; a three-seater, two two-seaters, and a *poltrona*; one two-seater and two *poltrone* (figure 8.5). The corners between adjacent units that face one another are filled in with the Square coffee table. Each table has the same dimensions in plan as the single-seat *poltrona*, and the sofas are multiples of this unit's dimensions; the repeated module ties the room together.

Reinforcing the impression of coherence, all of the furniture was upholstered in the same beige fabric, the effect of which was highlighted in *Domus* by color photographs.[6] The room, whose three nooks offered ample space for different generations of the family to sit together and at some distance from one another at the same time, was also outfitted with multiple copies of Zanuso's 275 table lamp. The furniture and lighting give the impression that every part of the room is attended to, without *punti morti*, as Ponti wrote of the Zanuso apartment (discussed in "Soggiorno").

The living room for a Mr. Cappa, completed in the same period, illustrates the method of planning the room on a grid (figure 8.6).[7] This basic approach is one that Zanuso had employed during the late 1950s in his designs of factory buildings for Olivetti. Among the drawings for the Olivetti factory in Brazil, in the Zanuso archive, are floor plans, evidently drawn in collaboration with the technicians who were responsible for the machinery in the assembly sequence. On this type of drawing, each individual machine is depicted as a dark silhouette with circulation space around it. The machines for assembly, printing, finishing, packaging, and other operations, each within its designated circulation space, are precisely related to one another and to the architect's column grid (figure 8.7).

As applied in the domestic sphere, however, Zanuso's use of the module and grid is not sterile or automatic. The Square system's intrinsic capacity for variation ensures that the furniture

Figure 8.5 Square seating and table in Bay apartment, 1963. Photo Giorgio Casali © Fondo Giorgio Casali, IUAV Archivio Progetti, Venice.

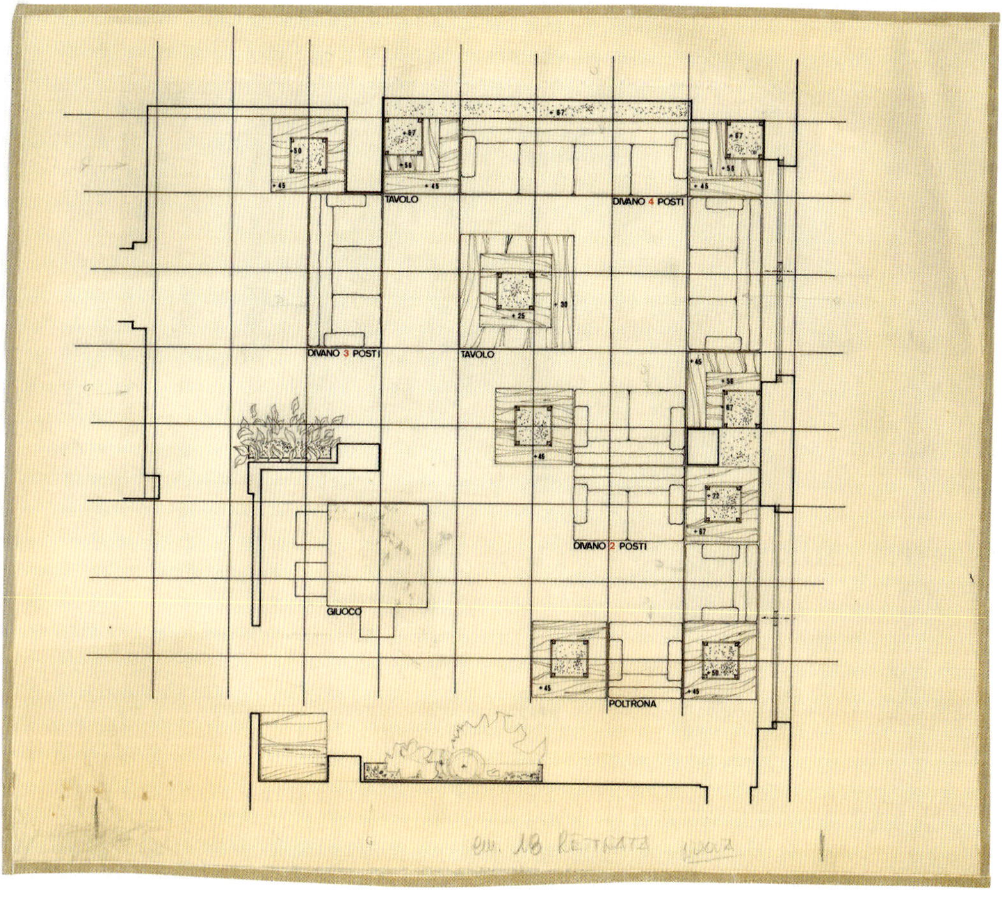

Figure 8.6 Drawing of living room plan with Square sofas and tables, Cappa apartment, 1963. Fondo Marco Zanuso, Archivio del Moderno, Balerna.

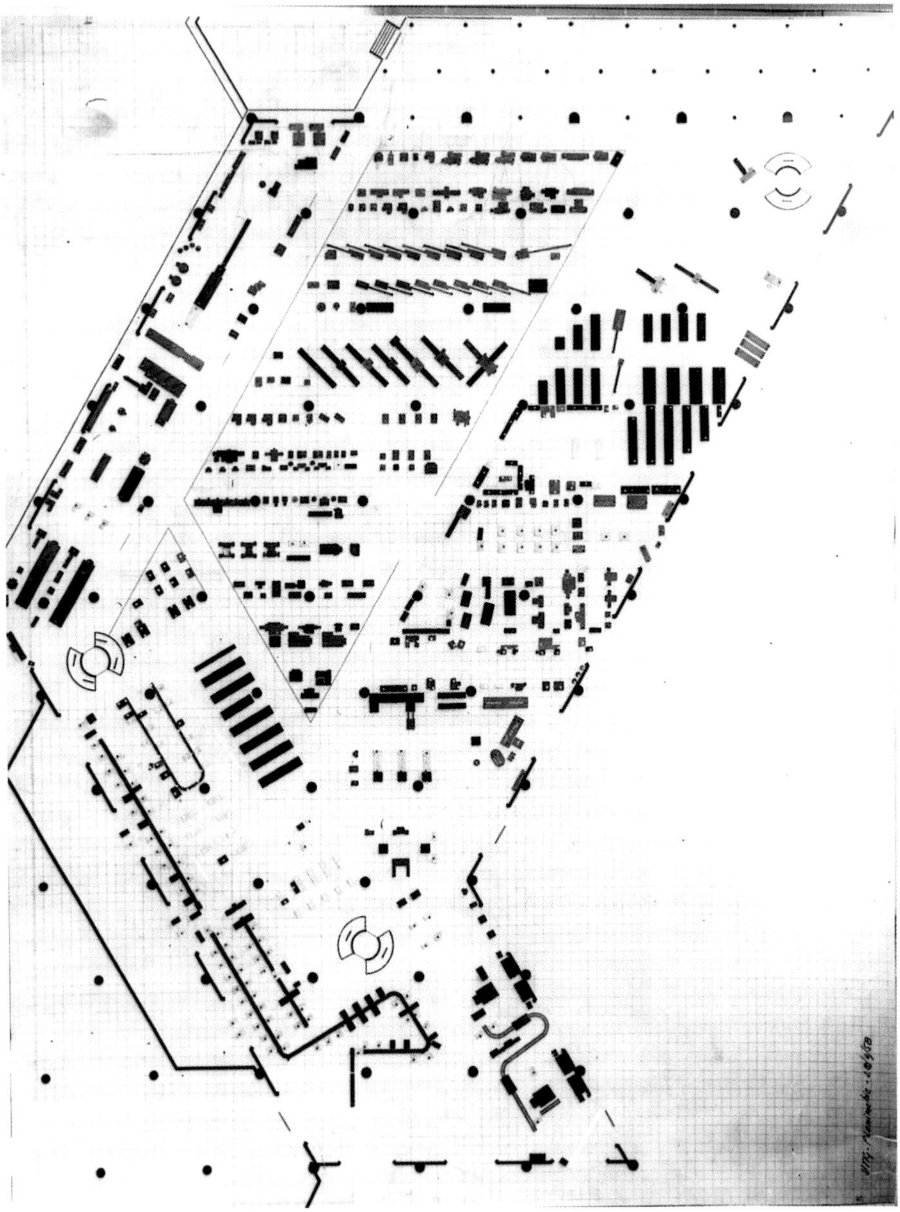

Figure 8.7 Layout of manufacturing sequence on building grid, factory for Olivetti at São Paulo, Brazil, c. 1960. Fondo Marco Zanuso, Archivio del Moderno, Balerna.

layout is not static or heavy, while details such as the slight tilt of the Square sofa's back and the clear space between the seat and the floor give it the impression of relative lightness for a sofa. The detailing of the Square table is such that it, too, appears to hover above the floor. With Square, Zanuso achieved a mass-produced system that could organize space and create interior architecture.

As noted above, feature articles in *Domus* in early 1946 addressed the furnishing of apartments at diverse income levels, for different kinds of families, forming a lexicon of sorts, formalized in the Quaderni di Domus series (see "Studio"). Zanuso's living room design circa 1950, and the way that room was interpreted when the apartment was published in *Domus*, were attentive to similar goals. The furnishing of a small apartment entailed the accommodation of functions in easily distinguished areas of the room.

The *ragazze* suite in the Zanuso apartment was furnished from the beginning in the manner of the *soggiorno* in 1962, with low tables, seating at right angles, and the Oluce lamp providing the basic structure of a space for repose. By the mid-1960s, the postwar crisis was no longer keenly felt. Magazine features on furniture were not as concerned with coming to the "rescue" of the consumer. However, Zanuso's innovation in the design of apartment interiors by mass-produced pieces found an audience among those of his peers who continued to focus on that theme in the mid-1960s. Zanuso was one of several architects who designed a room for *La casa abitata* (The inhabited house), an exhibition dedicated to mass-produced furniture, in 1965. His designs for Techniform, including the bookcase discussed above (in "Ingresso"), figured prominently in his contribution to that event.

The principal curators of *La casa abitata* were the architect Giovanni Michelucci, the art historian and critic Lara Vinca Masini, the architect Pier Luigi Spadolini, and an organizer of the Milan Triennale, Tommaso Ferraris. Briefly stated, the curators' aim was to call on architects to demonstrate furnishing solutions for everyday spaces. In the catalog statement, this seemingly mundane request was motivated in remarkably emphatic language. The curators saw the everyday environment as an important issue; in their view, everyone had a right to live in a home where they felt secure. The matter was made more urgent by the role of a home base of this kind in forming a functional society. The introductory text in their catalog refers to each person's entitlement "to his inviolable and secret private life" as nothing less than the origin of society itself, and goes on to observe that architecture and urbanistic discourse have ignored this issue while focusing on other debates.[8] The curators' text echoes themes that were initially circulated in published essays by Giuseppe Pagano (see "Cucina").

The curators pointed to a number of problems faced by typical middle-class families. Many households lived in rental properties and other situations where traditional architectural interventions were not an option, yet market housing for middle-income households was too often impersonal, suited to the needs of the masses but not individuals. The curators expressed skepticism about whether an exhibition could capture the kind of perspective one might have on one's own furniture and home. In reality, they wrote, present-day life was given meaning by change: the arrival of new family members or transition from one stage of life to another could make a furniture arrangement obsolete, or furniture might gain meaning through its association with phases of life or with life changes. A true quest for wellbeing entailed a process of individual "thought"; by contrast, advertising and "propaganda" only promoted addictive behaviors.[9]

Operating on the premise of homemaking as a sovereign right, the curators explained, they put objects in rooms, not in isolation, in opposition to typical exhibitions of such objects that showed them individually. Zanuso and the other 14 architect contributors were each assigned a room in Palazzo Strozzi in Florence and asked to produce work with a degree of generality that would not represent a specific room but more an idea about a room for a certain range of circumstances.

Zanuso's designated room in Palazzo Strozzi was a square, roughly 480 square feet (50 sq m) in area, with an asymmetrically placed wide door on one short wall opposite two smaller doors near a pair of windows (figure 2.4). His first design move, according to his own short description of the installation, was to place a dining table on axis with the main door—he does not give a reason for this opening gambit in the text. Chairs followed, placed around the table and in some views moved to other parts of the open-plan space.[10] The space was otherwise divided by a diagonal path between the main door and the more distant of the smaller doors, creating larger and smaller triangular areas. To one side of the path were a cluster of divans and an armchair around a low square table. To the other side was the dining table and, closer to the windows, a play area for children. An installation of mechanized projected light added a measure of visual complexity to the scene.

Roughly in the middle of Zanuso's layout, closer to the windows than to the main entrance, the children's play area was bordered by two partitions, each made of five bookcases connected together to form a shallow curve. The dining chairs were Lambda, the dining table Dinner, the living room furniture Woodline, and the children's furniture included the K1340 (or K4999) child's chair, made from injection-molded plastic, which could be sat in or stacked.

In remarks published in *Domus* after the event, Masini wrote that a key feature for her in Zanuso's installation was the set of curved banks of walnut shelving, five units each, that separated each zone of the room from the others, such as the children's play area from the *soggiorno*.[11] As Masini describes characteristics of their design and placement, certain details interest her: the height of the shelves, tall enough to divide spaces but not imposing; the placement of five units in a row, not straight but softly curved; the choice of surface finish, introducing a backdrop to whatever activity may be before it. This addressed the premise of the exhibition as a showcase of approaches that could be applicable in a range of middle-class households.[12]

Masini picked up on the implicit lexical quality of the furnishing scheme when she described Zanuso's room as an "anthology of signification," groups of pieces signaling the locations of dining, reading, or playing. A single *poltrona* and ottoman in one area contrasted with the multiple seats in another, reinforcing the distinction between the quieter and the more sociable spaces. In this respect, Zanuso's room recalls the functional approach of his apartment in 1950. At the same time, the shapes and properties of these designs contribute to the tone of their spaces. The children's chairs, copies of Zanuso's K1340, produced by Kartell, are made of plastic and can be stacked in piles or ziggurat shapes, which animates their part of the room in contrast to the comparatively staid metal Lambda chairs in the dining area.[13]

Zanuso's design showed a more casual approach than the room proposed by Angelo Mangiarotti, which was more rigorously pragmatic in its use of a modular wall system, which the curators termed "pareti attrezzati" (equipped walls); a variety of different service objects could be accessed or stored there. Zanuso's room adhered more to the mundane than the room proposed by Achille and Pier Giacomo Castiglioni, who showed how an assortment of objects could be used to express a personal outlook. Their mass-produced objects included a long table with chairs, as in a generic dining room. The table was set with Castiglioni tableware designs, and above the table hung one of their lamps. Next to the table, near one end, a tiered sideboard sat beneath a shelf, held on brackets, that held houseplants. In addition, a number of unusual objects were propped or hanging from the walls, including a tapered ladder made of stainless steel and a jagged fragment of charred wood, once used to make buried supports for ancient houses in Rome, next to a Castiglioni wall clock.

Whatever their differences, the schemes by Zanuso, the Castiglioni, Mangiarotti, and the others were differentiated from projects that fell in two other categories by their use of mass production, as Masini observed. In one category were the exhibits of Leonardo Savioli and Leonardo Ricci, which shaped their rooms with novel curved walls. Savioli's featured curved wall surfaces made of concrete, to be built on an armature or chassis within the city. Ricci's room was similarly concerned with a new language of interior form, imagining a cellular approach. The third tendency, represented by Ettore Sottsass, emphasized an arrangement of colored shapes within the room, on walls and furniture pieces, composed with an eye to aesthetic "tension" in the interior.[14] Sottsass's room, captured by Giorgio Casali in color images, bears a resemblance to interiors by De Stijl, the Bauhaus, or, in Italy, to work by Giuseppe Terragni, for instance the meeting room in the Casa del Fascio, in which the walls featured abstract painted forms by the painter Mario Radice. There are some similar forms in Zanuso's room and Sottsass's palette of physical forms, such as the square grille that appears in Sottsass's window shade and in some of Zanuso's designs; but the differences, in particular the different relationship between furniture and walls, are striking. Sottsass pays close attention to the construction and division of wall planes, for example in the frieze of colored tile that wraps from one surface onto another, turning the corner to delineate the space of the room and to charge the negative space around the intervention (figure 8.8). By contrast, Zanuso seems to focus mainly on positioning furniture in space; he would engage ceilings (as noted above), but apart from paintings hung on the walls, the vertical display surface was not a site of interest in many of his

Figure 8.8 Ettore Sottsass, installation in *La casa abitata* exhibition, Palazzo Strozzi, Florence, 1965. Photo Giorgio Casali © Fondo Giorgio Casali, IUAV Archivio Progetti, Venice.

design interventions. This is a point of method and sensibility that merits further investigation (figure 8.9).

La casa abitata is an essential reference for differentiating the sensibilities of Zanuso and other architects at the room scale; meanwhile, as one in a series of exhibitions, journals, and architects' projects with a shared focus on industrial design in the interior between 1945 and 1970, it is an informative point of reference for understanding the continuity of the discourse on mass production and everyday life from the 1930s to the 1960s. *La casa abitata* was initially proposed as a new biennial of interiors, but there was never another edition after 1965. When Zanuso and other architects first entered and reentered practice after the end of World War II, they had focused on *arredamento*, furniture and the furnishing of interiors; but after the social unrest and intellectual critiques of 1968, and perhaps due to other events as well that would change the tone of the discourse on architecture in Milan, almost no one would publicly espouse the belief that architects' designs could reach a nationwide middle-class public through mass production.

In the Zanuso family apartment, the courtyard-side wall of the *ragazze-soggiorno* was broken by the niche with the desk in it and by the second niche, the small window seat with a cushion (plates 30, 31). The small terrace provided a place for a pause, or a cigarette, steps from the girls' living room. Their terrace, the only one on the apartment level, was an amenity that Zanuso included in many of his apartment designs. Terraces feature prominently in two of his apartment building designs from the early 1960s that, at the time, marked the high point of his investigation of prefabricated design: the condominium buildings on Via Laveno and Via Solaroli (today on Via Adelaide Coari), built in the early 1960s. If a theme expressed in the Square system discussed above is the implication of Zanuso's object designs in his architectural designs, the Via Laveno and Via Solaroli projects, as they were called at the time, speak to the question of how his *building* designs could assimilate strategies of his object designs.

Zanuso used a constructive system for both buildings, which in each case entailed a reinforced concrete core along with a steel framing system that combined proprietary joint designs with readily available off-the-shelf steel members, making progress on the agenda of prefabricated building that was advocated by a number of Milanese architects during the 1950s and 1960s, which Zanuso

Figure 8.9 Marco Zanuso, installation in *La casa abitata* exhibition, Palazzo Strozzi, Florence, 1965. Photo Giorgio Casali © Fondo Giorgio Casali, IUAV Archivio Progetti, Venice.

followed closely.[15] That system, called FEAL VAR-3, designed by the engineer and construction entrepreneur Giovanni Varlonga, provided for non-load-bearing exterior walls, which allowed the architect to freely adjust the position of walls in relation to the structural grid, analogous to the possibilities of Le Corbusier's Dom-ino paradigm of concrete slabs supported by columns pulled back from the slab edge.[16] Zanuso did not just use the system to make this pair of buildings; he explored the system's capacity for the development of perimeter walls, which made for an abundance of terraces. Solid walls alternated with balconies to give each apartment an adjacent outdoor space; on Via Laveno these extended outward, while in the Via Solaroli project, where the building had a smooth cuboid shape, the terraces were inset, as on the curtained volume seen in figure 8.10 at center right.

The dimensions of Varlonga's open-plan interior could be set freely around the steel columns. Preparatory drawings held in the Zanuso archive show that Zanuso took advantage of this flexibility to design floor plans around the dimensions of his own furniture pieces, such as Woodline and Lambda, which appear in a photograph of an apartment interior (figure 8.10). Zanuso's architecture was often either made of pieces that had qualities in common with industrial design objects, as in his factories, or responded in its dimensions to the aggregation of smaller objects, anticipating the movable pieces. Either approach is analogous to the manner in which, in Zanuso's Viale Gorizia building, he had constrained the architecture to a rigid and monochrome abstract geometry in order to provide a backdrop to mural artwork (see "Letto"). Among various architects who designed for mass production, Zanuso placed a distinct emphasis on methods and strategies for producing architectural qualities through serially produced things. His projects show his consistent concern with careful coordination of one kind of thing with another, or one kind of system with another, resulting in an object that sustains complexity without sacrificing coherence.

The desk in the *ragazze-soggiorno* was a board covered with green fabric set on sawhorses (plate 30). The sawhorses resemble those in a desk used by Zanuso in one of his offices, pictured in a photograph from the early 1960s, most likely the office he occupied on Via dei Bossi, a couple of blocks from the Olivetti headquarters in Milan, before moving to a space in the Via Laveno building. Other objects on the desk include a Cubo ashtray, Bruno Munari's

Figure 8.10 Interior, Casa FEAL condominium building on Via Solaroli, Milan, 1965. Photo Publifoto. Archivio del Moderno, Fondo Marco Zanuso, Balerna.

design for Danese; an Olivetti typewriter, likely a Lettera 22, the same model as Billa Zanuso's typewriter seen in the *studio*; and a monograph on the Bauhaus.

Perhaps the book, along with the drafting table that appears in the published floor plan of the 1967 apartment (but not in the photographs), belonged to the eldest daughter, who would become an architect. The apartment was relinquished by the family following the death of Billa Zanuso in 2012. The furniture was divided by the Zanuso children; today the paintings hang on their walls. The coffee tables sit in their living rooms, piled with their books, often with seating designed by their father, the chairs facing each other or set at right angles.

Vedute

Marco Zanuso had the attention of critics and mentors for his entire career, from his appearances in early postwar surveys of Italian architecture alongside older architects who had begun practice before World War II to the solo exhibition on his work at the Milan Triennale in 1999.[1] As noted above, the reception of the work of Zanuso and other Italian architect-designers of his generation took on a negative tone in the 1960s, as architecture critics responded to a shift in the wider culture from the optimistic outlook of the postwar reconstruction to the acknowledgment of the bitter realities of uneven development amid a seeming prosperity. This last chapter of the book turns to the final task of reflecting on just what kind of relationship to culture and society is expressed in Zanuso's apartment design. To begin with, I look again at how the reception of Zanuso and his work was haunted by the notion that the architect-designer was a "problematic" form of practitioner during the 1960s in order to clarify the terms in which Zanuso's work in particular, exemplified in designs for his own apartment, speaks directly to a form of social engagement that emerged precisely in the moment of Italy's industrial expansion.

In the mid-twentieth-century literature on the architect-designer, which reads like a balance sheet of opinion, an early standout voice is that of architect-critic Vittorio Gregotti. In an essay published in *Casabella* in 1957, when Zanuso was roughly ten years into his professional career and Gregotti was very young, Gregotti described Zanuso as the quintessential architect of that moment.[2] Among Gregotti's criteria were Zanuso's acquaintance with current formal languages in architecture, his talent for finding the salient solution for a given functional need, and his capacity to design an object at any scale.[3] A decade later, in a survey of Italian architecture Gregotti wrote that the modernist project of remaking the world through the design of objects was at an impasse, with architects drawn to an aesthetic ideal based on efficiency yet weighted down by a sense of responsibility toward the wider economy and culture that conflicted with the modernist stance.[4] Gregotti's pessimism in 1968 was not specifically about Zanuso but about architecture in general, yet he was clearly disenchanted with the values implied by the attributes he had praised in 1957.

A similarly ambivalent observer was the architect Guido Canella, who in 1963 characterized Zanuso as the "most problematic" of Italian architects. Canella expressed admiration for Zanuso's seeming familiarity with the world of industrial methods and technology, which called to mind a "naturalist" in an industrial wilderness, but he thought Zanuso's personality tended to deflect attention away from the social dimension of the design object. Canella singled out armchairs such as Martingala, a *poltrona* which, however novel its materials, seemed to Canella to be destined for new living rooms just as conventional as the old ones. Canella suspected that well-off couples would settle into quiet conversation after dinner in Zanuso's chairs and sofas just as in any upper-middle-class *soggiorno*.[5] A similar tension figures in Billa Zanuso's stories of evening dinners in homes like "casa Z," as she called it in a story in *Nostra signora di Milano*: the men at a dinner party in one story form a circle of conversation after the meal, smoking and debating for hours while their wives observe them quietly, intervening only to reassure or to express agreement.[6]

By the end of the 1960s a reaction against the claims of functionalist design was expressed in broader and stronger terms. Modernist architects such as Walter Gropius or Ernst May, who had called for architects to act as agents of social beneficence, had been hero figures for many postwar Italians, including Zanuso; yet the critical response in Italy around 1968, a year of widespread popular protests against governance and social policy on university campuses and in cities across Europe, declared these models to be useless. Critics such as Paolo Portoghesi and Virgilio Vercelloni (mentioned above in "Ambiente") portrayed postwar architecture as, at best, the addition of "quality" to a city with structural *inequalities*. Architecture was material for profit-oriented market forces, incapable of becoming a vehicle for social change. These fixed ideas afforded little scope for enthusiasm about the architect-designer.

Essays in the catalog *Italy: The New Domestic Landscape*, published in conjunction with the 1972 exhibition at the Museum of Modern Art that introduced Italian design to a broad international audience, articulated with particular clarity an analogous judgment of design as a discipline. The curator of the exhibition, Emilio Ambasz, divided Italian designers into three categories. One type was the "conformist," who focused on "the aesthetic quality of single objects," including explorations of color and novel materials, remaining true to preexisting forms of things. Such designers considered their work to be autonomous, "responsible only to itself." By contrast, the "contestatory" designers either refused to design anything or produced design in stridently unconventional forms. Finally the "reformist" avoided the extremes of the other types but was caught in a paradoxical effort to reshape the social pattern while remaining invested in the underlying system that reinforced it. Ambasz placed Zanuso and most of the designers in the "reformist" designers' camp.[7]

Such negative judgments of design as a subordinate of architecture or a powerless discipline may have turned otherwise interested scholars away from Zanuso's work, according to the architect Manolo De Giorgi, who speculated in a 1999 essay that Zanuso has not been more prominently featured in the historiography of Italian architecture because of the widespread idea that design, entailing habitual compromises, is the source of an "unpardonable contamination" in his architecture.[8] In response to this putative anti-design bias, it is worth recalling that design figured in some of the first histories of modern architecture, as in Nikolaus Pevsner's 1936 book *Pioneers of Modern Design*, which identified the source of modern architecture in the Great Exhibition in London of 1851.[9] Pevsner argued that the incoherence of objects on display at the Crystal Palace, badly conceived goods made in new materials, assisted by machines, had motivated William Morris—and after him Louis Sullivan, Frank Lloyd Wright, and others—to make the earliest characterizations of modern form; the values of modern architecture originated in the responses of these so-called "pioneers" to the offending products, which included objects for everyday use in the home. The problem that the pioneers overcame, how to assimilate new materials and methods to regular production, was the same problem that Zanuso faced after 1945. The 1968 critiques that disparaged architecture and design for their seeming naiveté about capitalism represent, perhaps, the need for a new kind of "pioneer."

The scholarship on Zanuso that has emerged in the twenty-first century has approached his work on the terms set out by the architect and his peers, extending the literature that began in Gillo Dorfles's 1971 book *Marco Zanuso, designer*, with Zanuso's objects considered individually and in comparison, demonstrating the complexity of the objects, the depth of thinking that had brought them into being, and the characteristics that identified them as works of art. François Burkhardt's 1994 book *Marco Zanuso* further emphasized Zanuso's deep and extensive research into design types. More recent scholars have made extended analysis of Zanuso's designs in relation to organicism and landscape, the way the object engages the user by way of basic perceptions and other topics with a broader resonance in architecture and design history.[10]

Burkhardt asked in a more recent essay whether and how Zanuso might be relevant to young architects in the digital era;[11] but his remark in 1994 that further study was needed into the relationship between Zanuso's design work and architecture still holds true. I have sought to show in this book how Zanuso mobilized the furniture and furnishing schemes in his apartment designs toward the ends of *architecture*. I refer in particular to modernism's imperative of shaping the spaces of everyday life across social classes. Faced with documentation of numerous designs in the Zanuso archive, it is almost too easy to revert to a reckoning of specific achievements. For example, the hinge of Grillo, a compact telephone set that the Zanuso office designed for Siemens a few years later, led by Richard Sapper, was such a salient design that it was cited in patent applications as late as the early 2000s.[12] This illustrates Zanuso's commitment to the thorough solution of design problems, which was noticed by Vittorio Gregotti in his 1957 article about Zanuso: "his contribution is precisely the thought of an action that is in itself, by its own determinate nature, qualitative," Gregotti wrote.[13]

Something more is needed as an answer to the postwar critiques, for their insistent focus on the architect and designer's capacity to bring about change was leveled at the profession as a whole, not at issues that the designer confronted on the drafting table. In my view, an adequate answer to the question of Zanuso's influence must discover and clarify the relationship between these two frames of reference. On one hand is the designer's lack of power to achieve the modernist imperative of social change, which led some critics to declare in effect that the whole modernist project of architecture was pointless. On the other hand are not only the echoes of ideology between postwar architectural practice and its prewar modernist counterpart but also the new motivations and working relationships that a designer could discover amid industrialization.

From the vantage point of today, the "enclosure" of the architect and architecture in rigid economies of production has only increased, along with the progress of global capitalism, since 1968; and the situation is perhaps even more alarming to architects now, notably in a "digital" era (to Burckhardt's point) but also at a moment when many architects are aware that the ambient economic framework not only governs what they can make or do without extraordinary means, but also fixes in advance a quantity of collateral harm, through extraction or resource depletion, that any such project produces. Rather than either take the critiques of the architect-designer at face value or try to ignore them, let us ask instead how this architect fared within the condition of open-eyed entanglement in advanced capitalism in postwar Milan.

If Zanuso was a reformist, what did the work of that project look like? What was he able to do with the resources that were available to him? Could a design object be "good," even in a situation that limited his reach, demographically speaking—and if so, how?[14] Or perhaps this should not be a question of "good" or "bad" but involves a broader spectrum of value. For the remainder of this last chapter, I turn to what the example of Zanuso's family apartment suggests in the way of answers to these questions. First, his choice to publish his apartment for design declared his commitment to the very public problem of the home. The apartment as such has traditionally not been at the forefront of types of project that define the architect's professional identity. The relationship of its internal spaces to overall volume or massing, which are important aspects of the freestanding architectural work, are normally not under a tenant's control and beyond the scope of his architect. But in Italy, the apartment, not the single-family home, was the most common dwelling type.[15] Zanuso and his editors recognized that his home was an authoritative but widely relatable example of how to confront the problem of dwelling at that particular place and time.

Zanuso's design of his home drew from the perspectives of both architect and designer. As noted above (in "Soggiorno"), in fact Zanuso was able to intervene in the configuration of walls and the structure of the roof of his apartment at Piazza Castello, 20. But an apartment lends itself to the shaping of spaces by means of furniture, mostly independent of the configuration of the walls and building envelope. Zanuso's practice of designing furniture and appliances unlocked levels of the problem of the home that ordinarily lie beyond the scale at which an architect operates. At the same time, his designs express the priorities of architecture within design and furnishing. I will return to this point below.

A second instructive aspect of the apartment in the attic of Piazza Castello, 20 is the way the architect prioritized the needs of its occupants. Zanuso's working method on the Olivetti factories was described by one architecture critic as design "a posteriori," meaning that Zanuso did not bring a preconceived formal schema to the project but instead *discovered* the form through dialogue with the client and consultants.[16] Zanuso's apartment design, too, could be called a design "a posteriori." According to the "Socratic dialogue" method of planning the apartment design, attributed to Zanuso by Eugenio Gentili Tedeschi in an article about the Zanuso apartment (discussed in "Letto"), the architect began by interpreting his family's requirements of the objects. He would turn to the inventory of furniture pieces only after defining the family's needs as clearly as possible.

The "lexicon" of expressive functional groups, exemplified in the *lessico dell'arredamento* articles and Quaderni di Domus series in which ideas circulated among Milanese architects, was a medium in which to approximate the meeting of needs through furnishing schemes. The lexicon provided a stable framework of function satisfaction that could withstand variation in the manner in which an instance of a functional group (such as a table and dining chairs) or functional object (such as a place to rest clothing while dressing or undressing) served its purpose. This framework accommodated not only Zanuso's designs but also inherited pieces.

The pair of *marinaia olandese* chairs, for example, were placed to either side of the matrimonial bed and took on a new set of roles after being relocated from the living room in 1958. These chairs bear out Eugenio Gentili Tedeschi's remark that (in paraphrase) an old piece could retain some measure of its original capacity to fulfill the function for which it was constructed. When taking into account how to use it, different factors could be considered, including a desire for a souvenir from the past.[17] Gentili Tedeschi also refers to the architect's choice to keep the exposed wooden timber in the soggiorno as an acknowledgment of the age of the building at Piazza Castello, 20. One might also relate the use of the antique chair in the Zanuso bedroom to an idea that entered the architectural discourse in 1966, Aldo Rossi's notion of the architectural "archetype," which possesses a timeless adequacy and can "structure the city" even as its use changes in the course of centuries.[18]

A third feature of Zanuso's response to the problem of dwelling was his embrace of variability. The successive versions of the apartment that he published were each in part a response to life events, such as the birth of the youngest child (figure 9.1) or the transition of the older girls to their lives as university students and young adults. Functional furniture groups were introduced, relocated, multiplied, or reconfigured by the architect. The children needed more space; the architect moved the master bedroom from one end of the apartment to the other. The children grew more autonomous; he gave their room its own "study" by incorporating two desks. As Billa Zanuso developed her writing practice, the architect captured the *studio* in a room that could be isolated by closed doors.

The way Zanuso's apartment operated as a platform for living is consistent with what the curators of *La casa abitata* wrote in 1965 about the apartment as an architectural type at that moment: from a social, psychological, and economic point of view, when it comes to constituting the home, what matters is variation and variability. The scenes and events in a family's history are not registered in static fixed spaces but in provisionally furnished rooms and in the spontaneous modification of such rooms.[19]

The idea of the dwelling as a platform also resonates with the idea of the "open" that appears in the title of this book, borrowed

Figure 9.1 Marco Zanuso and Susanna Zanuso, c. 1960. Image from Fondo Paolo Monti, owned by BEIC and located in the Civico Archivio Fotografico, Milan. Servizio Paolo Monti. La Fondazione BEIC è titolare dei diritti d'autore dell'Archivio Paolo Monti.

from Umberto Eco's *Opera aperta* (*The Open Work*).[20] My intention is not to suggest that Zanuso's apartment is a simple instantiation of Eco's "open work."[21] In the most general definition, an open work is, above all, a framework in which meaning can be made. In some examples it possesses an ambiguity that invites or compels a reader to complete the work, and in other instances it refers to a sign with an indefinite number of interpretations. In a chapter of *Opera aperta* on "The Open Work in the Visual Arts," the main theme is the "informal" in art, and the focus is on painting and sculpture.[22] By invoking this term I refer to more than one aspect of Zanuso's apartment design, including the way his approach both relied on the lexicon of furnishing based on iconic functional groups and allowed for variation in the manner of emulation of a given group, a type of object, or a conventional room.

A fourth aspect of Zanuso's response to the problem of dwelling is his insistence on the use of contemporary materials and methods. He could rely on the lexicon as a source of functional and semantic codes, but his signature is particularly evident in the way he combined rigorous planning with a frank interest in new materials, or the outcome of innovation in modes of manufacture. From one design to another within a given type, his designs often bear little resemblance to one another. The manner in which each one emulates the function of that object is variable. Zanuso was known to say that the interior space of any given time period, including the present, had its own particular character that imposed demands on its objects.[23] To some observers, Zanuso's objects seemed to capture not only the novelty and interest of new materials and process but also, and perhaps to a greater extent, the untested or uncertain aspects of those novelties. Carlo De Carli, writing about the Zanuso apartment for *Interni* in 1967, referred to Zanuso's designs as *oggetti umani*, comparing these domestic things to human companions. The furniture pieces were given a humane dimension by this "innately talented" designer, De Carli wrote, but they also struck an observer as "disorderly," as in the endearing way that a friend can be difficult to be around.[24]

Zanuso described his role in design as an effort to "interpret" the new ways of making things and in that way to express current conditions; and he did not hesitate to place industrial-world materials in the living room.[25] His forays in this direction were in keeping with Giuseppe Pagano's notion of confronting the industrial realm in order to tame it (see "Cucina"). A chair design by Zanuso might take cues from a familiar furniture piece while also having feet and legs made of steel; an appliance might be made entirely of plastic, placed in a room with furniture made of wood, rattan, cloth, and leather. De Carli's leeriness toward Zanuso's objects may reflect his outlook as an authority and advocate for artisanal and craft practices, focusing on wood, rattan, ceramics, and other such materials; but in calling Zanuso's furniture pieces "disorderly" he may have alluded to the opposite of the "civility" that was the goal of design according to Pagano.

Another aspect of Zanuso's approach, related to the embrace of variability, is the way his furniture objects possess intrinsic physical traits that make them amenable to combination and recombination in furnishing plans. The pieces are visibly symmetrical or formed of fairly regular geometric shapes that would lend themselves to patterns of aggregation in the plan. The objects often incorporated artifacts or traits that came from the materials or manufacturing process, such as a shape, a texture, or other striking quality. For example, the radiuses of the curves in the bent sheet metal of Lambda were constrained by the sheet metal bending machinery. Such quirks led to intrinsic tactile qualities that sometimes also implied potential relationships to other objects. The chair Lambda and table Dinner are made of materials that bring different qualities of temperature, texture, weight, and color to the room, but they are outcomes of the study of the same problem, the transition from a supporting leg to the supported horizontal surface. Another example is Zanuso's children's desk, which responds to the legs of the standard *chiesa* chair with its own round legs.

The analogousness of Zanuso's objects is a trait of his architecture as well as his design works. He developed the furniture piece as he would a building, by drawing it in plan, elevation, and section; as noted above (in "Studio"), Lambda, Dinner, and the Brionvega factory all emerged during a period of investigating the transition from vertical support to horizontal surface. Zanuso's furniture pieces are in other cases strictly governed by proportional relationships that allowed them to be combined in various ways. His designs for Arflex (later Techniform), including the sofa and side table in the *ragazze-soggiorno* and the side table and sofas from the Square system (demonstrated in the Bay apartment), were based on the same square dimensional module.

Analysis of the Zanuso apartment also brings to light ways that he brought distinctly architectural qualities to interior space.[26] One such motive is a holism of the object: the drive toward the resolution of the object into a visually cohesive totality. The objects that are linked by visual analogy or modular similarity lend themselves to the formation of rooms that cohere in spite of being composed of different pieces. The formal relationships between any two individual pieces may not be as evident as they would be if they all had the same or similar shape, but fleeting resemblances among them, in which a given piece might resemble a few others or share a detail or a module, confer the sense of a whole upon the object, functional group, sequence of spaces, or complete environment.[27]

Zanuso leaned on these relationships to use the furnishing plan to control the shape of inhabited space through the object and its relationships to other objects, as well as through relationships among furniture groups, circulation paths, and walls. The synergy between the design of objects and the design of the floor plan is particularly effective in the *soggiorno*, where the symmetrical placement of furniture normalizes a room with an irregular shape.

These attributes of the Zanuso apartment are suggestive of his response to the problem of dwelling as it presented itself in early 1960s Milan. Motivated by the imperatives of modernism, anticipating the decisive role of the mass market product in shaping the home, Zanuso expanded his practice to encompass the design of furniture and appliances. In this way he could claim and defend the project of dwelling for the architect. His method entailed defining the occupants' needs and articulating these with respect to a familiar lexicon of functional home furnishings. The furnishing plan, made of semantically coded functional units and subordinated to the occupants' needs, provided a stable framework that could accommodate change in the manner or the place of emulation of any functional object or group. The objects that Zanuso designed for mass production had strong formal characteristics that lent themselves to aggregation and provided for a renewal of the expression of functions within the furnishing plan or furniture group. These same characteristics allowed the architect to create coherent furniture groups and plan designs that could sustain familiar architectural qualities, above all a strong sense of organization based on relationships of orthogonality, symmetry, or modularity that could confer the sense of a whole even on a heterogeneous set of objects.

The result of Zanuso's insistence on qualities of analogy across objects and formal patterns in the *arredamento* was a casual-looking but coherent interior that was inviting to the moving observer and lent itself well to interpretation through photography. In the published images through which we can revisit the Zanuso apartment today, the relationship between the project and photographs is one of mutual reinforcement. Furnishing, and the movement of furniture, were constitutive in the creation of these views, while photography, by capturing the furnishing scheme by freezing a state of the moving pieces, gave substance to each scheme as a work of design.

The photographers did not simply document the distribution of furniture pieces. Among the photographic negatives captured in 1958 by Giorgio Casali are various clues to the artifice behind each depicted furnishing scheme. Casali used a Linhof Technika 4 × 5 view camera that made large-format images on glass plate negatives.[28] This type of camera, commonly used for landscapes as well as for architectural photography, entails a slow process but produces a high-resolution negative. Casali's images were edited, just like the texts that would accompany them. A tear in the wallpaper, a patch of plaster, and a stray cord are visible in images that are printed in this book, which were drawn from the negatives, not the published versions. Casali's published images were also cropped slightly. At the edge of one negative, one can see the shade of a lighting fixture (figure 9.2). If one looks carefully, shadows in several images speak to the use of artificial lighting.

The photographs by Ugo Mulas that are included in this book are similarly pulled from his negatives. The images are published here uncropped in keeping with Mulas's eventual rejection of cropping as a tool; the edges of his 35 mm and 6 × 6 cm film negatives, which were intentionally excluded from the published images, are visible in this book. On his contact sheets at the time, however, Mulas used a felt tip pen to indicate the edge of each print.[29] The versions of these photographs that appeared in *Abitare* and other publications were cropped according to his instructions.[30] An article in the magazine *La signora ABC*, November 1963, shows the apartment through the cropped versions of several of Mulas's photographs (figure 9.3).

For both Casali and Mulas, a photograph was a pictorial view with an emphasis on something that was central in the scene, in compositions that often made use of internal framing elements such as doorways. Although the edges of furniture sometimes appear in the published images, these are views that focus

Figure 9.2 Glass plate negative of Giorgio Casali photograph 47-167. © Fondo Giorgio Casali, IUAV Archivio Progetti, Venice.

La Signora ABC

... presenta la casa dell'architetto Zanuso

La casa della scorsa settimana apparteneva ad uno scapolo, l'architetto Rogers, ed era una dimora tutta moderna. Questa, di un architetto pure milanese e ben noto, è l'abitazione di una famiglia con due figli. E' assai interessante perché risolve due problemi nei quali molti hanno occasione di imbattersi: adattare alle necessità della propria famiglia una vecchia costruzione esistente e utilizzare mobili d'altri tempi, accostandoli a mobili d'oggi. Come mostrano le fotografie, anche gli elementi costruttivi di un edificio di cinquant'anni fa possono apparire, quasi, un fatto decorativo.

L'ingresso: la parete divisoria è formata da una serie di scaffali componibili sormontati da lastre di cristallo. Per terra una stuoia.

La sala da pranzo è a doppio uso: quando la tavola non è apparecchiata, diventa tavolo da studio; così si spiegano anche gli scaffali-libreria che la separano dall'ingresso. Sulla parete, una pittura astratta convive con un quadro caravaggesco.

In alto a sinistra: nella stanza da letto, soltanto i mobili essenziali, « vecchi » e sobrii. Nella parete di fronte al letto, tre porte che conducono una nel bagno e due ad armadi-camerini.

Il soggiorno: ha il soffitto a padiglione e i grossi travi del tetto entrano nell'arredamento come sostegno della lampada o piano d'appoggio. Le poltrone e i divani, bassi e comodi, sono stati disegnati dallo stesso Zanuso. In altra parte della sala, un trumeau impero, un tavolo e una sedia dell'800, una serie di stampe, cose « vecchie di casa ».

La camera delle bambine: librerie svedesi, sedie da chiesa e scrivanie disegnate da Zanuso per la produzione in serie. Anche qui, la grossa trave in vista e le finestre ricavate in serie sotto il tetto, che sono gli elementi unificatori di tutto il disegno dell'appartamento.

Figure 9.3 Photographs by Ugo Mulas of the Zanuso apartment, as they appeared in a spread in *La Signora ABC*, November 1963. Fondo Marco Zanuso, Archivio del Moderno, Balerna.

attention on a few central subjects such as the chairs, lamps, tables, and doorways close to the centers of the photographs.

A pair of useful concepts for thinking about the photographic interpretation of the Zanuso apartment are the *veduta* and the vignette. In the *vedute* made famous by Giovanni Battista Piranesi in the eighteenth century, edges of his prints were handled in an intentional way that makes them appear to be spontaneous. The centers of his views of recent architecture in Rome, viewed in printed etchings, might show a subject such as the Spanish Steps or the twin church buildings at Porta del Popolo; but the left and right edges tend to show fragments: slivers of windows, a corner, a cornice cut off where the plate ended.[31] By including the cut buildings at the edges of these images, Piranesi leaned on an analogy between the printed drawing and a physical window that offers a limited view of a reality, tacitly asserting that the depicted objects were not isolated fragments but parts of a broader built fabric.

By contrast, a vignette, originally defined as a painted image with a blurred area between its content and the surrounding blank paper, by definition has no edge, no sign of a reality that extends beyond the frame. For the viewer of a vignette, the center is unequivocally the point. The photographs partake to various degrees of these two ways of thinking about the Zanuso apartment. The published images are collected vignettes that call attention to contents, especially to furniture pieces and groups, carefully related to one another. Casali, cropping his images, and Mulas, marking his negatives with a felt tip pen, composed the furniture and other features into vignettes. In a series of photographs the apartment is presented as a coherent whole glimpsed part by part, as in the *vedute* of Rome; yet in each series the viewer experiences one thing after another, as in an episodic narrative that leaves the reader to decide how, if at all, to assemble the pieces.

Acknowledgments

An Open Work is a product of a research project with at least three beginnings. For my introduction to Marco Zanuso's work and for initial feedback on my first efforts to write about this architect, I am thankful to Kenneth Frampton, who pointed me to Fondo Marco Zanuso at the Archivio del Moderno (now in Balerna), affiliated with the Accademia di Architettura in Mendrisio, and who advised my dissertation on Zanuso. Thanks also to Mary McLeod, Reinhold Martin, Felicity Scott, and Paolo Scrivano for their feedback on my dissertation and their encouragement in the ensuing years.

I am grateful for the very existence of the Archivio del Moderno; grateful to its directorate, Letizia Tedeschi and Nicola Navone, to Annalisa Viati Navone and to all the staff members who welcomed me time after time and enabled my extensive access to drawings, photographs, and other documents. Their kindness and professionalism are an enduring source of motivation. I am particularly grateful to Elena Triunveri, who supported my research during the last five years with tireless patience and collegial friendship. Thanks also to Micaela Caletti for her assistance with materials for this book.

The photographs that appear in this book are crucial to the project as documentation that has allowed me to encounter the Zanuso apartment in its many configurations and to formulate and test hypotheses about Zanuso's design process. For access to photographs of the Zanuso apartment by Giorgio Casali, Ugo Mulas, and Gian Battista Colombo, I am indebted to the Archivio Progetti of the IUAV in Venice and grateful for the meticulous, timely assistance of Sabina Carboni, Teresita Scalco, and Antonella D'Aulerio as I navigated the Fondo Giorgio Casali. I am deeply grateful to Carmela Mulas and Valentina Mulas for their kind permission and to Alessandra Pozzati for her assistance at Archivio Ugo Mulas. I am fortunate to have met Susanna Colombo at Archivio Giancolombo, who kindly showed me examples of her father's work. I am also grateful to have received permission from the estate of Aldo Ballo and Marirosa Toscani Ballo and from the owners of Paolo Monti's archive in support of this publication. Thanks as well to the staff in the archives at Triennale di Milano and Politecnico di Milano for their kind assistance with photos and documents. Every effort has been made to identify copyright holders for permissions of images reprinted here; in case an omission is discovered, please contact the publisher.

I could not have included these edifying materials in the book without substantial support for permissions costs. A grant from the

Graham Foundation for Advanced Research in the Visual Arts was decisive in bringing this book to life. To Sarah Herda and to James Pike, thank you. Additional funds for permissions and printing came from Rice School of Architecture and from the Creative Ventures Subvention Fund at Rice University.

In addition to research in the Fondo Marco Zanuso and in photographic archives, I had the privilege of access to materials in the Study Center for Architecture and Design at the Museum of Modern Art in New York, and to examples of Zanuso's televisions held at the St. Louis Art Museum. Thanks to Paul Galloway and Genevieve Cortinovis at their respective institutions for facilitating these enlightening encounters.

For my account of Piazza Castello and the geography of Milan and Lombardy, I am grateful to Massimiliano Maderna at the Cittadella degli Archivi, to Luca Dossena at the Biblioteca Trivulziana Archivio Storico Civico, and to Alberto Di Bello at the Civico Archivio Fotografico for their benevolent assistance in the respective archives of the city of Milan. I appreciate the partnership of these institutions that gave kind permission to publish drawings and photographs from their collections for educational purposes. I am also grateful to the estate of Giovanni Dradi for permission to publish a detail of his exquisite bird's-eye view drawing of Milan. For site visits to buildings by Marco Zanuso beyond Milan, I am grateful to Gerolamo Patrone, who showed me several apartment buildings in Arenzano, and to Luca Guido, who drove me to projects in the Veneto. Thanks also to Lorenzo Ciccarelli, who informed me about Zanuso's projects in Le Marche.

I am deeply grateful to Federica Zanuso, Lorenza Zanuso, and Susanna Zanuso for encouraging me in this project and for sharing their recollections of their father and their family life. Thanks as well to Marco Zanuso, Jr., for his account of his childhood apartment and his kind permission to see the summer home in Sardinia that was designed by his uncle and namesake.

To consult archives, meet people, and visit sites over four years while preparing this book, I made several research trips that would not have been possible without the generous funding I received from Rice School of Architecture. Thank you, Dean Igor Marjanovič, for supporting my research. I am also grateful for the assistance of Rice students John Maldonado, who helped to format the manuscript for submission, and above all Elliot Yamamoto, who drew the floor plans that illustrate this book with meticulous, indefatigable attention to detail.

For the second beginning of *An Open Work*, which compelled me to seek out these archives and individuals, I am grateful to Thomas Weaver, who commissioned this book for the MIT Press, for his encouragement to pursue this book's unconventional approach and for his patient and insightful critiques that helped to refine my proposal. I am also indebted to the peer reviewers whose thoughtful responses shaped the project in profound ways. This book would not have seen the light of day, however, if not for the third beginning in which Victoria Hindley, with Gabriela Bueno Gibbs, put it on the path to production and graciously tolerated my inexperience as a first-time author.

A special thanks to Matthew Abbate, also of the MIT Press, for his thorough, detail-oriented, sympathetic editing that brought clarity and polish to the final manuscript. I am grateful to Jennifer Shade Wilson and Christopher Nicholson at the Center for Academic and Professional Communication at Rice University for their advice on individual chapters, and to Jerrell Jones and Francine Arizmendez of Fondren Library, who assisted with digital files.

Among the many people who stand out for their miscellaneous acts that helped me to believe in myself and my subject through the long, often solitary process of research and writing, I am especially grateful to Mohsen Mostafavi, Romy Golan, Heather Woofter, and Javier Agustín Rojas for their material gestures of good will. I also deeply appreciate my colleagues at Washington University in St. Louis and at Rice who encouraged me in my pursuit of this project. Thanks to Eric P. Mumford for mentoring me and to Robert McCarter for inviting me to give a public lecture about Zanuso and introducing me to important Italian contacts. A heartfelt thanks to Stephen Leet and Susan Bower Leet, generous friends with whom I discovered a shared love for Italian architecture and design, and who so often made me laugh. I am grateful to be teaching at Rice at time of writing, as a historian who learns every day from brilliant architect, designer, and theorist faculty colleagues.

My affinity for postwar Italian architecture and design is driven by a love of the objects and building designs as works of art. I feel a great appreciation for architects like Marco Zanuso who sought to push the limits of what was possible and imagined that by so doing they could help others to transcend circumstance and make a place for themselves among the wonders of the modern world. A quest to belong is part of my own family history as well. I am grateful for the support of my family, including my parents, my brother Andrei Blakely, and especially my grandmothers Alice Blakely Brink and Maudie Howell Taylor, who understood more than most of us the substance of hoped-for things.

Notes

All quotations from Italian-language sources are translated by the author except as noted.

Ambiente

1. Virgilio Vercelloni, *Atlante storico di Milano, città di Lombardia* (Milan: Officine Grafiche di A. Lucini, 1989); Dante Isella, *La Milano dei navigli: Passeggiata letteraria* (Milan: Officina Libraria, 2017).

2. See for example references in Lucy Maulsby, *Fascism, Architecture, and the Claiming of Modern Milan, 1922–1943* (Toronto: University of Toronto Press, 2014), 71, 89.

3. See Angelo Lunati, *Ideas of Ambiente: History and Bourgeois Ethics in the Construction of Modern Milan 1881–1969* (Zurich: Park Books, 2020).

4. "Giovanni Battista Bossi, Architect," ArchINFORM.net https://www.archinform.net/arch/25833.htm (accessed February 8, 2025).

5. Giovanni Antolini, *Progetto sul foro che doveva eseguirsi in Milano, del architetto professore Giovanni Antolini: in 24 tavole in rame, 1801–1802*, consulted via National Gallery of Art Library in Washington, Grega and Leo A. Daly III Fund for Architectural Books. Antolini's project is discussed in detail in Carroll Westfall, "Antolini's Foro Bonaparte in Milan," *Journal of the Warburg and Courtauld Institutes* 32 (1969): 366–385.

6. *Regolamento edilizio del Comune di Milano* (Milan: Tipografia di Luigi Giacomo Pirola, 1889); *Progetto di regolamento edilizio-stradale e per l'ornato pubblico della città di Milano* (undated). Both documents are held in Fondo Ornato Fabbriche, Archivio Storico Civico e Biblioteca Trivulziana, Milan.

7. *Regolamento edilizio del Comune di Milano*.

8. "Gadda, Giuseppe," Treccani.it https://www.treccani.it/enciclopedia/giuseppe-gadda_res-8db4137c-87ed-11dc-8e9d-0016357eee51_(Dizionario-Biografico)/

9. *Regolamento edilizio del Comune di Milano*, 35–36.

10. Zanuso's design is included in Edgar Kaufman Jr., *Prize Designs for Modern Furniture: From the International Competition for Low-Cost Furniture Design* (New York: Museum of Modern Art, 1950), 73.

11. "Prefazione," in *Politecnico di Milano, Annuario anni accademici dal 1934–1935 al 1936–1937*, Milano 1935–XIII Archives of Milan Polytechnic.

12. See Mathilde Baffa, Corinna Morandi, Sara Protasoni, and Augusto Rossari, *Il Movimento di Studi per l'Architettura* (Bari: Laterza, 1995).

13. Paul Ginsborg, in *A History of Contemporary Italy* (Harmondsworth: Penguin, 1990), describes a gradual emergence of a middle class in his social history of the period from 1945 to the 1980s.

14. Manfredo Tafuri, *History of Italian Architecture, 1944–1985*, trans. Jessica Levine (Cambridge, MA: MIT Press, 1989), 11.

15. Giò Ponti, *Milano oggi* (Milan: Edizioni Milano Moderna, 1957).

16. Paolo Portoghesi and Virgilio Vercelloni, "L'occhio vuole la sua parte: L'edilizia milanese tra qualità e quantità," *Controspazio* (July-August 1969), 6–23. See also Vittorio Gregotti, "Italian Design, 1945–1971," in *Italy: The New Domestic Landscape*, ed. Emilio Ambasz (New York: Museum of Modern Art; Florence: Centro Di, 1972), 315–340, and Manfredo Tafuri, *Architecture and Utopia: Design and Capitalist Development*, trans. Barbara Luigia La Penta (Cambridge, MA: MIT Press, 1976), among other essays.

17. Described in François Burkhardt, *Marco Zanuso* (Milan: Federico Motta Editore, 1994), and in Roberta Grignolo, "Marco Zanuso tra tecniche di produzione e tecniche di progetto," in Marco Zanuso, *Scritti sulle tecniche di produzione e di progetto*, ed. Roberta Grignolo (Mendrisio: Academy Press; Milan: Silvana Editoriale, 2020), 1–74.

18. Varlonga's system is described in detail by Stefania Mornati in "Construction and Business Industrialization in Italy in the Second Post-War Period: The FEAL," in *Iron, Steel and Buildings: Studies in the History of Construction: The Proceedings of the Seventh Annual Conference of the Construction History Society*, ed. James W. P. Campbell et al. (Queen's College, University of Cambridge, April 5, 2019), 171–184.

19. Ernesto Nathan Rogers, "Milan, Design Renaissance," *Vogue*, September 15, 1949, 154–157, 183.

20. For a narrative of this period, see Leonardo Benevolo, "The Beginning of Modern Research, 1930–1940," in Ambasz, *Italy: The New Domestic Landscape*, 310–312.

21. Francesco Monotti, "Riforma delle esposizioni," *Quadrante* 2 (June 1933), 13.

22. The principal articles referred to here are "Alloggio in soffitta," *Domus* 244 (1950), 2–6; "Alloggio in soffitta: L'appartamento di Marco Zanuso a Milano," *Domus* 358 (1958), 11–17; Eugenio Gentili Tedeschi, "Marco Zanuso: La nuova sistemazione del suo alloggio a Milano," *Abitare* 7 (1962), 12–14; and Carlo De Carli, "Gli oggetti umani di Marco Zanuso," *Interni* 3 (April 1967), 1–10. The Eco della Stampa clippings, which trace Zanuso's wider profile in the press, are held in the Marco Zanuso archive at the Archivio del Moderno in Balerna, Switzerland.

Ingresso

1. See, for example, the apartment for Michele Zanuso, "Appartamento in condominio a Milano," *Abitare* 7 (1962), 22–26.

2. See Stefano Santini, "Marco Zanuso a Jesi," *Progetti Ancona* 1 (1998), 14–18.

3. The original layout and functions of building entrance and courtyard are recorded in the ground-floor plan drawing in the permitting drawing set. Fondo Ornato Fabbriche, Archivio Storico Civico e Biblioteca Trivulziana, Milan.

4. "Alloggio in soffitta," *Domus* 244 (1950), 2–6. The author is not named but was likely editor Giò Ponti.

5. Marco Zanuso, "La casa ideale," *Domus* 176 (1942), 328–332. Luciano Crespi has explored the relationship of several of Zanuso's projects to landscapes in "Interno, esterno, mentale. Il paesaggio nell'opera di Zanuso," in *Marco Zanuso architettura e design*, ed. Luciano Crespi, Letizia Tedeschi, and Annalisa Viati Navone (Rome: Officina Libraria, 2020), 41–52.

6. A potential blurring of the boundaries between walls and furniture is implied by the way *mobile* and *immobiliare*, the Italian words for furniture and real estate, respectively, contain a common root, as if some weight is given to the property itself, large or small, alongside the distinction between "movable" and "immovable."

7. Ponti had been Zanuso's instructor at the Milan Polytechnic in his final year of studies. It was one of Zanuso's most successful academic performances, according to his academic records. In addition to publishing articles on many of Zanuso's major projects in Milan in *Domus*, including the office building on Via Senato, apartments on Viale Gorizia, and others, Ponti referred to Zanuso's office both the young architect Cini Boeri and the German industrial designer Richard Sapper in the 1950s. Each would be a principal collaborator in the Zanuso office for many years.

8. See, for instance, Ponti's "Project for an Italian Embassy," in Fulvio Irace, *Giò Ponti la casa italiana* (Milan: Electa, 1988), 70.

9. Reyner Banham, "Exposed Power," in *The Architecture of the Well-Tempered Environment* (Chicago: University of Chicago Press, 1969), 239–242; and "Design by Choice," *Architectural Review* 773 (1961), 43–48.

10. Marco Zanuso, "La 'Maison Lumière' realizzata da Le Corbusier a Marsiglia," *Vetroflex* (January-March 1953), 22–25.

11. See Mario Manieri, *Morris, architettura e socialismo* (Bari: Laterza, 1963); Giancarlo De Carlo, *William Morris* (Milan: Il Balcone, 1947); Giulio Carlo Argan, *Walter Gropius e la Bauhaus* (Turin: Einaudi, 1951).

12. Lara Vinca Masini, "Marco Zanuso: Mobili per il soggiorno," *Domus* 426 (May 1965), 35–37.

13. A more upscale version of the same chair, called Maggiolina, was put into production in 1972 by Zanotta.

14. Zanuso's Tripolina was most likely made by the Italian company Paolo Viganò in Tripoli, Libya, based on a design first patented by British engineer Joseph Beverley Fenby in the 1870s.

15. "Alloggio in soffitta," 4.

16. "A Program: Domus, the House of Man," *Domus* 205 (1946), unnumbered first page of English digest.

17. Carlo De Carli, Vittorio Gandolfi, Vito Latis, Renzo Mongiardino, and Mario Tevarotto, "Pronto soccorso," *Domus* 205 (1946), 6–24.

18. Vittorio Gandolfi in De Carli et al., "Pronto soccorso," 7–10.

Soggiorno

1. "Regolamento Edilizio del 22 maggio 1889 N. 35901/257 TIP IX del 1889," cited on permit documents for Piazza Castello, 20, dated May 13, 1957, document PG 85194/1957 12-1-C Riforma Locali. Cittadella degli Archivi, Comune di Milano.

2. "Alloggio in soffitta," *Domus* 244 (March 1950), 2–6.

3. "Alloggio in soffitta."

4. "Alloggio in soffitta," 2.

5. "Alloggio in soffitta," 2.

6. "Alloggio in soffitta," 4.

7. "Materie plastiche nell'arredamento di un ufficio," *Domus* 273 (September 1952), 25.

8. "Alloggio in soffitta," *Domus* 341 (April 1958), 11–17.

9. "Divan" in American English refers to a couch without a back or arms; it may be used as a bed. By contrast, *divano* in Italian refers to a sofa or ottoman.

10. Guido Canella, "Zanuso il più problematico degli architetti italiani," *Fantasia la rivista della donna* (November 1963), 66.

11. Leonardo Ferrari, "La poltrona ideale," *Maria Chiara* (December 1959), 27–28.

12. Observed by Eugenio Gentili Tedeschi in "Marco Zanuso: La nuova sistemazione del suo alloggio a Milano," *Abitare* 7 (1962), 14.

Studio

1. Marco Zanuso, "Two Chairs," in *Zanuso: The Dunhill Industrial Design Lectures of 1971* (Melbourne: Trevor Wilson Co. for Industrial Design Council of Australia, 1971), 26–34.

2. Kenneth Frampton, writing in 1999, speculated that Zanuso may have borrowed this solution from Amancio Williams, whose bus station Zanuso may have seen in Argentina. "Il progetto di Zanuso: Una tettonica per tutte le scale," in *Marco Zanuso architetto* (Milan: Skira, 1999), 30–35.

3. Zanuso, "Two Chairs," 26.

4. Sapper, whose lamp Tizio, produced by Artemide, can be made out at the bottom of a sheet of sketches for Lambda, would go on to work in a similar vein with fabricators and producers in Milan. On the working relationship between the two, see Richard Sapper, "Quindici anni di lavoro felice," in *Marco Zanuso: Architettura, design e la costruzione del benessere*, ed. Antonio Piva and Vittorio Prina (Rome: Gangemi, 2007), 120–122. See also Jonathan Olivares, *Richard Sapper* (London: Phaidon Press, 2016).

5. Zanuso, "Two Chairs." Documentation in the Zanuso archive includes a quote from Biffi Officina Elettromeccanica in Milan for 20 chair prototypes, 10 in each of two sizes, specifying welded steel, heat-treated legs, and three options for surface treatment. Fondo Marco Zanuso, Archivio del Moderno, Balerna.

6. Marco Zanuso, "La casa ideale," *Domus* 176 (1942), 328–332.

7. Marco Zanuso and Paolo Chessa, "La casa prefabbricata: Il modulo," *Domus* 205 (1946), 26–27.

8. Zanuso, "Two Chairs," 27–28.

9. Zanuso and Chessa, "La casa prefabbricata: Il modulo."

10. "A Milano, al diciottesimo piano," *Domus* 421 (1964), 29.

11. "A Milano, al diciottesimo piano," 29.

12. Marco Zanuso, "La casa," in Zanuso, *Scritti sulle tecniche di produzione e di progetto*, ed. Roberta Grignolo (Mendrisio: Academy Press; Milan: Silvana Editoriale, 2020), 75–80.

13. "Lessico del arredamento 5: lo studio," *Domus* 189 (1943), vii.

14. "Lessico del arredamento 5."

15. Lorenza Zanuso, "Marialisa (Billa) Pedroni Zanuso: Milano 20 Agosto 1920–Milano, 8 luglio 2012," ASPI Archivio storico della psicologia italiana, https://www.aspi.unimib.it/collections/entity/detail/376/ (accessed January 21, 2025). See also "La signora di moda—La Billa una e tre," collected in Rassegna Stampa 10 Triennale di Milano 1954 Prefabbricazione e Industrial Design. The journals to which Billa Zanuso contributed articles included magazines like *Arianna* which were edited with a wide audience of Italian women in mind, often homemakers. *Artecasa*, *Noi Donne*, *Novità*, *Gioia*, *Amica*, and *Fantasia* were among the magazines that featured Marco Zanuso's designs on many occasions, including his furniture pieces that gave structure to spaces in the home, particularly kitchens and bedrooms, often with advice from the architect on how to think about such spaces. These articles were collected by Zanuso's press clippings service, Eco della Stampa, and are held in the Fondo Marco Zanuso at the Archivio del Moderno.

16. "Anna" was cowritten with Cesare Zavattini, who had been screenwriter of De Sica's celebrated *Ladri di biciclette* (*Bicycle Thieves*), 1945, and *Miracolo di Milano* (*Miracle in Milan*), 1950. *Ieri, oggi, domani* (*Yesterday, Today and Tomorrow*) starred Sophia Loren and Marcello Mastroianni and was awarded an Oscar for best foreign film in 1965.

17. Billa Zanuso, *The Young Freud: The Origins of Psychoanalysis in Late Nineteenth Century Viennese Culture* (Oxford: Blackwell, 1986).

18. Lorenza Zanuso, interview with the author, March 12, 2024.

19. On the Michele Zanuso apartment, see "Appartamento in condominio a Milano," *Abitare* 7 (1962), 23–26. The building is described in Christian Sumi and Annalisa Viati Navone, *Giulio Minoletti: Architetto, urbanista e designer* (Mendrisio: Mendrisio Academy Press, 2014). On the Bay apartment, see "Un appartamento al diciottesimo piano," *Domus* 405 (1963), 27–41.

20. Ponti's Superleggera was a derivation of the *chiavarina*, the lightweight, cane-seated nineteenth-century classic from Liguria. See chapter 2 of Catharine Rossi, *Crafting Design in Italy* (Manchester: Manchester University Press, 2015).

Cucina

1. For a discussion of Zanuso's approach to kitchen design, see Roberta Grignolo, "Marco Zanuso e l'integrazione 'sinergetica,' dal design all'architettura" (1–40), and Alberto Bassi, "Marco Zanuso e il progetto integrale dell'ambiente cucina" (185–194), in *Marco Zanuso architettura e design*, ed. Luciano Crespi, Letizia Tedeschi, and Annalisa Viati Navone (Rome: Officina Libraria, 2020).

2. Roberta Grignolo offers a meticulous analysis that situates *La cucina* in relation to 1930s proposals, in her introduction to Marco Zanuso, *Scritti sulle tecniche di produzione e di progetto* (Mendrisio: Academy Press; Milan: Silvana Editoriale, 2020).

3. Marco Zanuso, *La cucina*, Quaderni di Domus 3 (Milan: Domus, 1945), 7.

4. Zanuso, *La cucina*, 7.

5. Giuseppe Pagano, "Civiltà industriale," *Casabella costruzioni* 175 (1942), xxvi.

6. Pagano, "Civiltà industriale."

7. Materials on the *Mostra internazionale della produzione in serie*, in particular the brochure for the exhibition, can be accessed online via the Milan Triennale library.

8. Giuseppe Pagano, *Tecnica dell'abitazione* (Milan: Hoepli, 1936), 9.

9. Floor plan of Villa Scotti, on microfilm, FMZ mfarch 001 Scotti Premeno 011b, Fondo Marco Zanuso, Archivio del Moderno, Balerna.

10. "Cucina," *Artecasa* 18 (1961), unnumbered pages. Cini Boeri, who was working in the Zanuso office at the time, is credited in publications as a coauthor of the project.

11. Richard Sapper describes a moment in the design process behind the house near Lake Como that Zanuso designed for Sapper, who had left the office by that time, and his family. At one point, Zanuso revised the design completely after a long conversation with Sapper's wife. Richard Sapper, "Quindici anni di lavoro felice," in *Marco Zanuso: Architettura, design e la costruzione del benessere*, ed. Antonio Piva and Vittorio Prina (Rome: Gangemi, 2007).

12. On the Emergency Capsule, see Emilio Ambasz, ed., *Italy: The New Domestic Landscape* (New York: Museum of Modern Art; Florence: Centro Di, 1972), 190–199. Zanuso mentioned the Schütte-Lihotzky kitchen in *La cucina*, 7–8, as a pioneering example of research in efficient spatial planning.

13. "L'arredamento che strizza l'occhio," *Staff*, June 15, 1972, 75–77.

14. "A Milano, un appartamento al diciottesimo piano," *Domus* 403 (June 1963), 13 unnumbered pages. Zanuso installed the ELAM kitchen in his own apartment during the 1980s, according to Zanuso's daughter, Lorenza Zanuso, in a conversation with the author. The E5 kitchen is still in production today.

15. The other condominium building was that on Via Laveno in the San Siro district. See Pier Carlo Santini, "Marco Zanuso una casa a Milano," *Ottagono* 1 (1966), 79; Fabrizio Oliva, "Due edifici gemelli d'abitazione a Milano," *Architettura cronache e storia* 11, no. 123 (1966), 566–571.

16. "Un frigorifero," *Stile industria* 1 (1954), 8. The author was most likely Alberto Rosselli.

17. Marco Zanuso, comments in a short description from the catalog of the tenth Triennale, Industrial Design exhibition, tenth Milan Triennale, 1954, https://www.bdl.servizirl.it/bdl/public/rest/srv/item/17979/shortlink

18. Catalog of the tenth Triennale, 135.

19. The coffee grinder was published among a selection of kitchen appliances in *Stile industria* 24 (1959), 27; drawings of the unit were consulted in Marco Zanuso's archive, FMZ archive MZ-D Macina Caffè "Carossello," Fondo Marco Zanuso, Archivio del Moderno, Balerna.

20. Zanuso made a practice of naming collaborators in his office who worked with him on published products; he credited the young architect Alberto Scarzella as a cocreator of the tile. Ubaldo Castelli, "In ricordo di Alberto Scarzella Mazzochi," February 2017, https://rivista.inarcassa.it/en/-/in-ricordo-di-alberto-scarzella-mazzocchi (accessed January 10, 2025).

21. The shape of the tile elicited different kinds of interest in London, where it was part of the exhibition *Selected Examples of Italian Industrial Design*, curated by Marco Zanuso and held at the Italian Cultural Institute in Belgravia in summer 1955. After an erroneous image of the tile was published in the *Daily Telegraph*, an article in the journal *Art Club* (issue no. 3) clarified its true shape with a geometric diagram that was republished in a mathematics journal the following year. H. M. Cundy, "2647. A Mathematical Tile," *Mathematical Gazette* 40, no. 334 (1956), 285.

22. *Domus* 305 (April 1955). The decorative potential was highlighted when the tile was featured on the cover of *Domus* in a painted study for a three-color installation by Giuseppe Ajmone. The author of the article, which was unsigned (possibly written by director Giò Ponti), attributed a refreshing playfulness that added a "function" of play to the object.

23. *Casabella* 216 (1957), 61–65.

24. *Selected Examples of Italian Industrial Design* (London: Italian Cultural Institute, 1955).

25. "Decima Triennale di Milano," *Edilizia Moderna* 53 (1954), 15.

26. "'L'industrial design' italiano fattore di sviluppo economico," *Il Giornale di Vicenza*, December 2, 1970. Zanuso sought to explain the necessary formation of the industrial designer to an audience of manufacturers. Eco della Stampa file, Fondo Marco Zanuso, Archivio del Moderno, Balerna.

Bambine

1. Interview with Lorenza Zanuso, March 2, 2023.

2. In a short story by Billa Zanuso, for instance, a character considers the rumors she has heard that the domestic she has just hired, her first one, will probably steal from her. Over six watchful months, she notes that the maid does not steal anything in spite of ample opportunity. Relieved, she gives the maid two sweaters. The maid begins to steal from her. "E ha ragione," the narrator says, "and she is right"—conceding her own enjoyment of, and access to, luxury. "Signora di lusso," in *Nostra signora di Milano* (Milan: Lerici, 1962), 32–33.

3. "Alloggio in soffitta," *Domus* 244 (1950), 4–5. See also Marco Zanuso, "La casa ideale," *Domus* 176 (1942), 328–332.

4. An attribution of this lamp to Zanuso is unconfirmed, but the use of steel and the lamp resemble the designs of the lighting design firm Stilnovo.

5. These appear in a photograph held in the Milan Triennale archive: item TRN_IX_06_0327 Archivio Fotografico, Triennale di Milano, https://front-triennale.caveaudigitale.com/oggetti/50620-ix-triennale-abitazione-alloggio-n-7-elementi-di-appartamento-marco-zanuso-camera-per-due-ragazzi-letto-pieghevole-con-materassini-in-gommapiuma?i=19

6. A caption in the 1950 article "Alloggio in soffitta" mentions this chair among furniture "vecchi di casa" and gives its date as 1889. The *chiavarina* was a colloquial name that referred to Chiavari, a town on the Ligurian coast just east of Genoa where several companies had manufactured the chair since 1807, when the first model was designed by an artisan named Giuseppe Gaetano Descalzi.

7. Zanuso had toured recent school buildings on a trip to England around the same time, paying close attention to prefabrication possibilities, including the Hertford County Council schools, Bristol aluminum school, and Hunstanton

School. His sketches are recorded in his Notebook 65, held in the Fondo Marco Zanuso, Archivio del Moderno, Balerna.

8. On the experiences of Maria Cristina Mariani Dameno (Cini Boeri, 1924–2020) as a woman in a predominantly male profession, and on her role as an architect in Marco Zanuso's office between 1952 and 1963, see Cecilia Avogadro, *Cini Boeri: Architetto e designer* (Cinisello Balsamo: Silvana, 2004), and Catharine Rossi, "Furniture, Feminism and the Feminine: Women Designers in Postwar Italy, 1945–1970," *Journal of Design History* 22, no. 3 (September 2009), 243–257.

9. Another example that touched the Zanuso office indirectly was the construction of a new institutional building in the QT8 experimental quarter in the San Siro area, in northwest Milan, founded by Elda Scarzella Mazzocchi to provide temporary shelter to young unwed mothers. Alberto Scarzella Mazzocchi was the architect of that project, "Villaggio della madre e del fanciullo," built in the 1950s; in the early 1950s he worked in Zanuso's office and he is credited as co-designer of the tile SZ1. See "Amare il fanciullo per bene educarlo," *Corriere della Sera*, March 6, 1955, 2; "Fiori d'Arancio ieri al Villaggio della madre e del fanciullo," *Corriere della Sera*, July 14–15, 1958, 4.

10. "Italy: The Lady Magnate of Milan," *Time*, June 7, 1971, https://time.com/archive/6838995/italy-the-lady-magnate-of-milan/ (accessed January 12, 2025); Alberto Bolzani, "Anna Bonomi e il suo impegno per le 'Carline,'" *Corriere della Sera*, June 6, 2017, 15.

11. Cini Boeri, "Pensionato femminile a Milano," *Edilizia Moderna* 68 (1959), 23–27.

12. Boeri, "Pensionato femminile a Milano."

13. The exhibition was organized by the Association of Fine Arts of the province of Como, held at Villa Olmo. "Commento di Bruno Zevi," in *Colore e forma nella casa d'oggi*, exh. cat. (Como: Associazione Belle Arti della Provincia di Como, 1957), unnumbered pages.

14. Boeri, "Pensionato femminile a Milano."

15. *Asilo nido* refers to a child care center.

16. "Un asilo a Gubbio," *Domus* 362 (1960), 15–24.

17. Carlo L. Ragghianti, "Arte italiana al 1960," *Sele Arte* 48 (1960), 88–100.

18. Ragghianti, "Arte italiana al 1960," English digest, p. VII.

19. Ragghianti, "Arte italiana al 1960," figs. 139–144.

20. Ragghianti, "Arte italiana al 1960," figs. 129–132.

Letto

1. "Pronto soccorso," *Domus* 205 (1946), 7–9.

2. Marco Zanuso, "La casa ideale," *Domus* 176 (August 1942), 328–332.

3. Zanuso, "La casa ideale," 328.

4. The work was tentatively identified by the Lucio Fontana Foundation in correspondence with the author, based on a photograph, as *Concetto spaziale, I muri*, 1957, made of pastel and holes on canvas, gray and brown, 100 × 80 cm, cited in *Catalogo ragionato di sculture, dipinti, ambientazioni* (Crispolti, Skira, 2006) with the number 57 G 50.

5. Fontana's Le Carline chapel decorations are described in Cini Boeri, "Pensionato femminile a Milano," *Edilizia Moderna* 68 (1959), 23–27. Fontana was also the artist collaborator on one of Zanuso's very first projects, the Sacrario dei Caduti (1938), a memorial antechamber (since demolished) designed by Zanuso, Giovanni Albricci, Mario Tevarotto, Luigi Mattioni, Gianluigi Reggio, and Mario Salvadé and constructed within Milan's Fascist headquarters building, designed by their professor Piero Portaluppi. See *Casabella* 157 (1941), 45.

6. For a broader discussion of art-architecture collaborations, see Romy Golan, "From Monument to Mural Nomad: The Mural in Modern European Architecture," in *The Built Surface: Architecture and the Pictorial Arts from Romanticism to the Twenty-First Century*, ed. Karen Koehler (Aldershot: Ashgate, 2002), vol. 2, 186–208.

7. These details about the origins of the Via Senato building are related in Alberto Macchiavello, "Zanuso inventore del Lady," *Amica*, April 15, 1962, 63–67.

8. Allan Ballantyne, "Italian Scrapbook," *Architectural Review* 111, no. 662 (February 1952), 83–91.

9. The equipment is itemized in Piero Bottoni, *Antologia di edifici moderni in Milano* (Milan: Editoriale Domus, 1954), 30.

10. Sharon Hecker, "Servant of Two Masters: Lucio Fontana's Sculptures in Milan's Cinema Arlecchino," *Oxford Art Journal* 35, no. 3 (2012), 344.

11. Marco Zanuso, "Architettura e pittura," *Edilizia Moderna* 47 (1951), 46.

12. Documented in Bottoni, *Antologia di edifici moderni in Milano*, 171. See also Giò Ponti, "Astrattismo per una facciata," *Domus* 267 (February 1952), 2–3.

13. Giò Ponti, "Ai pittori astrattisti per collaborare con gli architetti moderni," *Domus* 268 (March 1952), 86–87. The producer, active for many years in the Milan region as a specialist in wall finishes and pavements, was Fulget Fratelli Capoferri, based in Bergamo. It is worth noting that Fulget was a frequent advertiser in journals such as *Domus*; but questions about mercenary motives on Ponti's part are dispelled, for the most part, by a sample of his passionate polemics about architecture and decoration, in which the Viale Gorizia building played a part, for example in "Astrattismo per una facciata."

14. Giò Ponti, "Architettura forma di una sostanza," *Domus* 267 (February 1952), 1.

15. Ponti, "Astrattismo per una facciata," 2–3.

16. Giò Ponti, "Tutto al mondo deve essere coloratissimo," *Edilizia Moderna* 48 (1952), 81–82. "The true tradition, the one I adore, the one of which innovators are the keepers, has always been colorful and sanguine," Ponti writes (81).

17. Zanuso, "La casa ideale," 331.

18. Zanuso, "Architettura e pittura," 43–48.

19. "Hervé," *Domus* 284 (July 1953), 39.

20. On Ballocco, see *Visione logica ed estetica: La ricerca di Mario Ballocco* (Milan: 10 A.M. Art, 2017).

21. Paul Damaz, *Art in European Architecture; Synthèse des Arts* (New York: Reinhold, 1956). Damaz was a Portuguese-French architect who had emigrated to the United States to work on the United Nations Building with Le Corbusier. For a discussion of the "Synthesis of the arts" movement in Europe, see Romy Golan, *Muralnomad: The Paradox of Wall Painting, Europe, 1927–1957* (New Haven: Yale University Press, 2009).

22. Gillo Dorfles, "Una nuova biblioteca per architetti," *Edilizia Moderna* 48 (June 1952), 53. Zanuso's linoleum showroom was praised in similar terms by Olga Gueft in "On Displaying without Displays," *Interiors* (December 1952), 92.

23. Mario Ballocco, "Viviamo il colore," *AZ arte d'oggi* 2, no. 2 (February 1950), 1.

24. Mario Ballocco, "Arte funzionale," *AZ arte d'oggi* 2, no. 3 (March 1950), 1. The "concrete art" movement was a loose network of which a nearby center was in France, around the French sculptor André Bloc. Gianni Dova and Mario Ballocco were associated with the Italian affiliate, Movimento Arte Concreta, which had many vocal advocates of the integration of painting, sculpture, and architecture. Gillo Dorfles, a painter and critic, was a particularly eloquent and prominent advocate.

25. Bruno Munari, "Arte e industria: L'arte concreta ha la possibilità di portare un contributo vantaggioso per l'industria e per la società," *AZ arte d'oggi* 2, no. 4

(April-May 1950), 3. The English translation of the title would be "Art and Industry: Concrete art has the possibility of an advantageous contribution to industry and society."

26. For Ballocco's commentary on the Fiera exhibition, see Mario Ballocco, "Sala delle arti e dell'estetica industriale," *Edilizia Moderna* 48 (1952), 78.

27. Marco Romanelli, *Gino Sarfatti opere scelte/Selected Works 1938–1973* (Cinisello Balsamo: Silvana, 2012), 442 (standing lamp).

28. Eugenio Gentili Tedeschi, "Marco Zanuso: La nuova sistemazione del suo alloggio a Milano," *Abitare* 7 (1962), 12–14.

29. Gentili Tedeschi, "Marco Zanuso," 13.

30. Gentili Tedeschi, "Marco Zanuso," 13.

31. Gentili Tedeschi, "Marco Zanuso," 14.

32. "L'antiquariato oggi," *Abitare* 7 (1962), 4–10.

Ragazze

1. Quoted in Gillo Dorfles, *Marco Zanuso designer* (Milan: Editalia, 1972).

2. The former Achille Castiglioni studio remains at Piazza Castello, 27 at time of writing: https://www.fondazioneachillecastiglioni.it

3. See, for example MIM and Arflex exhibits from the "Eurodomus" exhibition at the Genoa trade fair, in *Domus* 440 (1966), unnumbered pages.

4. Most of the early 1960s apartments were designed with Cini Boeri in the Zanuso office; by 1967 Boeri had established her own office and begun to design variations on the same types of furniture pieces as well as innovative further iterations under her own name.

5. Cini Boeri is credited as collaborator in published versions of this project.

6. "A Milano, un appartamento al diciottesimo piano," *Domus* 403 (June 1963), 24–39.

7. Published in *Domus* 403 (June 1963), unnumbered pages.

8. Lara Vinca Masini et al., *La casa abitata: Biennale degli interni di oggi, Firenze, Palazzo Strozzi, 6 marzo-25 aprile 1965* (Lissone: Arte Grafiche Meroni, 1965), unnumbered pages.

9. Masini et al., *La casa abitata.*

10. Marco Zanuso's description of his intervention is published in the exhibition catalog along with illustrations of his room.

11. Laura Vinca Masini, "La casa abitata," *Domus* 426 (May 1965), 36. One wonders about the acoustics of such a scenario, however.

12. Masini, "La casa abitata."

13. Zanuso discusses the Kartell chair, which was stacked in a ziggurat form in his installation, in "Two Chairs," in *Zanuso: The Dunhill Industrial Design Lectures of 1971* (Melbourne: Trevor Wilson Co. for Industrial Design Council of Australia, 1971), 26–34.

14. Masini, "La casa abitata," 31.

15. See Costantino Corsini and Giorgio Wiskemann, "Indagine alla FEAL," *Stile Industria* 28 (August 1960), 28–35.

16. Letizia Tedeschi discusses the "lecorbusian" aspect of Zanuso's FEAL projects in "Marco Zanuso, progettare senza dogmi: Il contributo degli artisti," in *Marco Zanuso architettura e design*, ed. Luciano Crespi, Letizia Tedeschi, and Annalisa Viati Navone (Rome: Officina Libraria, 2020), 136–138.

Vedute

1. For example, Carlo Pagani, *Architettura italiana oggi* (Milan: Hoepli, 1955); see also "L'Italie," *L'Architecture d'Aujourd'hui* 41 (June 1952), edited and introduced by André Bloc.

2. Gregotti mentioned Ettore Sottsass, Roberto Menghi, Vito and Gustavo Latis, and Achille and Pier Giacomo Castiglioni, who had begun their careers within a few years of Zanuso, as other members of the same group. Gregotti, "Marco Zanuso, un architetto della seconda generazione," *Casabella-Continuità* 216 (1957), 59–60.

3. Gregotti, "Marco Zanuso, un architetto della seconda generazione."

4. "The ghost of national progressive reality often evoked by Italian architects after 1950 was still a symbol of the narrowness of an elitist culture incapable of accepting real isolation or becoming an authentic mass culture." Vittorio Gregotti, *New Directions in Italian Architecture* (New York: George Braziller, 1968), 47–48.

5. Guido Canella, "Zanuso il più problematico degli architetti italiani," *Fantasia la rivista della donna* (November 1963), 62, 64.

6. See, for instance, the description of gender roles in the short story "A posto," in Billa Zanuso, *Nostra signora di Milano* (Milan: Lerici, 1962), 13–14.

7. Emilio Ambasz, "Introduction," in *Italy: The New Domestic Landscape* (New York: Museum of Modern Art; Florence: Centro Di, 1972), 19.

8. Manolo De Giorgi, "Un vedutista lombardo del XX secolo," in *Marco Zanuso architetto* (Milan: Skira, 1999), 16.

9. Nikolaus Pevsner, *Pioneers of Modern Design: From William Morris to Walter Gropius* (London: Faber, 1936).

10. See the essays by Burkhardt, Maddalena Scimemi, and Luciano Crespi in *Marco Zanuso architettura e design*, ed. Luciano Crespi, Letizia Tedeschi, and Annalisa Viati Navone (Rome: Officina Libraria, 2020). See also Christian Sumi, "Forma e tettonica: Una radio, tre televisori e sei stabilmenti industriali," in the same volume.

11. François Burkhardt, "L'interpretazione dell'opera di Marco Zanuso e i suoi mutamenti nel tempo," in Crespi, Tedeschi, and Viati Navone, *Marco Zanuso architettura e design*.

12. Patent #US3551607A, filed in 1967 under Zanuso's name, patented in late 1970, cited by 28 subsequent patents. See https://patents.google.com/patent/US3551607A/en-

13. Gregotti acknowledges that he is repeating a remark made by Giulio Carlo Argan, who wrote the statement referring to Marcel Breuer. As quoted by Gregotti, the Italian sentence is: "Il suo contributo è appunto il pensiero di un'azione che è essa stessa, per la propria determinatezza, qualitativa." Gregotti, "Marco Zanuso, un architetto della seconda generazione," 60.

14. An instructive example along these lines is the art historian Paolo Fossati; in *Il design in Italia* (Turin: Einaudi, 1972), he draws a distinction between "Italian design" and "design in Italy" and inquires into their relationship.

15. While single-family homes were not uncommon in Italian architecture journals, such projects were often secondary residences or private villas as opposed to homes for middle-class residents.

16. Roberto Guiducci, "Una progettazione 'a posteriori': La fabbrica Olivetti di Marco Zanuso a Buenos Aires," *Casabella-Continuità* 229 (1959), 20–25. Guiducci was the head of the technical office of Olivetti while Zanuso was designing factories for the typewriter maker. The receptiveness to the technical situates Zanuso in the tradition of *constructeur*, in a line that includes Jean Prouvé, Robert Maillart, and others who worked at the intersection of architecture and engineering. One can also place in this category the architect Renzo Piano, who authored a textbook with Zanuso and worked in the Zanuso office during the development of the Italian factories for Olivetti in the 1960s. Roberto Lucci, Renzo Piano, and Marco Zanuso, *Elementi di tecnologia dei materiali come introduzione allo studio del*

design (Milan: Tamburini, 1967). On the relationship of Zanuso and Piano, see Lorenzo Ciccarelli, *Renzo Piano before Renzo Piano* (Rome: Quodlibet, 2017).

17. "Il modo con cui vengono esercitate le differenti funzioni (sedersi, coricarsi, leggere, studiare, riunirsi per conversare, ecc.) va continuamente modificandosi e di volta in volta occorre utilizzare mobili che meglio rispondano allo scopo. Avviene così che un mobile, indipendentemente dal suo stato di conservazione e dal suo pregio estetico, conservi in proporzione più o meno ridotta la capacità di adempiere agli scopi per cui è stato costruito." Eugenio Gentili Tedeschi, "Marco Zanuso: La nuova sistemazione del suo alloggio a Milano," *Abitare* 7 (1962), 12–14.

18. "One is struck by the multiplicity of functions that a building of this type can contain over time and how these functions are entirely independent of the form. At the same time, it is precisely the form that impresses us; we live it and experience it, and in turn it structures the city." Aldo Rossi, *The Architecture of the City*, trans. Diane Ghirardo and Joan Ockman (Cambridge, MA: MIT Press, 1984), 29. Rossi worked in Marco Zanuso's office briefly around 1960.

19. Giovanni Michelucci, Domenico Benini, Tommaso Ferraris, and Pier Luigi Spadolini, in the foreword to the exhibition catalog, Lara Vinca Masini et al., *La casa abitata: Biennale degli interni di oggi, Firenze, Palazzo Strozzi, 6 marzo–25 aprile 1965* (Lissone: Arte Grafiche Meroni, 1965).

20. Umberto Eco, *Opera aperta* (Milan: Bompiani, 1962); in English, *The Open Work*, trans. Anna Cancogni (Cambridge, MA: Harvard University Press, 1989).

21. The publication of *Opera aperta* in 1962, the same year in which Zanuso had his renovated family apartment photographed by Ugo Mulas, may suggest a common sensibility or parallel responses to similar ambient forces; the investigation of the historical relationship merits further attention but is beyond the scope of this study. Eco himself defined the "open work" in different ways.

22. Eco developed the "open work" principally in relation to literature and music. Architecture is not discussed in "The Open Work in the Visual Arts," but architecture in relation to linguistics and structuralism was a topic in the Italian literature of the early 1960s, with many contributors, including Gillo Dorfles and Eco, contributing essays on related themes to various artistic and literary journals. Among publications in this discourse was issue 82–83 of *Edilizia Moderna*, a survey of Italian architecture published in 1963, edited by Vittorio Gregotti. The issue featured a portfolio of architectural projects whose irregular, rhizomatic, or aggregative forms were interpreted as an "informal" architecture. Drawings of a factory for Olivetti, designed by Marco Zanuso with Edoardo Vittoria, were among the featured projects. Umberto Eco contributed an essay on international expositions to the following issue, *Edilizia Moderna* 84, published in 1964. Zanuso evidently did not know Eco and may not have been familiar with his work, though the architect and the young literary critic moved in overlapping circles in Milan's arts communities.

23. Zanuso discussed the problems of popular taste in a recorded discussion with a collector and gallery owner in 1962; the transcript was published in the same issue of *Abitare* as Gentili Tedeschi's article on the Zanuso apartment. Zanuso said, for example, "A dining room from long ago evidently was inserted in an environment with values spatially and volumetrically seventeenth-century, corresponding to different relationships, profoundly different, from those that determine the spaces in which we of today live. It does not seem possible to me to reconstruct a seventeenth-century atmosphere in a place with 3.3-meter [10½-foot] ceilings." Marco Zanuso et al., "L'antiquariato oggi," *Abitare* 7 (March 1962), 8.

24. Carlo De Carli, "Gli oggetti umani di Marco Zanuso," *Interni* 3 (April 1967), 1–10.

25. In the transcript of a 1962 interview, Zanuso is recorded as stating that "among all, Mies van der Rohe is possibly the only architect of production; the artist who knew how to express this world profoundly; who in the use of the module, in the joint, in the material succeeded in bringing together for the spatial emotion spatial and volumetric architectonics, that 'material of industrial design.'" Zanuso added on the same page, "Louis Kahn, too, expresses in his architecture the integral motive of functions that is typical of design." Gillo Dorfles, Alberto Rosselli, Silvano Tintori, and Marco Zanuso, "La responsabilità degli architetti," *Stile industria* 36 (1962), 25.

26. Careful study of the Zanuso apartment lends support to Giampiero Bosoni's assertion that furniture and small spatial arrangements in the home were a fundamental medium for Zanuso. See Giampiero Bosoni, "La filosofia dell'arredamento di Marco Zanuso: Un altro percorso dal progetto degli interni al design del mobile in Italia (1939–1951)," in Crespi, Tedeschi, and Viati Navone, *Marco Zanuso architettura e design*, 169–184.

27. *Oxford English Dictionary*, "wholism (n.)," July 2023, https://doi.org/10.1093/OED/1125635526.

28. According to an archivist at IUAV Archivio Progetti, where the Giorgio Casali archive is held.

29. These markings are visible on the contact sheets, held in the Ugo Mulas archive in Milan.

30. According to Alessandra Pozzati, archivist at Archivio Ugo Mulas.

31. See for example Giovanni Battista Piranesi, *Veduta della Piazza del Popolo*, from *Vedute di Roma*. Object number 37.45.3(49), Metropolitan Museum, New York, https://www.metmuseum.org/art/collection/search/362729 (accessed July 18, 2025). Note: *veduta* is roughly the Italian equivalent of the English "view."

Index

References to pages with visual material appear in italics. Architecture, design projects, and texts authored by Marco Zanuso appear in boldface.